MAK
WORLDS

Nicolae Sirius

Parallel Universes

ISBN 979-12-201-0247-6
First edition: December 2020

PARALLEL UNIVERSES

INTRODUCTION

The author proposes a new and interesting analysis, offering new insights to deepen the meaning of the construction of the Great Pyramid and the Giza complex in general. He shows that in order to properly study and look for an understanding of the greatest and most mysterious monument of the Ancient World we must have a broad view that encompasses the entirety of our human experience: mathematics, numerology, astrology, biology, physics and human history through the ages.

Matteo Olivieri

PART 1

One of the most subtle concepts on which was structured the design of the Great Pyramid- attributed to Khufu, the second pharaoh of the Fourth Dynasty of ancient Egypt- was worked out on a kind of mathematics that is entirely different from the mathematics used before and after that period. The designer entrusted with that task displayed skillfully within the walls of the pyramid, as a mean of measurement, a mysterious puzzle about transcendence and parallel universes.

This could be viewed as something entirely unrealistic, taking into account all that has been written about the Great Pyramid. Since there is nowhere indicated or at least suggested anything like this.

How then could this be proven as such?

A thousand years after the Great Pyramid is assumed to have been built, in a papyrus attributed to the Egyptian scribe Ahmose (1650 BC), is for the first time maintained a simple method for measuring the pyramids. The said papyrus, removed from the tomb of Ahmose and purchased in Luxor, Egypt, by the Scottish antiquarian Alexander Henry Rhind in 1858, rests now in the British Museum.

To get the length of the seked* the scribe wrote, it has to be divided the base of the pyramid by 2, and the result obtained further divided by its height. Based on that information were drafted various sekeds, like the one below, in the attempt to depict the structure of the unit of length, known as the Royal Cubit, used for the survey of the Great Pyramid; as the original one could not be found.

  *Seked is the Egyptian term for calculating the slopes of a pyramid.

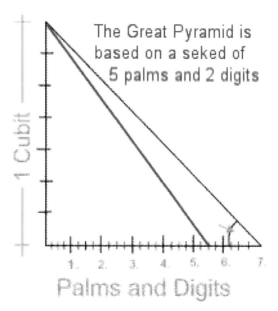

Seked 5.5 (ratio 7:11 - height to base) - The Great Pyramid Ratio
Copyright: David Furlong

Such a piece of information is obviously of great historical significance and has remained unchallenged so far. In this work- as part of the same field of measurements- will be presented an elusive kind of evidence, that precedes in time the one just maintained. Which otherwise is key to decoding the role of the Great Pyramid. What else should be added in this context, as being equally important, is that we could have accessed that knowledge. Why we haven't, or more precisely why are we unaware of it at this point in time, is to be dealt with by presenting a few relevant facts, stagged as a sum of steps. Beginning with the so-called Pythagorean theorem, in which the Greek thinker, Pythagoras, proved that the square of the hypotenuse in a right triangle is equal to the square of the other two sides.

Yet, as seen in the presentation below, the designer of the pyramid of Khufu applied a different formula. Dividing first the sides of the right triangle by π.

Such an approach may appear irrelevant, taking into account that π, from the time of Archimedes (287BC- 212BC), has mainly been described as the ratio of a circle's circumference to its diameter.

Admitting, however, that there would be good-will for taking on board a new intricate mathematical formula to pursue its result, that inevitably would raise a delicate question. Why wasn't this handed down if it was known to be of any good?

To this, the designer unfolds a logical answer, although described in a very unorthodox way.

The length of the sides of the right triangle used by the designer in his computation is the binary 33,44,55. That divided by π (3.1415926535898), as seen in the image below, reveals a unit of measurement double the size of the Royal Cubit.

33 : 3.14 = 10.50
44 : 3.14 = 14.00
55 : 3.14 = 17.50

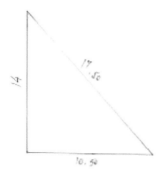

What importance has this result? The designer divided the length of the unit of measurement once more.

10.50 : 2 = 5.25
14 :2 = 7
17.50 : 2 = 8.75

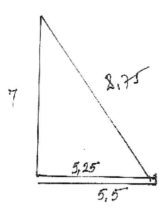

The unit of measurement obtained is almost identical to the Royal Cubit. (See image above: Seked 5.5, Copyright, David Furlong). Only that the designer indicates that exactly that has to be squared.

7 x 7 = 49
5.25 x 5.25 = 27.5625
8.75 x 8.75 = 76.5625
49 + 27.5625 = 76.5625

As at this point, it is not possible to at least figure out what relation is between the above result and the Great Pyramid or why was necessary the use of π, it will be pursued first the hidden link between 76.5625 and the speed of light.

Back in 1983, the meter was re-defined, and its length described as 'the path travelled by light in vacuum during a time interval of 1/299 792 458 of a second.'

(3) The Physical Measurement Laboratory of NIST

With the new measurement in place, the circumference of the Earth was re-defined, and the world of science heralded that light could encircle the Earth almost 7.5 times in one second.

(299792458 : 40075000= 7.48)

A great result like this is or at least assumed to be the outcome of a long string of experiments, which might somehow describe science as a sum of knowledge that has evolved in time. Although there is enough to wonder why the method for building the pyramid of Khufu remained unrecorded. As a matter of fact, that is not the only one. Other ancient cultures left behind works which prove to have been realized by making use of advanced technology. What happened to that technology is a big question. It might be that it was engulfed by cataclysms. But to demonstrate this, there is a need for evidence. Which, despite all efforts so far, proved to be scarce.

Fortunately- as this might be the most appropriate word

in this context- there is one thing, a hidden one though, that could elucidate this enigma. And that is the encoded format displayed as a mean of measurement within the walls of the Great Pyramid. Whose builders, whoever they were, possessed an intricate kind of knowledge, which they mastered to such a degree, that enabled them to search beyond the speed of light. The Royal Cubit, used for that survey, was as well calculated in a way that shows high class and subtlety in the field of measurements.

Some details about the Royal Cubit* (*seked), derived from the historical data of ancient Egypt, are presented in various works such as Building the Great Pyramid by Franz Löhner.

"The ancient Egyptians used cubits, palms and fingers as units for measuring. The cubit was divided into 7 palms and a palm into 4 fingers which resulted in 28 fingers for one cubit."

"1 finger = 1.87cm (Yeba or Zebo)
1 palm = 7.48cm (Shesep or Shep)"

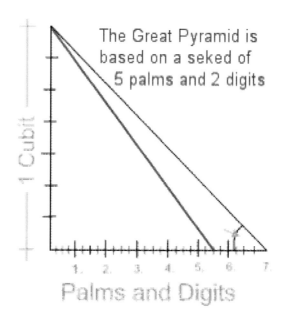

Seked 5.5 (ratio 7:11 - height to base) - The Great Pyramid Ratio
Copyright, David Furlong

Having a closer look at the dimensions of the Royal Cubit, described above, one may get a clue regarding the designer's reason to divide the sides of a right triangle by π. The Earth's circumference divided by 76.5625 yields the length of the Royal Cubit.

40075000 : 76.5625 (1000000) = 0. 52342857142857

In other words, one million Royal Cubits, multiplied by 76.5625, equals the circumference of the Earth at the equator.

0.52342857142857 (x 1000000) x 76.5625 = 40075000

What can be added here and eventually proven is that number 76.5625, obtained by using the 'older version' of the Pythagorean theorem and used to determine the length

15

of the Royal Cubit, is the key number in determining the measurement of the pyramid, including its height and the perimeter.

Aside from this, 76.5625 was used for encoding messages displayed within the structure of the pyramid. And there is a reason for this. Namely, that, this number, together with π, could be used to calculate the speed of light, which, as we will see, was encoded within the Burial Chamber. Or, such knowledge, could not have been mastered except by a sophisticated culture. Because, only to make head or tail of the speed of light, the builders needed electronic devices in the first place. Why this knowledge was not handed down is the question.

Legends of Ancient Egypt, as well as modern research, indicate that the pyramid was built by ordinary people and that, the unit of length for that survey was designed as something simple and based on choice. Resembling the forearm of a man. And as the pharaoh Khufu commissioned the pyramid, it was assumed that the unit of length was designed to depict his forearm. In the end, that was thought to meet the logic. Keeping in mind that in the past kings could indulge themselves in deciding what unit of length could have been used for their domains.

As it turns out though the length of the Royal Cubit was calculated to hint at the intricate nature of measurements at the subatomic level. The very place the human body, like anything else in the universe, emerges from and it returns to. Or to achieve that, one needs a profound understanding of transcendence for which, it looks like, there was more research in the remote past than it is now.

2. THE OLDEST FORM OF TRANSCENDENCE

Among all cultural aspects handed down from generation to generation, one stands apart. And that is the concept of transcendence. That, in a way, would not surprise anyone, since from the beginning, one of the main questions human being has wrestled with has been what happens with the Soul after the body enters extinction. The answer that has reached us is that the self never dies. A conclusion, I assume, judged upon a range of mystical experiences.

What is interesting to note is that at the time the Great Pyramid was projected, the builders debated the same concept. On this occasion, though, the transcendence of the Soul was described in an intricate, complex, language of mathematics. For that, the designer used (ontological*) data related to transcendence. That data, the designer claimed, was gained from a Solar God.

Ontological data, in this work, is a reference to the sum of knowledge the designer of the Great Pyramid claimed to have gained from a Solar God.

The said Solar-God is not descried in elusive terms that would bring to mind a religious dogma. It probably meant, in the parlance used among the builders of the pyramid, a knowledgeable traveller. Similar, somehow, to what the ancient Greek historian, Herodotus (484 - 425 BC), inferred in his work. Namely, that long time in the past, the Egyptians had a visitor of some kind. A God, he indulged to say. Who taught them all sorts of things. That, to some extent, comes in line with what the designer of the Great Pyramid said. Not to maintain that he even structured the design of that work on the sum of knowledge he acquired.

Unfortunately, from all those things surrounded by a veil of mystery, that might have gravitated within the borders of the Giza Plateau at the time the Great Pyramid was built, it only survived a legend about a famous pharaoh. Who, willing to have a Burial Chamber built within the most exquisite pyramid of all, exhausted his empire to have at any cost his wish achieved.

It is how we came to know- which otherwise is a note of great surprise- that such an elaborate monument was built by simple people, though able to quarry with no other means but copper chisels and hammers million of blocks of rock, up to 70 tones in weight. Transporting them from the immediate quarry or from hundreds of km away, as to finally be lifted, for the requested design, with a maximum degree of accuracy.

The irony is that, when all that said appeared to have remained unchanged, history turned its other side, as if intended to show that it is not the foam of an agitated ocean. And that, deep inside it, the real story of pharaoh Khufu has remained as if frozen in time. Not to maintain that such a story is at a different level. Related to some heavenly events, such as the Sothic cycle, which was encoded within the design of the pyramid.

Some argue, as if there is no alternative in seeing things beyond that, that ancient people could achieve such knowledge by merely observing the celestial movements. To prove that, though, anyone knows that it is not possible. And that because even generation after generation would spend day and night gazing into the empty sky, could not get a correct measurement of the Sothic cycle. As that stretches on more than one thousand four hundred years.

Simply put, direct observation could not have validity for everything. The most eloquent example is the size of the Sun. To the necked eye, it appears like a ball in the sky. Although the Sun is one hundred nine times bigger than Earth. Or, this became known to science only a few decades ago.

It might be that, people who lived in the remote past gained that sort of knowledge from an unknown source to us. Keeping in mind that on some artefacts that are about 40.000 years old, it is engraved some data the designer of the Great Pyramid claimed to have gained from a Solar God.

The small artefacts are not made of gold or crystal to arise great interest. Much more, the messages encoded on them are in a dot format. Or in a line format. That would indicate simple models of writings. This is probably why some people consider them a form of cultural development just in its first stage.

Only that such a thing should be carefully considered because that format is used as well in the most advanced technology of our time. The computing program uses no more than a binary: 01. To this, we will come back. What can be underlined here is that from Old Europe we do not have legends and tales of more than a few thousand years. In contrast, in the old culture of Egypt, there are legends and stories with a religious meaning, which could be related to the knowledge possessed by the builders of the Great Pyramid.

At this point in time, though, it cannot be proven when the Great Pyramid was built. What is known for sure is that more than two thousand years ago, great thinkers such as Pythagoras and Herodotus, who studied or travelled to

Egypt, tried to find out who built the three pyramids from the Giza plateau. Meeting for that the Egyptian priesthood, supposed to have the most relevant evidence about the past of that culture. Though nothing said about that would reach the target.

Closer to our time, it was invested anything possible to elucidate that matter. Unfortunately, no proper explanation could be provided. With this, the story about the Great Pyramid would have ended if there was not left behind in an encoded format an enigmatic kind of calculations. Based on which could be proven that the builders took part in sophisticated debates, similar to some extent to the modern space-time theory and the 'Big-Bang' concept.

For that kind of work, the Royal Cubic appears to have played a central role. Describing the link between each of these three operations.

A) the speed of light and π

B) the circumference of the Earth and the constant 76.5625

C) the speed of light and the square of the circumference of Earth

The decoding process of such things is not an easy task. And it could not be done except by following in the builder's footsteps. By saying this is not, however, argued that the historical evidence is useless or that it could be ignored. Practically, it all began with the historical evidence as a front runner. Fragmented as it is. But that is not enough to decode the concept of transcendence woven within the design of the Great Pyramid.

Based on historical data, the length of the Royal Cubit is said to be 52.36 cm. The same historical evidence, though, describes the length of a rope of 100 cubits as 52.24 meters.

"Because the hieroglyph for 100 (Khet or Chet) is a rolled-up rope some archaeologists think, that measuring ropes of 100 cubits were used (= 52.24m)." Building the Great Pyramid, Franz Löhner

Why then this discrepancy?

One can simply point out that in almost all cultures, the unit of length had varied over time. It might have been under a new king or due to constant developments in an empire. That fact, obviously, could not be denied. What can be argued here is that, such measurements were, on the one hand, demanded and, on the other hand, they were not based on sophisticated calculations. Simply put, they were related to some rules imposed, for example, by a king.

The two units of length of the quoted above, on the contrary, they are windows into the way the builders of the Great Pyramid mastered data related to our Solar System. As we could see, the designer divided first the Earth's circumference at equator, to get a unit of length for his survey. And the result was an unexpected one: one million Royal Cubits multiplied by 76.5625 yields the Earth's circumference at the equator.

40075000 : 76.5625 (1000000) = 0.52342857142857

The next calculation is not less exquisite: the Earth's circumference from the North Pole to the South Pole, divided by the same constant, 76.5625, yields one million cubits with the length of 0.5224 meters. Identical to the length of the cubit used for the extent of a rope of 100 cubits.

40003000 : 76.5625 (1000000) = 0.5224

These two units of length, though, hint at the hidden depth of a form of reality, we never inquired into in the way the builders of the Great Pyramid did.

In old times, in Egypt, the beginning of the year coincided with the appearance of star Sirius at the horizon. Since the brightest star in the visible sky, as the legends tell, made its appearance, annually, in the same place. An event followed by the flooding of the Nile river, that was taken probably to mean the relation between Heaven and Earth and was used to herald the beginning of a new agricultural year.

What is to be observed as well is that the Egyptians measured time not only from one year to the other; but in cycles of four years. Known as 'Sothic cycles'. Each of these periods stretching on precisely 1461 years. That length of time, divided by the constant 76.5625 and the small cubit (at a reduced scale) yields the time in a year.

$$1461 : 76.5625 \times 0.052244 = 365.25$$

The fact that the small cubit was used to determine the length of ropes of one hundred cubits (52.24 meters) indicate that those ropes were used for agricultural purposes. Which means that back in time, it was known that the succession of the seasons was due to Earth's movement around the Sun. And that the crucial role in this precession was played by the tilt/axes of the Earth. How long ago was that, or why this knowledge was not handed down, are still questions to be answered.

The Royal Cubit, as we will see, was used together with another form of measurement for encoding data within the design of the Great Pyramid.

3. THE EARTH SEEN FROM ABOVE

For almost two hundred years since the research on the Great Pyramid began, a few issues have remained the main objects of dispute. One of them, which is the most controversial, is related to the height of the pyramid. The two examples presented below are a small fraction of the enlisted work on that:

"When newly completed, the Great Pyramid rose 146.7 m (481.4 ft), nearly 50 stories high." In the second example, we get a very different view on the same. "Its height was 480 feet and 9 inches, and its base 764 feet square; in other words, it was higher than St. Paul's Cathedral, on an area the size of Lincoln's Inn Field. 145.45 m."

Copyright: Height Of The Great Pyramid, The Physics Factbook, Perkha Ahmed -- 2003

The discrepancy highlighted in the examples above has at its core one main reason. An unfortunate one, it must be said, if that would, however, fit any criteria. For, at the time the first measurement was in place, the top of the pyramid was missing. As it happened, a sudden rain of fresh opinions appeared to have fired up the mind of researchers, and the battle for who was the most competent to deliver the correct answer on that matter began. Some have suggested that the result of a great earthquake was to blame. Others considered that the appalling state of looting of the external layer of the walls of the pyramid, that took place in the previous centuries, was the main factor.

Sir Flinders Petrie, a pioneer in the field of Egyptology, trying to elucidate this matter, did estimate the height of the pyramid based on its perimeter. Pointing out that if the measurement is carried out in cubits, then the edge divided by its height yields a good approximation of 2π.

$1760 : 280 = 6.2857142$

To demonstrate what let him consider that the builders were aware of such computation, he provided another exquisite example to support his argument. "The King's Chamber walls are determined by the same π proportion which rules the exterior of the Pyramid."

(SKETCH OF HISTORY AND DESIGN OF GREAT PYRAMID, p. 94)

Only that such an argument could as well produce a thin wave of controversy. Many beginning to whisper that, as long as the Royal Cubit, the physical object, was not found, no one can claim its exact length. To further present similar examples in this regard is possible, though this would not solve our problem. Mainly because the belief that the pyramid was built a few thousand years ago and that it is the work of simple people has been like a landmark. And not many are ready to abandon that idea. How 'simple' were those people, one may wonder, as long as the greatest minds of our time could not explain how the pyramid was built. More recent research, to which is ideal to pay attention, indicates that there was a range of manipulations that affected the top evidence of historical data of old Egypt.

"The few surviving king lists are fragmented, omit certain controversial reigns, such as those of Hatshepsut and Akhenaten, and list several contemporaneously reigning dynasties (at times when the kingdom reverted to local rule in Upper and Lower Egypt) as if they reigned consecutively. Consequently, Egyptian chronology is far from exact."

Edith Watts, The Art of Ancient Egypt, made available by the Metropolitan Museum of Art.

Objectively speaking, there is not a great surprise that parts of the Egyptian historical data were altered. Such practices were probably a norm in any culture of the past. In our time, they are, perhaps, more diverse and even more troubling. About the Great Pyramid, I assume, was created intentionally or by ignorance a distorted view—that of being no more than a mortuary place. At the same time, his owner, the pharaoh Khufu, described as a cruel prince who tortured his empire to work for him as slaves.

The good part of this story is, that, whoever built the pyramid left behind knowledge which could not be altered. That, in part, is because the Great Pyramid, as well as the other two pyramids sumptuously perched on the Giza Plateau in Egypt, known by the name of their owners Khufu/Cheops, Khefre and Menkaure, are connected to each other like π (3.14) to the circumference of a circle. Having encoded within them the most sophisticated story on transcendence.

Was, then, this truth replaced with imaginary stories about an apparent mortuary role the pyramids supposedly played or, there was something else?

What we know from the little fragmented available historical data, is that Khufu's pyramid was built first. Then, the pyramid of his son, Khefre. And that, the last of the three pyramids was commissioned by Menkaure, the son of Khefre.

Paradoxically, the story of transcendence, the pyramids are endowed to carry, begins with the pyramid of Menkaure, it continues with the pyramid of Khafre, and it ends with the story of the exit from the cycle of incarnation, coded in the Burial Chamber of the Great Pyramid.

Surprisingly, none of the encrypted formulas, based on which the pyramids have been designed, is to be found in any of the known Egyptian papyri. Or at least known to have enriched the collective memory of our ancestors. Which could raise a real question about the time the pyramids were built. And the knowledge possessed by its builders. Since the height of the Great Pyramid, for example, was worked out as the frame of a universal clock. Who then knew this?

Legends tell that, at the time of its completion, the Great Pyramid was 280 cubits high. And that the length of the Royal Cubit used for that survey was about 0.524 meters. As a result, the height of the pyramid was considered by almost all Egyptologists as 146.72 meters above the ground.

What the designer shows is entirely different. There were indeed used 280 cubits, but the height of the pyramid was worked out to describe the passing of time, having the Earth circumferences- at the equator and from pole to pole- resembling the hands of the clock.

To be able to demonstrate that, the designer used the constant 76.5625 and length of the two cubits. Since they describe the Earth's circumferences.

$76.5625 : 0.5234 \times 0.5224 = 280$.

Then he went about the mean of the two cubits.

$0.5234 + 0.5224 = 1.0458$ Divided in two is $(1.0458 : 2)$ 0.5229.

That result was used to get the height of the pyramid.

76.5625 : 0.5229= 146.41 meters.

Why then did he need to do this?

Based on the Solar calendar, there are three years in a row of 365 days and a leap year of 366 days. That means a Sothic cycle. Which stretches on 1461 years.

Already maintained the Sothic cycle divided by the constant 76.5625 multiplied by the small cubit, does herald the number of days in a year.

1461: 76.5625 x 0.052244 = 365.25

To obtain three years in a row, of 365 days, and a leap year of 366 days, calculated in rapport to the height of the pyramid and the Earth's two circumferences, the designer envisioned a subtle model. The height of the pyramid divided by the units of length at a reduced scale; since they describe the Earth' circumferences.

146.41 : 76.5625 x 0.005224= 366

146.41 : 76.5625 x 0.0052344= 365

The same result could not be obtained if the height of the pyramid would have been projected at 146.72 meters, as claimed.

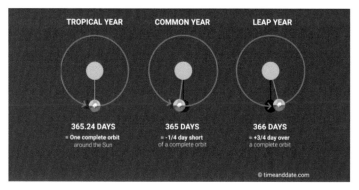

Copyright: Vigdis Hocken

At this point, we may argue that we have a clear idea about the versatility and use of the Egyptian cubit at the time the Great Pyramid was built. And could as well plead that the cubit has on its back a vast, yet complex history, tested in the physical world. There is, however, something else in this saga of measurements. Something more profound. Which one needs to handle as to be able to decode the story of transcendence and parallel universes encoded in the work of the builders. That is about the data, the designer claimed to have gained from the so-called Solar God. Which, surprisingly, is based on a system of measuring identical to our unit of length: the Meter. And it looks like the designer could understand as well that matter before making the design of the pyramid. That assumption is based on the fact that if the measurement would have been carried out in Royal Cubits alone, then we could not understand why the Burial Chamber was placed 43 meters above the ground, or why the length of the sarcophagus is 1.98 meters, for example. Since the ontological data converted in Royal Cubits has no meaning. It is precisely the way around. Converting Royal Cubits into meters.

To illustrate this with an example.

There is the belief that the pyramid was completed in 23 years. As a result, almost all calculations related to the amount of work became somehow associated with that number. How many hours a day the builders worked. How many days in a year. Or, how many stones were cut, lifted, and put in place during the day. Some specialists in the field ignored such an idea. Pointing out that it would have been impossible in that amount of time to erect the pyramid, taking into account the building compatibility of that period. In reality, the completion of the pyramid has nothing to do with that number. That is a code. A loose meaning, if we want to interpret it, would be 'the pyramid was built for eternity'.

How, then could this be justified?

To have access to the data, the designer claimed to have gotten from a Solar God, he was entrusted with a code. The Indian sages of old described that code as a sonorous substratum that maintains the equilibrium of the Universe. Hebrew Prophets claimed to be the Word of God.

Some scientists, who tried to research on anything that would allow them to gain a better insight about the hidden part of our life, travelled in the last decades to India and Tibet, as within the religious culture of these countries, there is a permanent study on the nature of mind. They as well made inquire into the old religious aspect from Old Europe, Hebrew, Sumerian, and so on. Yet, the research could not lead to something conclusive. Why that?

What it is known about the most famous mystics is that they have trained themselves to navigate the nature of mind, and had as well a full control over the functions of the body. That way is assumed, they could access that Mystic sound. The designer of the Great Pyramid argues that the Mystic sound is the core of the Soul. Who acts as a software; displaying that (ontological) encrypted data in the cells/genes of the body.

One hundred years ago, such news could have infuriated the religious figures. Thanks to science, we are somehow familiar with the notion of 'code' these days. As almost anyone uses such a thing to open a computer, an email, a bank account, and so on. We know as well that all forms of computing are based on encrypting programs. The 'code' described here as the Mystic sound, is a composite of 23 units of sound, structured in six words. That is used to unlock the 'ontological' data. That data is made up of matrices of numbers, all binary and trinary, which turn out to be encrypted data about our Solar system, and, probably, beyond. Since the builders of the Great Pyramid speak of a parallel universe. They used those matrices in their work to describe the concept of transcendence. The 'Older Version of the Pythagorean theorem', with which this story began, it is part of the same data.

   To have a better understanding of this matter, it will first be presented a few relevant facts, beginning with the code of the Mystic sound, which was described as the code of life principle. To enlighten that, or to make that number visible in the structure of things they possessed, in Southern part of the Great Pyramid, for example, was built a small pyramid, used for religious ceremonies, which is 23 times 23m. Close to Abydos, in Egypt, was uncovered the remains of 14 ships, which were buried side by side. Each of them is 23 m long. (2950-2775 BC).
   What should be underlined here is that 20.000 to 40.000 years ago, this matter, related to the so-called Mystic sound, taken as the sonorous structure that maintains the equilibrium of the Universe was known. It came almost to a halt some ten thousand years ago. And again could be achieved by a few sages and prophets in the last few thousands of years.
   In this work, it is discussed first how the builders of the Great Pyramid handle this matter. Since they could master the mathematical structures of those matrices, and displayed two of them in the design of the pyramid. That data will be compared with similar things from other cultures.
   The two matrices maintained above were researched by a

few sages from various cultures such as Hebrew and Greek. One of those matrices was known as 18 stages of enlightenment. Since this is a matrix of 18 binary on vertical. The other is composed of 14 trinaries on horizontal. Interestingly, these matrices have remained in the old culture of Egypt, though, as it turns out, they became simple graphics used by artists to describe the proportion of the body. That was in the Third, Five, and Six Dynasties. Not in the Fourth, when it is assumed that the three pyramids from the Giza Plateau were built.

I underlined this, not to leave the impression that here is presented a fairytale. It all started with the code of ontological data, which the designer encoded first at the foundation of the Great Pyramid. For that, he multiplied 23 by 76.5625, which was obtained by using the Older Version of the Pythagorean theorem. So, these two numbers are part of that encoded data.

23 x 76.5625= 1760. That means 921.21 meters, which is the perimeter of the pyramid.

One may assume that this was a well-thought formula; keeping in mind that the designer could not have accessed and eventually understand the ontological data if he was not given that code. As a result, he would not have been able to calculate the constant 76.5625 on the Older Version of the so-called Pythagorean theorem, and then access the Earth's circumference to get the length of the Royal Cubit.

To draw a conclusion on that, might be a good idea. But, in doing that we would inevitably touch the border of speculation. Since these sorts of things could not correspond to the mathematical expression, two plus two is four. What can be noted, and, could otherwise count much, is that the designer paved a way of communication between him and the Solar God. A simple look at the formula on which he calculated the speed of light, would tell us more about this.

$$76.5625^2 \times 1866.9 \times 5.234^2 = 299792459.$$

In the above calculation can be noticed a bunch of numbers multiplied to get 299792459, which is a meter higher than the speed of light heralded by science. By using the constant 76.5625 and π, in a specific way, it could be obtained the same result.

However, the designer tried to break that down to show how he could get there and why. For that, he projected what may appear to be at first glance a few alien calculations. Using the length of the Royal Cubit as if the invisible diameter of a circle ($0.52342857142857 \times \pi$) and the Earth's circumference, and played the two circles against each other.

$$0.52342857142857 \times \pi \ (\times \ 1000000) : 40075000 = 0.04103304690403$$

The result multiplied by 76.5625 hints at the value of π. Which means that at the time the Great Pyramid was built the correct value of π was not only known by used to determine the length of the unit of measurement which was in perfect 'alignment' with the circumference of the Earth.

$$76.5625 \times 0.04103304690403 = 3.1415926535898$$

I made this accolade because I imagine that the reader would prefer along with these calculations a good narrative, beginning with the time the pharaoh was born. His life as a young man. The circumstances he was crowned. And further contouring the intrigues at the court. All described in great detail, with what might be considered the most sumptuous or relevant aspect that would be thought as part of that period. Ending with a stellar ceremony about transcendence, accompanied by religious songs of an afterlife.

The reasons for not doing that is simply because what we know about the pharaoh Khufu is very questionable. It might be that, as it results from the quote presented below, we are dealing with two pharaohs bearing the same name. One, probably, from the pre-dynastic Egypt- who debated the exit from the cycle of life. The other, closer to our time. Who at the time he was born, the pyramids of Giza were there.

"An inscription on the so-called Inventory stele from the 18th dynasty (1578-1335 BC), found in the Temple of Isis from the Late Period (700-500 BC), built on the remains of the eastern chapel of the southernmost satellite pyramid of the Great Pyramid, clearly mentions that Khufu found the pyramids and the Sphinx already existing on the Gizah plateau, and restored the Temple of Isis."

Ian Onvlee, Mystery of Pyramids, Part I, page 9

To see if this is the case it will further be compared the measurements of the Burial Chamber, presented by Egyptologists, with data the designer crafted to create a hidden meaning of that chamber. The word 'hidden' may sound unrealistic. As in the Burial Chamber, there is no more than a sarcophagus. So, it can be described, at least metaphorically, as an almost barren place.

In his work A Miracle in Stone: The Great Pyramid of Egypt, Joseph A. Seiss claimed the dimensions of the Burial Chamber as follows.

"This room is an oblong square, four hundred and twelve inches long, two hundred and six broad and two hundred and thirty high."

Retrieving that measurement into the unit of length identical to our metric system we get: the length of the chamber 10.4648 meters, and the width 5.2324 meters, respectively.

The speed of light, divided by the square of the length of the Burial Chamber, yields the square of the width of the Burial Chamber.

$299792458 : 10.4648^2 (x\ 100000) = 27.37$

$(5.2324^2 = 27.37)$

In other words, one hundred thousand times the square of the length of the Burial Chamber, multiplied by the square of its width, yields the speed of light in a second.

PART 2
THE SOLAR BARGE

There is, as it was worked out as such, a subtle link between the Solar Barge, the Burial Chamber of the Great Pyramid, and the code of life principle. The said link is staged to describe a story in the language of number. The most important one known to date; which could ultimately shed light on the real role of pharaoh Khufu in this world. In the pyramids built after Khufu departed from this world, there are some texts which describe "the king's desire to unite with the sun-god re…"

It goes without saying that legends and myths, which otherwise are the oldest creative aspects of life, flourished first within the border of small communities. Due to diverse circumstances, they became part of new cultures, where, intentionally or not, at least to some extent, their meaning was altered. At first glance, it can be noticed that almost all of them are imbued with religious meaning. Under that religious dogma, though, structured to support the main idea, some of those legends and myths prove to be endowed with a thin layer of knowledge that could have scientific validation. The elusive story of the well-known Egyptian Solar Barge, sailing permanently across the sky, is such an encounter.

The said story, which had been known within the border of the old culture of Egypt for thousands of years, would have remained unchanged to this day, had the Solar Barge of pharaoh Khufu been not discovered. That happened in 1954 when, while doing some routine work at the foot of the Great Pyramid of Giza, the renowned Egyptologist Kamal El Mallakh stumbled upon some debris, which prompted him to have a closer look around. Then, drilled a hole through one of the rocks in front of him, that, to his understanding, was there to protect something and, ultimately, placed a small video camera through the hole he drilled.

To his own surprise, he realized that under his feet, in a pit, there was the Pharaoh's Solar Barge. Though, not as anyone would have expected, ready to sail down the Nile or towards the starry nights, enabling the pharaoh to meet the deity RE, as the legends told. The barge was dismantled and all its parts stacked in piles.

One may incline to think that the size of the pit in which the barge was due to be entombed was a regretful miscalculation. And that, those in charge not being able to find another solution in due time, though filled with remorse and shame dismantled the boat in as many parts as possible, placed them there, and hurriedly sealed the pit.

It can as well be assumed that the priesthood did intentionally that. Since the pharaoh used to perorate that as soon as he would exit the cycle of life, he would travel in his Solar Barge across the sky until he would meet the Solar God. If this story bares any form of truth, it might mean that the priesthood was worried that the subjects would spend much of their time gazing at the sky, eager to witness such an event. And being convinced that their expectation would end up in a bitter disappointment, the priesthood decided to entomb the barge in secret at the foot of the pyramid, as soon as the pharaoh would pass away. Then inform the subjects that they would be able to see the Solar Barge only when it would appear at the horizon signalling the return of the pharaoh. That might have worked wonders. Not because the subjects that way could have been deluded, but because the pharaoh's reputation would have remained intact.

These kinds of things are very workable. Needless to say, that they are most of the time in the drive of our mind. Ready for modelling the reality in which we live. However, what is bizarre here is that the religious story of the Solar Barge derives from work on math. Known is that the ancient stories were structured around a thin layer of symbols embedded in allegorical descriptions, as that way a great deal of information could easily be summed up. The Solar Barge, though, as briefly maintained in the previous chapter, had its design structured on ontological data and it might mean that the builders kept that secret, since, so far, no one had at least a vague idea about this.

2.

When the barge was discovered, it was not noticed anything in particular. The barge was built from wood. Like any other barge. The only thing confirmed was that the barge was structured from 1224 parts. The smallest is about 10 cm and the longest 23 meters. Another thing maintained was that the barge was dismantled and its parts stacked in 13 piles. Which, again, would not present any particularity.

How then could be proven that the design of the barge

was done on 'ontological' data the designer claimed to have gotten from a Solar God?

As can be seen in the image below, the pit in which the barge was put to rest was covered with 41 slab stones. Each in part, based on an estimation made by a Japanese team from Waseda University, weighing between 17 to 20 tones. For which there was needed more than a crane to remove them.

That means, or at least it could be assumed, that the builders planned that at their work should have access only an advanced culture, which would intend to decode the message encoded in the design of the barge. This fact would fundamentally contradict the legends that the pharaoh Khufu claimed that once reborn, he would enter the same body and continue to run his empire.

In a word, the design of the pyramid is about the transcendence of the Soul. And the design of the barge, as we will see, was worked out to match that. That mathematical display, in essence, was addressed to an elevated audience.

The first of the 41 slabstones from the pit in which the Solar Barge was placed, removed. Egypt Excavates. Ancient King's 4,500-Year-Old Ship, Published June 23, 2011
Copyright: Associated Press

The Royal Barge of Khufu (Cheops), 43.6 m (143 feet) long, 5.9 m (19.5 feet) wide
Copyright: Anthropology 316 - Introduction to Nautical Archaeology

What should be done when it comes to a decoding process as the one we are talking about here is to follow the hidden part of the story. Its poetical description, for example.

The movement of the barge, in the religious version, is an encounter about permanence: death and resurrection. The barge swings permanently from Sunrise to Sunset, then from Sunset to Sunrise.

The place from which this movement is witnessed is the Earth. And the encoding process was structured in the language of math.

How that was done?

The number of parts the barge was dismantled into, the number of piles those parts were placed in, the number of stone-slabs used to cover the pit, and the length of the barge- which is 43.6 meters- are code-numbers. We will take them one by one to see what role has each number in part in this story.

According to NASA, the average distance to the Moon is 384400 km.

A circle with diameter 1, is 3.14159265...

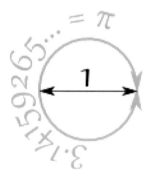

Copyright: www.mathsisfun.com

Imagine then that you enlarge circle upon circle. Until you get the distance to the Moon.

384544 : 100π= 1224, the number of parts the Solar barge was built from.

Simply put, 1224π x 100 is the distance to the Moon.

The average distance to the Sun, based on science, is 149817600km.

149817600 : 1224 x 100 = 1224

In other words the square of 1224 x 100 is the distance to the Sun.

1224^2 x 100 (the distance to the Sun).

Some would try to refute this in the idea that a number like 1223, which is just a unit smaller than 1224, multiplied by π would match almost the same result. Though, what we discuss here is very different.

If one of these numbers related to the Solar Barge is different, then the whole concept fails. Because all these numbers were calculated.

Much more, and probably the most essential element of this story, is that the designer infers and let us know a formula, from which results that the same number, 1224, is the code of a parallel universe. Why did he try to tell us all these? What can be noticed is that the designer started to bring our attention to a story of transcendence. Yet, while doing that he points out that the ontological data he gained and used in his work is part of our heritage. In other words, he intended to let us know where we should search if we want to find out what is our role on Earth.

In this context, it must be said that the story of transcendence, and the role of the Solar Barge sailing permanently between Sunset and Sunrise, initially was not a religious concept. It became in time.

Those hundreds, or thousands of gods as a manifestation of faith, have a sort of motivation, though it should be understood why they appear in religion in the first place. The 'Solar God' was associated with the Sun as the source of life. What is surprising, though, is that the same knowledge, the designer claimed to have obtained from the Solar God, was acquired by sages from different cultures. Only that in any culture the name of god is different.

The most interesting part of that knowledge appears to be the story of transcendence, which unveils in the language of math two elements. One is eternal: the Self—the other mortal: the body.

It is implied that the soul penetrates the material realm to provide data. And it lives in the body for a while. At the end of the journey, the soul departs. How, then, could the designer describe this in the language of math?

Any part of the design of the pyramid, as well as those that compose the Solar Barge, is a hint at ontological data. The word, 'ontological' might not be very pleasing to hear. As it is not poetical or casual, and it could not be as clear as a picture in front of us. The reason for being used here is that this word has some connotations in various forms of research on the nature of human being and beyond. Such as an argument about the existence or nonexistence of a god, for example. As it is presented in Stanford Encyclopedia of Philosophy.

"Many classical philosophical problems are problems in ontology: the question whether or not there is a god, or the problem of the existence of universals, etc."

This work, though, is not about my beliefs. Or just a metaphorical narrative about the existence of an entity with knowledge infinitely more sophisticated of those achieved by the human being. Here is presented some evidence, which proves to be the work of an advanced culture.

To describe the prim step of the ascension of the soul, the designer pointed out at the relation between the soul and the Mystic sound, of which we spoke, and said to be the code of the ontological data. To open the ontological data, there is a specific duration, measured, obviously, in units of time. The designer converted that amount of time and used it to describe the length of the sarcophagus since that is the last resting place of the pharaoh, who claim to exit the cycle of life. Or this is another indication that this pyramid could not have been built a few thousand years ago, because there is nowhere at least suggested that, then, there were used electronic devices to measure time.

The pyramid was probably a place for training. Debating and practicing things about transcendence. In the Great Gallery of the pyramid, as further will be presented, there are encoded, as a mean of measurement, the same elements discussed in the Indian religion: karma and ascension. The difference in the way this is presented proves that the builders were masters of hidden knowledge, that allowed them to survey the Solar system.

The Earth's circumference is one million Royal Cubits multiplied by 76.5625. According to NASA, the farthest distance to the Sun is 152093407000m. By dividing the farthest distance to the Sun one billion times 76.5625, yields the internal length of Khufu's sarcophagus.

152093407000 : 76.5625 x 1000000000 = 1,98m

This calculation brings us closer to the meaning of the Solar Barge. In that story, the barge is described as sailing permanently between sunrise and sunset. Then return. That movement, surprisingly, was calculated.

In a day there are 86400 seconds. The time needed for the Mystic sound to unlock the ontological data is 198 seconds. The length of the Solar Barge is 43.6 meters.

86400 : 198(x10)= 43.6.

In this context, could be argued that the 'Solar Barge' is a hint at the Mystic sound (the one said to maintain the equilibrium of the Universe) which travels permanently between the source of life and us. Which, probably, made its way in religion much later, and having a different meaning.

When we speak of the dimensions of a building, then, obviously, we rapport the measurement to the unit of length. Here, though, it is a story corseted in the design. To complete this narrative, it will further be presented various forms of evidence of the remote past that might make us consider that once upon a time, we were aware of this knowledge. Why then we lost that knowledge? Take as an example a diskette, on which is recorded something, and which could be overwritten.

The cultural stratum of our life is what contours our behaviour and knowledge. The other important aspect is that without accurate technology, we cannot make a significant step in understanding this ontological data. Even though let's say, we all so suddenly had access to the said Mystic sound. What we can do except to wonder about it? Let's admit, however, that in a while, some, more knowledgeable, would have the chance to open the ontological data. What they could do with it? Nothing! Because that is encrypted.

What should we do then?

PART 3
THE ROAD BETWEEN MYTH AND SCIENCE

It is the beauty of life when, as if out of nowhere, it brings to light a hidden puzzle: as the one, which, long before the Solar Barge was discovered, made the name of the Great Pyramid even more glorious.

That was in 1940 when a British Air Force pilot by the name Percy Groves noticed a particular occurrence in the shape of the pyramid.

It was before sunset and from the altitude where he was flying the pyramid appeared as an empty stage, half-covered by light while the other half engulfed in a silky kind of surreal shadow.

Intrigued by what so suddenly appeared under his eyes, and believed to be an anomaly, the pilot grabbed the camera and took a picture. After he developed the film, he intended to prove that what he saw it was not a mere occurrence and that the Great Pyramid did exhibit an eight-sided structure instead of four. As can be seen in the image below.

Image taken near sunset by British Brigadier General P. R. C. Groves, 1940

This hidden feature was known to the first Europeans explores, beginning with Sir Flinders Petrie, as Scott Creighton noted in his book The Sacred Chamber of Osiris. In the same book, he quoted the modern Egyptologist J.P Lepre concerning the same: "one very unusual feature of the Great Pyramid is a concavity of the core that makes the monument an eight-sided figure, rather than four-sided like every other Egyptian pyramid."

We may incline to think that the shape of the pyramid was worked out as part of a major religious concept, taking into account that the function of the pyramid was supposed to be, as legends tell, the last resting place of pharaoh Khufu.

That way can be assumed that the pyramid was designed as an eight-sided illusory base, resembling eight rays of light emerging- as seen in the image above- from the top of the pyramid, as if from the sun. A subtle design, one may say, intended to depict the deity RE; as he was thought to be the Solar God. Only that, the first image of the Solar God was found in the tomb of Nefertiti, the wife of Akhenaten, known as well as Amenhotep IV, who used to worship the

Solar God. The problem is not only that Amenhotep lived more than 1000 years after the time it was assumed the pharaoh Khufu lived, but what can be seen in the image below is not a form of worshipping.

Practically, what modern man think about the way people in the very remote past used to worship, if indeed they did, derives from ideas, legends, or religious encounters acquired from cultures that lived closer to our time.

Shrine stela depicting the pharaoh Akhenaten together with his wife, Nefertiti, and their children.

The rays, 'emanating' from the solar disk, seen in the portray above, are not a decorative part; they are a message in the language of numbers. Take, as an example, the sarcophagus. This object made some researchers wonder how big were the Egyptians a long time in the past. Which is a pertinent observation, otherwise. Since we all make assumptions or remarks based on feelings, the information we heard, or on what is in front of us. Yet, the sarcophagus, as said, was worked to allude to the duration the Mystic Sound takes to open the ontological data. Aside from that, it could be used to calculate the perimeter of the pyramid. It is, as well, related to the eight-sided base of the pyramid, that could clearly be seen only from space, (see the image above). All these worked out in a very intriguing way.

By extending the outer range of the sarcophagus, one hundred times, then multiplied it by eight, as many sides the pyramid has and, finally, dividing that by the internal length of the sarcophagus, it is obtained the perimeter of the pyramid.
228 x 8 : 1.98 = 921.21,
What then is the justification of such calculation?

The eight-sided shape of the pyramid was part of a concept researched and rehearsed like a play. If the external or internal length of the sarcophagus, for example, had been one centimetre longer or smaller, that infimum difference would have impacted the range of the base of the pyramid with one meter and the perimeter with four meters.
An external length of the sarcophagus of 2.29 meters, instead of 2.28m, heralds a perimeter of 925.2 instead of 921.2 meters.
2.29 x 100 : 198 = 115.65
115.65 x 8 = 925.2

Conversely, if the length is one centimetre smaller, then the perimeter of the pyramid would have been four meters smaller. This, precisely because all numbers are related between them. All of them are part of the ontological data. Therefore, they could not be changed. Much more, it goes without saying that the designer had to present his work to the pharaoh beforehand. Since the pharaoh was the one with the power to decide if the project would pass. We can imagine that the pharaoh would have had a change of mind, demanding the size of the sarcophagus to be altered. Would then such a thing be possible? Objectively speaking, yes, that could be done. But that would contradict anything the pharaoh claimed. Namely, his exit from the cycle of life. Which is woven in the design of the pyramid.

In our time, transcendence is viewed as a kind of journey into the future. Or into another dimension. The builders or the designer to be more precise used it to describe the return into the past. In different religions, the same matter related to transcendence and the so-called Mystic sound was viewed from a different angle. The Mystic sound was taken, which is not wrong, as the Word of God. And based on it was narrated a process of creation. But that probably meant in the view of whoever claimed it, that human being entered the cycle of life, based on specific data. The builders, on the contrary, let that apart and debated the return from the physical world to its source. This, at least, could be deduced from the code of the pyramid. Which hints at the One who provided knowledge of transcendence.

Previously was presented a few alien calculations, in which the length of the Royal Cubit was used to describe the diameter of a circle. That played against the Earth's circumference yielded 0.04103304690403.

That number multiplied by 76.5625 is π. And that was hidden in the pyramid. How then was done? The pyramid has four sides.

4 : 76.5625 = 0.05224897959184

This result is the radius of the circle in which the pyramid was structured. The four sides of the pyramid, as seen in the picture above, were divided into eight parts.

0.05224897959184 x 2π divided by 8 is 0.04103304690403
76.5625 x 0.04103304690403 = π.

In this structure is hidden the code of the Solar God.

As seen in the image below, taken by NASA in the northern part of Kazakhstan, there are artefacts displayed to be recognized only from hundreds of kilometers above the surface of the Earth, which could be used in decoding the puzzle presented in this work.

This square of 101 mounds is about "40 feet across and 3 feet high"…"covering more terrain than the Great Pyramid of Cheops/Khufu".

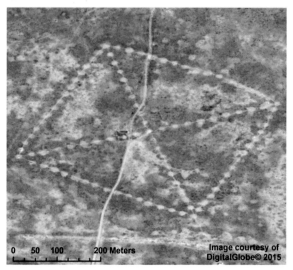

Image courtesy of DigitalGlobe

What brings the attention over this matter is the number of geo-glyphs. And the place.

The steppe of Kazakhstan, some 12000 years ago, when

this geo-glyph of 101 mounds is said to have been built, it was probably a place where shippers tried to make a living from their work. Why then so simple people would have bothered to create such artefacts?

The walls of the Burial Chamber of the Great Pyramid are built from 101 stones. And the length of the base of the pyramid divided by the length of the sarcophagus, known to be the last resting place of the pharaoh, yields the same number.

230.30 : 2.28 = 101

Surprisingly, the code of the Solar Barge, as we will see, is 101. Was then at the time the Great Pyramid was built anything in the sky, taken as a Solar Barge? And the designer encoded in the barge made from wood and entombed at the foot of the pyramid something related to this? The question is pertinent since the designer hints at a parallel universe.

However, it is at least safe to say that whoever structured that square of 101 geo-glyphs in the steppes of Kazakstan, knew that it could entirely be seen only from the sky. The same could be said about the eight-shape format of the Great Pyramid, which could entirely be seen only from the air, and only at a specific time of the year.

Another curiosity, located as well in the steppes of Kazakhstan, is a 41 geo-glyphs shaped in the form of a cross, which, the same, could be seen entirely only from high up in the sky. What can be added in this context is that both numbers, 101 and 41, are part of the ontological data. The puzzling thing is not only that the code of the Solar Barge is 101, but the pit in which the Solar Barge was put to rest was sealed with 41 stone slabs. Each in part, according to Ahmed Kadry from the Egyptian Antiquities Organization, weights about 14 tonnes.

The other aspect of this matter is related to the importance of the steppes of Kazakstan. Of which is said to be the best place for landing a space-craft.

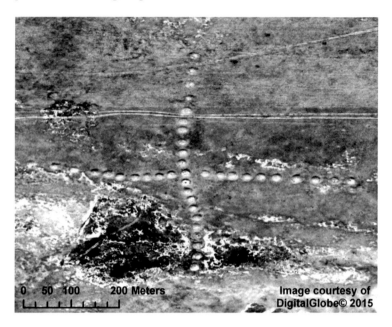

All that has been presented so far invites to proper research. Max Plank, a Nobel Prize Laureate in Physics did his part.

"As a man who has devoted his whole life to the most clear headed science, to the study of matter, I can tell you as a result of my research about atoms this much: There is no matter as such. All matter originates and exists only by virtue of a force which brings the particle of an atom to vibration and holds this most minute solar system of the atom together. We must assume behind this force the existence of a conscious and intelligent mind. This mind is the matrix of all matter."

PART 4
HIDDEN COMPUTED DATA

When it comes to symbols, mathematical formulas engraved on a piece of stone or some lines depicted on the walls of a cave, they are generally taken as a simple representation of the past. What is needed, and most of the times, unfortunately, entirely missing, is a bit of information on that particular matter, to begin with. The hieroglyphic writing of Egypt is such an example. It was brought back to life, after an absence of almost two thousand years, though all began without the slightest intention of dwelling on the lost meaning of that writing. That was during the Napoleonic campaign in Egypt in 1799.

In that atmosphere, which for sure was entirely unpleasant, a soldier saved from a building site a Stella- known today as Rosetta Stone, as it borrowed the name of the village where it was found. On this Rosetta is written a message in Ancient Egyptian (for which were used hieroglyphic signs), Demotic (the Egyptian language of that time), and Ancient Greek. The soldier had not at least a vague idea of what that writing would stand for, or that the message was bilingual. He presented the finding to his superior, Pierre-Francisco Bouchard, an army engineer, who, in his turn, informed Napoleon. As it is known, Napoleon was all the time accompanied by learned people. So, they discussed the importance of that writing, made a copy of it (lithography), and sent it to their compatriot Jean-François Champollion; known for his ability to master any language he would come across.

As it happened, just over one year, the British Empire defeated Napoleon, and the Rosetta Stone entered in possession of the winner. As no one could decipher what was written on it, they made a copy and sent it to Thomas Young, a renowned scholar from London, who began the translation.

The young Champollion recognized the Ancient Greek text on the Rosetta Stone and, as the message was a decree issued "on behalf of King Ptolemy V Epiphanes", he figured out that the hieroglyphical writing must reveal the same.
Only that, as soon the process of translation of that relatively small amount of words began, it proved to be a real hurdle. Not only because the transliteration could not be rendered in a relatively short time, but the young man himself was surprised by the unexpected difficulties, and at one point he made a halt. Thinking that would be impossible to render the encoded format of the hieroglyphs. As a simple sign would mean different things; depending on the context. At the same time, Champollion was stressed as news broke that Thomas Young would finish the translation before him.
In other words, now was the battle of the minds who struggled to decipher the hieroglyphic writing that belonged to the land they fought for.

The heaven favoured the French man to finish the translation, we may say, because the French were the ones to save the Rosetta Stone. However, at the end of that uneasy task, which stretched on no less than 23 years, the translation became a sensation; opening a fascinating field of study. Though full of obstacles, which were there as if to welcome those who dared to challenge them. And as not anyone was fit for such a task, one of the most distinguished Egyptologists, Sir Alan Gardiner, pointed out his sort of disappointment for the way various translations were rendered.

"But it must never be forgotten that the vocalizations thus provided are purely artificial makeshifts and bear little or no relation, so far as the vowels are concerned, to the unknown original pronunciations as heard and spoken by the Egyptians themselves."

Similar straightforward observations were made by Emeritus Professor, Kelly L. Ross. (The Pronunciation of Ancient Egypt, by Kelly L. Ross)

In reality, those pertinent viewpoints were not intended as real forms of discouragement for the learners of that elusive language. Instead, a rather benevolent sing to guard us, that the wheel of guessing would most of the time be in use as a substitute when the hieroglyphic writing passes through the process of translation.

All this time, it remained behind the curtains, almost entirely unnoticed, a more enigmatic matter from the old culture of Egypt. The 'mathematical language'. Of which could not be said much; since it is not similar to a language based on an alphabet. As it turned out, it was employed only by learned people to exchange information in an encrypted format.

The access to that kind of secret information requires, in comparison to hieroglyphics, a different form of decoding. Which, could, ultimately, reward us with an elaborate, precise and clear understanding of the measurements of the pyramids from the Giza Plateau. And, implicitly about the encoded format used for various stories that, as it turns out, derived from that work.

For that, and in the attempt to reveal the way that 'mathematical language' was employed, it will be first provided as an example: the hidden structure of the Solar Barge that belonged to pharaoh Khufu. Which is, as a matter of fact, crucial in cracking one of the most subtle mysteries related to transcendence.

The word 'mystery' may appear inappropriate in this context; since the pharaoh's barge is like any other barge: built from wood. And had no other means but to carry the pharaoh up and down the Nile. But why the barge was not recorded by the historical data?

In the inventory made, when the barge was discovered, there were enlisting all components of the barge. Yet, on no part of the structure of the barge was written the name of the pharaoh. It was not written, practically, at least one word or number. How then could be proven that within the design of this barge was encoded ontological data related to transcendence?

To begin with an example. Which long time in the past was not considered even appropriate for a discussion. As by then, no one could have imagined that the building block of life is sustained by a fragile entity. The Cell.

This became known in 1655. And it was due to Robert Hooke.

However, without the aid of the microscope, such a discovery could not have been possible. Let alone the improvement in recent decades on the same, thanks to advanced technology.

The reason for underlining these things is that the ontological data, is, as briefly maintained, the core of the Self. Which as well could not be seen with the necked eye. This is why there are endless debates on this.

In Egypt, the last pharaoh who had access to this knowledge was Amenhotep, the heretic, as they called him. The one who tried to abolish all sorts of religions and promote what he considered to be the most appropriate—a kind of religion, which is said to have only been on the time of pharaoh Khufu. Amenhotep's intention was good. But how can you convince an empire with hundreds of deities worshipped daily, that what they had done so far was wrong and what you propose them to do is wright?

Accepting that, the whole empire would have listened to Amenhotep and has done anything he said without reservation. That could not have stayed with them for good. Because religion, as we know it, it is not science. And if a god is described as loving, caring, forgiving, etc., then the believers would wonder why all this misery, inequality, war, that penetrated all stratum of our societies.

So, we can go around…debating who we are and what is our role on Earth. But if we cannot unlock what role the soul has, we cannot solve what is most important for us. As this matter, as the designer of the pyramid argues, is related to transcendence.

When the Solar Barge was discovered, it was noticed that the way the barge was dismantled was not random. And that there was in place a plan. Which appeared to be the simplest and the most natural. The parts of the Solar Barge were placed to indicate the easiest way the barge could be reassembled. Its parts were gathered in 13 pails. Giving the impression that it was done that way just to maintain a sort of order in the distribution of the parts.

However, when the length of the barge, the number of its parts, the number of piles, and the number of slabs the pit in which the barge was placed, were computed, the result was puzzling.

To begin with, it will be presented (first) two simple calculations.

1) The pit was sealed with 41 slab stones. Each in part about 17 to 20 tones, if we quote the experts from Waseda University of Japan.

Keeping in mind that in the design of the barge was encoded data about transcendence, it might not be a surprise to see that the number of stones divided by π is 13.

41: 3.14 = 13.

The only artefact that depicts the pharaoh Khufu is an ivory statuette of 76 millimeters. In which the pharaoh appears as a humble man. The statuette could have been calculated in relation to the height of his pyramid, at a reduced scale. 7.6 meters, for example.

Only that the pharaoh considered that such a colossal statue would undoubtingly shadow the importance of his work. Or would portray him as an ordinary ruler, not as a man of wisdom. And asked the designer for an alternative.

The answer came more or less as a surprise. The designer presented his master a unique formula:

a circle with a diameter 1. Its circumference is π.

π : 41 = 0.076 meters. Which hints at the height of Khufu's statuette.

What then is this 41?

It is said that God, long time in the past, sent a secret Word to a few sages. Each of them living in different lands. To be able to understand what that Word was about, the sages had to pass 18 stages. A real journey, through which they would master some knowledge as finally to become able to grasp the meaning of that sacred Word.

Some call that journey enlightenment and considered to be the highest achievement of a sage.

That Word is what the designer described as the Code of the ontological data. Which is, as said, a composite of 23 units of sound.

Greeks sages described that code as the Word/Logos on which was designed the Universe. The Indians, as already maintained, described It as the sound that maintains the Universe. Hebrew sages claimed That as the Word of God.

The two numbers, 18 (stages) and 23 (units of sound) are crucial elements in the decoding process of the Great Pyramid.

18 + 23 = 41

Based on this number could be calculated the height of the pyramid and the Royal Cubit. For this is used the relation between the constant 76.5625 (based on which was determined the length of the Royal Cubit) and 41.

76.5625: 41 = 1.867378

1.867378 x 28 (the number of part of the Royal Cubit) = 52.29 which means 0.5229 meters.

That was, as it was proven before, used to define the height of the pyramid. The pyramid is 280 cubits height.

0.5229 x 280 = 146.41 meters

From the subterranean chamber of the Great Pyramid, to the ceiling of the Burial Chamber, where the process of transcendence was said to take place, there are 78,26 meters. As seen in the design below.

18(x 100) : 23 = 78.26

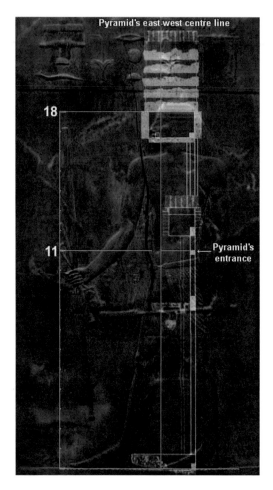

Pyramid's east west centre line

18

11 ← Pyramid's entrance

The merit of the designer of the Great Pyramid is enormous. Not only because he used the ontological data, for the design of the Great Pyramid, but because he structured it in such a way that it could be decoded.

The Solar Barge, as we could see, was meant to express the relation between two things: the sunrise and sunset.

However, the barge, in the end, was entombed. Here, too, would represent the relation between two things. Only that they lack movement.

The speed of light is 299792458. Under zero is 0.299792458.

0.299792458 x 43.6 = 13, the number of piles in which all parts of the barge was stacked, then entombed.

What in the end would this number tell us?

A number theory, called partition, describes in how many parts a number could be divided. Based on that theory number 4, for example, could be divided into 5 ways (as seen in the diagram below).

4
3+1
2+2
2+1+1
1+1+1+1

Number five could be divided into seven parts. And so on.

With this simple method, the designer revealed one of the most unexpected things. Number 13 could be divided into 101 parts. Pointing, this way, at the relationship between the Solar Barge and the Burial Chamber of the Great Pyramid, built from 101 stones.

On the one hand, it could be suggested that the pharaoh treated the Solar barge, like any other being, who has a soul. And decided to have his Burial Chamber resembling the soul of his beloved barge. As the story goes, he claimed to travel in his barge after he exits the cycle of life. By any means, the pharaoh was not a dreamer. Number 101 corresponds in this context, to the 'soul' of the Solar Barge. Which in its turn reflects the inner of the Burial Chamber, which is structured for the setting of transcendence.

Metaphorically, yes, it could be argued that the intent of the designer was to show that the soul of the pharaoh and the soul of his barge was in no way different. That ultimately would mean that anything has a soul.

But, things here are approached from a different perspective. The name of the barge is related to the Sun. The Sun's circumference is 109 times larger than the Earth.

109 x 40075000 (the Earth's circumference) is the circumference of the Sun: 4368175000

Which means that the length of the Solar Barge, 43.6 meters, is one hundred million times smaller than the Sun's circumference.

If the story would have ended here, we may have considered that all that the pharaoh claimed was but a tale. However, the pharaoh takes us on a journey to a parallel universe.

In ancient Egypt, the belief in the existence of Self after parting from its body was well researched. But like in any situation where some abstract elements are used to better describe a reality that hinges between what can be seen and what is behind the veil of immediate reality, here, too, things appear to show some inconsistency. The most known description on this suggests that the life force, known as BA, would remain close to the one who passed. Life-force is said to be the one that maintains as well the Self, known as KA. Both of them being spiritual entities. However, they as well believed that there is another entity, known as AKH, which could accompany the soul of the dead, if that one deserves, to another dimension.

The designer of the Great Pyramid, described all that in the language of math. Despite all odds, though, the narrative expressed in that language brings forward an elegant portrait of the three forms of existence, that would survive the body. As well as describing an inanimate thing- the Solar Barge- that has a soul. In doing that, the designer underlines why the barge was dismantled into 1224 parts, why the smallest part of that barge is 10 cm, the longest 23 meters, and why all parts were gathered in 13 groups.

Another important aspect of this matter is the exact length of each side of the base of the Great Pyramid. Specialists in the field confirmed that the

North and the South is 230.25 meters, and the

East and West sides, 230.36 and 230,39 meters, respectively.

Would this arrangement suggest anything?

The base of the pyramid is asymmetric. Some say that it based on calculations. Others consider that there was a mistake.

The science argues that the axis of Earth undertakes a slight swing between 22.1 and 24.5 degrees once in just over 40000 years.

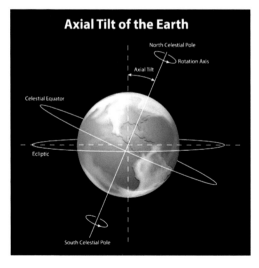

PART 5
PARALLEL UNIVERSES

In his book, Just Six Numbers: The Deep Forces that Shape the Universe, Lord Martin Rees, one of the leading astronomers and cosmologists, tried to demonstrate that "Our whole Universe is governed by just six numbers, set at the time of the Big Bang."

Each of the six numbers is said to indicate one of the key aspects of our Universe, such as dimension (in which we live), dark matter, the strength of gravity and so on.

How much we can understand from this demonstration is hard to say. Though we grant science for almost anything it provides to us. Surprisingly, the scientific approach about the beginning of life due to a spontaneous burst of energy was preceded by certain religious concepts in which the same number, 6, underlines the prim step in the manifestation of life in the Universe. On this occasion, though, all is said to be orchestrated by a conscious mind.

"Six is a number perfect in itself, and not because God created all things in six days; rather, the converse is true. God created all things in six days because the number is perfect", wrote Saint Augustine, one of the most influential clergies, in his work entitled The City of God. The book was written after the fall of Rome in 410, as to provide some answers to all sorts of accusations made by the Romans. Who claimed that the decline of their beloved city, thought otherwise to be eternal- was the result of the acceptance of the new religion, known as Christianity.

Saint Augustine intended to prove that Rome fell to invaders not because it embraced the new faith, but because, before Christianity, Rome used to worship unworthy gods. However, he was conscious that his argument could not have been entirely convincing, and then he tried to underline that even God may be dependent on certain things.

Long before the City of God was written, the Tibetans meditators appear to have dealt with a particular aspect of creation in which the same number, 6, plays an important role. In one of their oldest documents, known as the Stanza of Dzyan, is alluded that the Mighty One uttered the mystical sound AUM six times while proceeding from the first to the last stage of creation of the Universe. This religious concept, though, does not reveal the same mechanism seen in the first biblical statement, where the process of creation takes place in the first six days, and then, in the seventh, God takes a rest.

In the Stanza of Dzyan, the Mighty One, after uttering six times the mystical word AUM, tried to tidy things up:

'Again He gathered in the sound. He drew to higher levels the feeble spark of light. Another tone was heard, the sound of cosmic fire, hid in the Sons of Mana'.

Translation by A. A, Bailey

There is, however, a more sophisticated aspect in which the same number, 6, plays a crucial role. Which science could not explain. It is said that if a human cannot see a writing format in order to read it, then the hand's sense of touch can help them to understand. The Frenchman Louis Braille (1809-1852) who at four, as a result of an accident, lost his sight, continued the work of Charles Barbier, a soldier, who invented 'night writing', a parole system used at night by soldiers to pass on secret information. Louis Braille developed this system of language without lettering. A method in a dot format…and his hands 'told' him that everything could be expressed through six 'words'.

In Japan, this language was introduced during the Meiji period. But there something inconvenient took place. Japan had in use three kinds of writing: hiragana, katakana and kanji. For that, they tried to develop another 'Braille' system. Though on this occasion, they realized they could not use more than six words. And this because the blind people's hands 'told' them that they didn't need more than six to express their feelings, emotions, and thoughts.

Sure, one may ask if the number itself has any properties. The answer is that numbers have no properties. So, it is not the number itself. It is something else related to numbers. And that has been the object of study of mystics of old. For example, one of the major players, concerning the nature of Mind, Shaka-muni of India, known as the Buddha or the Enlightened man, left behind among many teachings a work entitled Sad-dharma Pundarika Sutram, rendered in English as The Lotus Sutra.

That title gave food for thought to many people. As the first word in the title is almost untranslatable. However, the last disciple of Buddha, known as Nagarjuna, translated that work into Chinese. And he was the one to reveal that "Sad, from the title of the sutra, means six. Or perfect endowment."

The Opening of the Eyes | WND I | Nichiren Buddhism Library

As the builders of the Great Pyramid were masters on numerology, we may wonder if the number 6, which in math is considered to be the first perfect number, was part of their investigation. The measurement of the Great Pyramid is, as we could see so far, structured to deal with transcendence. The constant π is related to transcendence. Many of our contemporaneous, would disagree, pointing out that π is related to the circumference of a circle and no more. Even though π can describe a circle with diameter 1.

3.1415926535 : 6 = 0.52359, the length of the Royal Cubit.

The problem is that some modern thinkers view people who lived in the remote past as simple dwellers able only to provide food for their existence. Pointing out, proudly, that thanks to a continuing process of evolution, we are in a better position these days. Arguing as well that the most famous pyramids were built by ordinary people and that the sophisticated concepts such as immortality, immutable laws, and karma- which was used to describe something behind the visible curtain of manifestation of life, which could not be perceived by the naked eye, were mere speculations. But if you pay attention to the train of thought of some renown thinkers, you may notice that they began lately to debate these concepts.

The Greek Anaximander (610 BC-546BC) inferred that we live in parallel universes. The philosopher Plato, of the same origin, asserted that the Universe in which we live is illusory, related to another Universe, of forms, that never changes. In other words, our 'mortal' Universe- which flourishes and dies periodically- is nourished by a Universe that never dies.

Anaximander and Plato were not dreamers. They knew something that has remained unrecorded. Practically, it can be proven that in the past, there was a source of knowledge, to which, it looks like, some had access. There are, for example, a few mathematical methods, which appear strange, and yet, they could be used for a more in-depth insight concerning the metaphysical concepts related to the manifestation of life.

To illustrate this with an example.

The Academy of Jerusalem…Torah from Zion Project, The New Israeli Genesis Exegesis, years ago, made the following remark in regard to whoever wrote the first biblical statement:

"Our understanding of their saying is that the letters and words of the first sentence of Genesis comprise a hidden "utterance" in which are encoded the principles of the Creation."

At the time when a work/concept, like the one related to the first biblical statement was written, it was taken into account a few things. One of them is the narrative. In this case, the argument about creation. Second in line is the format of the text. Which is represented by the number of words and the number of letters those words are made up. And third is its mathematical format. Why there were used seven words, and one of those words is untranslatable. Why those words were structured from 28 letters. Why the first part of the statement is made up of 14 letters. And so on.

That mathematical structure refers to a code of a specific 'utterance', which is said that was used by God in His pursuit of describing the hidden phenomena of life.

The first biblical statement (see below), translated from the Greek language by Ivan Panin.

2-20-1-21-10-22-- In beginning
2-20-1-- He created
1-12-5-10-13—God

1-22--***
5-21-13-10-13-- the heaven
6-1-22-- and
5-1-20-18-- the earth

The word in position two is underlined with the numbers 2-20-1 (therefore 23 as a sum), and it stands for He created (or creation).

The word in position four, in number, is 1-22 (as a sum is 23), which refers to something based on which the process of creation was worked out.

That, may indicate the Mystic sound. The code, the designer of the Great Pyramid referred at.

That code is a six-word formula, which is a sum of 23 units of sound. So, it could be argued that whoever wrote that first biblical line knew a secret, which was as well mastered by the builders of the Great Pyramid.

The six-word formula is a composite of 16 letters. Yet, if the letters that repeat once or more times in their original format are taken out, what then remains are four vowels, five consonants, and a cluster NG. Similar to a counting system in base 10.

As this six-word formula is made known eighteen times-described in religion as 18 stages of enlightenment-, that was taken as a sum. The number of words, 6, multiplied with the number of times, 18, gives 108. A number that became part of various concepts, beginning with the idea that the Soul is unborn, and indestructible. The number of feelings a body is endowed with. The number of books composed by a master. Or the number of steps that leads to a temple.

Here there are some examples, in which number 108 is used:

1) Atman goes through 108 stages.
('Ātma (/ˈɑːtmə/) is a Sanskrit word that is equated to inner self or soul. It is described in the Bhagavad Gita as being unborn, eternal, omnipresent, constant, and immovable.')
2) Yogis claim that we possess 108 feelings.
3) The Heart Chakra is said to have 108 energy lines.
4) Lord/God Krishna had 108 servants.
5) Upanishads were compiled in 108 distinct books.
6) Buddha's work, apparently, was comprised in 108 volumes.
7) The Chinese Buddhists and Taoists use a 108 bead mala- Su-Chu.
8) At the entrance of some of the Buddhist temples, there are 108 paved steps.
9) Some exoteric texts point out to the fact that Jesus Christ would have had 108 disciples, not including the apostles.

Here is presented the hidden part that led to those concepts: the schematic format of those 18 stages of enlightenment. Following this, it will be shown the second matrix, which is termed as "14 stages". Both of them were used in the design of the Great Pyramid. These matrices, as we will see, are complex. But for a proper demonstration, they are first presented as a grid. Then, they will be upgraded.

The sign 0 indicates the beginning. The 0> refers to a small unit of time that takes place during that process. And the sign <> , depicts a pause.

Grid I (18 squares on vertical)
-0--
01
02
0>
01
02
03
<>
04
05
06
<>
07
08
09
0>
01
02
03
<>
04
05
06
<>
07
=76

The sum of all these stages, which signals the unveiling of a specific knowledge, which at first appears simple, is 76. The sum of all numbers that underline the first biblical word is 76.

2-20-1-21-10-22-- In the beginning

The code, which the designer of the Great Pyramid inferred to have it gained from a Solar God, and based on which was claimed to open the ontological data about our Solar system, is structured from 23 units of sound. The word Creation in the first biblical statement, which implies that the process of Creation was done on the power of sound, it counts to 23.

2-20-1-- He created

The sum number of the letters of an untranslatable word, in position four in the first biblical statement, which stands probably for "creation out of something unknown", counts as well to 23.

1-22--***

As the number of stages of enlightenment in which is made known the Mystic sound is 18, and the units of sound (that sonorous structure is made of) are 23, that was summed as 41.

18 + 23 = 41.

The name of God/Elohim, in the first biblical statement, counts to 41.

1-12-5-10-13—God

What can be noticed here? Greeks and Hebrew sages created what is known as Alphanumerics. The Hebrew alphanumeric has 22 letters. The first letter, Alef, with its number correspondent 1, and the last letter of the alphabet, Tav, with its numeric value 22.

The first and the last letters (1 + 22) of this alphanumeric suggests the closing of a circle. The logic behind this apparent simplicity was to hint at the word Creation, underlined with the number 23. Since the process of creation was thought to have been done on the power of sound.

In the Greek alphanumeric, Alpha has the numeric correspondent 1, while the last letter, Omega, 800. Here, the same, the first and the last letter were meant to describe a circle. 1 + 800= 801.

That hints at the numeric value of the famous statement, 'I am Alpha and Omega', attributed to God, which in number is 801.

Why did the Greeks do differently? In other words, why didn't they show that their alphanumeric is related to the Word of God?

To almost anyone these days, such things would appear as a kind of absurdity. What "I am Alpha and Omega" would in the end mean? One may wonder. And why should that be underlined with the number 801?

The two matrices (maintained above) describe a story related to transcendence. As the first matrix heralds the beginning of that story, associated with a process of creation, the second matrix deals with the exit from the cycle of incarnation.

Both of them were known in Old Europe. That could be judged on the information encrypted on artefacts.

The builders of the Great Pyramid used them for the survey of the pyramid. In the Third and the Six Dynasty, though, Egyptian artists used them to display the proportion of the human body, as described in 'Proportion and Style in Ancient Egypt' by Gay Robins.

"While figures were drawn on a grid of 18 squares, seated figures usually consisted of 14 squares from their soles to their hairline."

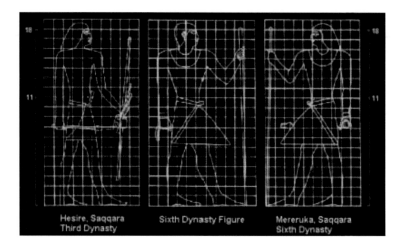

Hesire, Saqqara
Third Dynasty

Sixth Dynasty Figure

Mereruka, Saqqara
Sixth Dynasty

A subtle measurement of this kind was underlined as a hidden part of the structure of the Great Pyramid by Vincent Brown in his work Pyramid of Man.

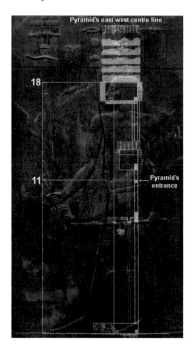

So far, it was presented only the format of a matrix, as a grid, which could be noticed that had an impact on some cultures of old. Yet, to see how sages dealt with a more complex matter related to the same, it has to be discussed the method they employed to solve that. That method has been handed down, but not entirely. It was known as the mirror reflection of a number. In other words, a number such as 12 would show its opposite side as 21. The process of turning a number into its opposite, though, was calculated.

This formula is similar to what in molecular biology is called palindromic sequences. Or, in mathematics, a palindrome. A Greek word made up of two words: 'pálin' which means again, and 'dromos', with the sense of 'running'. It might be that initially, 'palindrome' meant running 'back' (on the same road), and lately has been used to describe a word or a sentence which read backwards has the same meaning. Like the words "mom" or "dad". Some numbers display a similar format. Where the numeric value- when they are read from left to right or right to left- such as 11 or 33, remain the same.

Some mathematicians have tried their hand at finding out a method of turning each number into a palindrome. As there was no direct road to the heart of palindromes, they used a roundabout way, instead; as it can be seen in the example below.

Here, number 78 is used as a root number from which could be obtained a palindrome.

$78 + 87 = 165$

$165 + 561 = 726$

$726 + 627 = 1353$

$1353 + 3531 = 4884$

The ancients used a different method by which could be turned any number, instantly, into its opposite. From the same number, 78, given in the example above, ancient sages could get 78<>87. Metaphorically, it can be said that 87 is the reflection of 78. In reality, the set-number on the right side is calculated from the set-number on the left side. They did that to get access to the two grids of numbers (presented here), and see what information they can get from them. This, however, imply that they had some knowledge already about that, as they spoke about creation, transcendence, as well as about the exit from the cycle of life.

From science is known that there are needed two pairs of chromosomes for a being before entering the realm of life. One from mother and one from father. Though, 'Without the presence of the Self' as Erwin Rohde wrote in his book Psyche, 'the body cannot perceive, feel, and wish'. To this, he added a reasonable conclusion: 'Yet Self does not manifest these faculties and all the other actions by the psyche or through it'.

Having a closer look at the segment of a DNA (depicted below), one particular thing may ring the bell.

A	T	G	G	C	T	A	C
|	|	|	|	|	|	|	|
T	A	C	G	G	A	T	A
|	|	|	|	|	|	|	|

One is that "DNA, from this simple format, which resembles a ladder, turns into a kind of spiral, and then it continues its path until it reaches the structure of a chromosome."

U.S. National Library of Medicine

The second aspect, which is even more important, is that "The two strands can be pulled apart like a zipper, and because each base can only pairs with its complement, all the information of the double-stranded sequence can be obtained from a single strand."

Lisa Von Pay and Kevin Norris, the National Science Foundations

The builders of the Great Pyramid, turned those two grids into matrices, got the idea about what they would mean, and used them for the core of the story on transcendence and parallel universes. One of the things that has to be underlined here is that they could do that because the system of counting they used is binary. 01 to 09.

For the completion of the so-called mirror-reflection of a number, there are made the following steps. It is first divided the binary in two: base (left) and extension (right).

Number 12, for example, would have the base 1 and the extension 2.

To describe this movement, namely, how 12 turns into 21, it can be used this symbol<>, which could be called 'turn into'. 12 <> 21.

All binary abide by the same rule.

The procedure is initiated by number 9, which helps a set number re-store its data. To get that, number 9 is multiplied with the first number from right to left.

The first number from right to left in the set number 12 is 2.

9 x 2= 18

Then each of the digits of the binary 12 is added.

1+2= 3

Finally, the first and the second result are added.

18+3=21

In the same way 21 turns into 12

21:

9 x 1= 9

1+2=3

9+3=12

21<>12

This is the rule for all binaries.

For trinary (set of three numbers), the number is divided in the same way: base and extension.

297

9 x 79= 711

79+2= 81

711+81= 792

The revers of the 297 is 792

792=

9 x 29= 261

29+7=36

261+36= 297

792<>297

If a set number is already 'palindromic', like 525, for example, the method is the same.

525

9 x 52= 468

52 + 5 = 57

468+57= 525

525<>525

Modern science argues that the field of the electron has its 'mirror-reflection' somewhere else. Would numbers underline that unseen world as well? That would mean that the universe is a hologram of some kind. The way the ancient people used the counting system in all calculations related to knowledge on ontology- which describes the manifestation of life- indicates that they had an idea about this. The designer hints at one of these hidden things.

The first grid of 18 set numbers on vertical (see above) turns into this matrix (see below).

```
01 < > 10
02 <> 20
___ 0___
01 <> 10
02 <> 20
03 <> 30
   0
04 <> 40
05 <> 50
06 <> 60
   0
07 <> 70
08 <> 80
09 <> 90
___0_ __
01 <> 10
02 <> 20
03 <> 30
   0
04 <> 40
05 <> 50
06 <> 60
```

0
07 <> 70
=76......=760
760- 76 =684

The only statuette that describes Khufu is 76 mm. And the external length of the sarcophagus is 228 cm.

228 x 228 = 51984

The result obtained from the above calculation is 684.

76 x 684 = 51984

Radical from 51984 is 228.

What then is that 684? In other words, what does it stand for?

The sarcophagus was built to describe the relationship between the soul of the pharaoh, and the Higher Self.

Already discussed, the Egyptian religion of old argued that the soul is guided by an entity to a higher realm/dimension. Which implies a form of transcendence. Notice that, in the mathematical description of the designer, the unit of length is linked to this knowledge.

The constant 76.5625 was used to determine the length of the Royal Cubit. In the historical data, apparently, the length of the cubit is 52.36 cm. The result from the matrix above is 684.

76.5625 x 684/1000 =52.36.

Another intriguing thing is related to the code number of the Solar God. Which is 612. To calculate that number, the designer used all prime number from 1 to 100. The sum of all primes is 1060. To get 612, the designer used the same method presented in the matrix above. Why 612? And not another number?

612 + 612 = 1224, the number of parts from which the Solar Barge was built, in which pharaoh Khufu claimed to sail across the sky, until he would meet the Solar God: a subtle reference about soul and the Higher Self.

The beginning of that calculation remained encoded in the Bible. It is about Jesus and Peter while the later was fishing. Seeing that Peter was disappointed because he could not catch anything, Jesus gave him a hand and Peter could suddenly catch 153 fishes. This story puzzled many people. Wondering what that number would stand for.

Based on the narrative, Peter went fishing at night, and was not able to catch anything. Yet, when the Lord came... as Light, Peter put on him the fishing coat. In this context, the fishing coat plays a symbolic role. The Greek word for the fishing coat in number is 1060. Which is the sum of all prime numbers from 1 to 100 in the Sieve of Eratosthenes. So, it is the Sieve that resembles a fishing coat.

"The vesica that contains him represents the fisher's coat, for the Greek word is ελληνικά 1060, and since the width of this vesica is 612, its height is 1060."

Truth & Revelation by Moshyia de Broek .

In the Hebrew narrative, Jesus advised Peter to cast the net once to the right. As Peter followed the instruction, he got 153 fishes. Already presented, to turn a number into its opposite, there are some rules. The numbers on the right are calculated from the numbers on the left. And 'casting the net once to the right' is related to the order in which the calculation is done.

The prime numbers symbolize something indestructible. As they could not be divided. As it is the soul.

All prime numbers in this operation follow the order in which they are in the system of counting from 1 to 100. Here is the first result. As they are 25 primes, they are divided into seven groups. 4-4-4-1-4-4 4. Which is a palindrome.

In position 13 is number 41. The end results show the same key numbers discussed in this work: 414 and 198.

Here is the first setting:

02<>20
03<>30
05<>50
07<>70
=17 =170
170 - 17= 153

It could mean that in the remote past, these kinds of mathematical calculations were used for teaching. And they were embroidered in all sorts of narratives, which probably had a religious meaning as well, keeping in mind that the technique applied was based on knowledge claimed to had been revealed.

PART 6
HIDDEN KNOWLEDGE

A few thousand years before the Great Pyramid is said to have been built, in another part of the world, namely the Bay of Guayaquil, Ecuador, was concealed an artifact with the shape of a pyramid. Known as the Pyramid with the Eye.

Photo Copyright Project Avalon & Klaus Dona

It is said that this artefact was brought there by people who lived on the 'disputed' continent Atlantis. And that the artefact is about 12.000 years old. What is very interesting to note is that this artefact has a very specific design. The pyramid unveils 13 levels. On top of them, there is an eye. Very curious is the fact that when the artefact is shrouded in darkness, its enigmatic eye (as seen in the image below) shines.

A real wonder, which no one could explain since no one knows what material is that eye made of.

 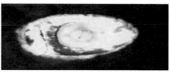

PhotoCopyright Project Avalon & Klaus Dona

On the bottom of the artifact, surprisingly, is depicted the constellation Orion accompanied by four letters/words.

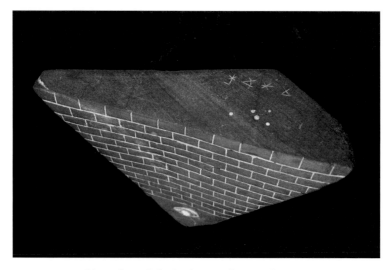

PhotoCopyright Project Avalon & Klaus Dona

These words/letters, as Klaus Dona confirmed, were translated by Kurt Schildmann, the President of the German Linguistic Association. Who concluded that they mean: "The son of the creator comes."

As well as Kurt Schildmann confirmed that this writing is at least 6000 years old; preceding Sanskrit writing. The curious fact is that those four letters are a composite of 13 lines.

Similar writings could be found in different parts of the world, which indicates that an unknown civilization preceded all our known civilianizations.

In the same place where the Pyramid with the Eye was discovered- namely in the underground tunnel in the Bay of Guayaquil, Ecuador-, it was found this big cup, accompanied by another 12 cups, much smaller. A set of 13 pieces. All made of jade.

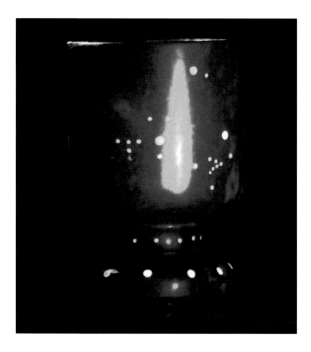

Copyright: Claus Dona & Project Camelot

Each of the 12 small cups has a slightly different size, and on each one is written a different number. On the big cup, there is designed a star constellation. Which becomes extremely bright in the absence of light. Or, to realize such a thing, there is a need for a special technique.

What else can be observed at this set of 13 cups is that the quantity of water held by the big cup, full to the brim, is equal with the needed amount of water to fill the 12 small cups to the brim. Showing this way that the set of cups was based on careful measurement.

Another important artefact found in the same place is a helmet (see the image below) made of granite. On it, a cluster of 13 dots in the central part, and an 'isolated' dot in the upper part of the artefact.

1) Unfinished helmet. 2) Finished helmet- covered in 'dark' light. Copyright: Klaus Dona & Project Camelot

Klaus Dona, who researched these artefacts, has suggested that the cluster depicted on the helmet- which in the absence of light becomes very bright- indicates the acupuncture places on the human scalp (Klaus Dona & Project Camelot- YouTube). That would mean, as the researcher concluded, that the role of the helmet was no other but to be used to revival the key energetic points of the head.

As these artefacts are very unusual, very sophisticated in

their intricate properties, and keeping in mind that no one knows where exactly or how they were made, it was assumed that they were crafted by people who lived on the continent Atlantis. The existence of this continent, which apparently was engulfed by waters in a single day, was confirmed by the Greek philosopher Plato. That might be true. As, among the artefacts found in the underground of Guayaquil, there is a stone-map (see image below), of which is said to be about 10 to 12000 years old. On it, there is depicted what has been considered to be the old maritime route, used in those days as a link between the small continent Atlantis and the place where the artefacts were found.

In the end, this does not exclude the fact that those arte-facts could have as well been worked out in the same place they were found. If that would have been the case, then a new string of questions would need to be answered. Such as: Who inhabited first that place? What else did they produce? Or, how did they interact with other cultures?

Obviously, it would be ideal to know such things. But how to find them out when 99% of our history has been lost for eternity?

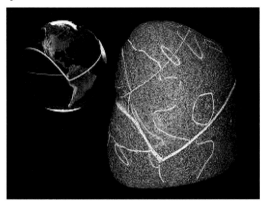

Copyright: Claus Dona & Project Camelot

Interesting to note is that number 13, of which is said to bring misfortune, was depicted in various ways on some of the most exquisite artefacts from a time and a culture that remained totally unknown to us. A more in-depth analysis of these artefacts would reveal why number 13 was taken as being inauspicious.

As can be seen, each of these artefacts has an extra element to it. The pyramid with 13 levels has an eye in the upper part. The helmet, has aside those 13 dots, in the upper part, an extra dot, isolated from the rest. The Big jar, accompanied by 12 cups needs water as the additional element to fulfil the reason it was made.

We may wonder what made those people work those artefacts that way, and what is their meaning, in the end. A direct, conclusive answer no one has. And yet, there are some bits of information that would enable us to get the meaning of those artefacts.

Many of us came across the famous saying "I am Alpha and Omega" attributed to God. And we just thought that it is no more than a narrative. A sage just described God as omnipotent. Nothing unusual, in the end.

Seeing the same saying worked out on the Greek alphanumeric that counts, in number, to 801, that might be taken as a peculiarity. And if we have to choose which of the two would provide for us a better understanding of that saying, we all will hint at the narrative. As that makes sense. The truth though is that the original meaning of that saying derives from the set-number 801. Which sounds absurd. How from a set-number to work out a saying? And much more, attributed to God.

The two matrices maintained before, one is structured from 18 binary. The other of 14 trinary. As it turns out, the two matrices are nothing but encoded data about transcendence and parallel universes.

In the second matrix, of 14 set numbers (297,414,198,90 9,356,356,359,198,913,247,356,247,198,801,000), in position 14, there is the set-number 801. The surprising thing is that all 14 set-numbers could be reduced to 801. I assume that the first who could decode that was the designer of the pyramid. How could he do that, and what then is that related to, are the good questions.

Based on modern science, as physicist Michio Kaku explains, when a universe reaches 13 dimensions becomes unstable. Only that, science argues that life on Earth came into being due to a burst of energy, known as the Big Bang. From the story on transcendence is understood that behind the veil of immediate reality, which we perceive, there is "an Intelligent and Conscious Mind", as the Nobel Laureate in Physics, the German Max Planck, put it.

The set number 801, as we will see, refers to a universe which has 11 dimensions. The number 1224, which is the number of parts in which the Solar Barge was dismantled into, stacked in 13 piles, then entombed, is a hint at a universe that is unable to further sustain life, as it reached 13 dimensions.

But first, let's see why all set numbers from the matrix of 14 set numbers could be reduced to 801.

We can say that a seed of a tree, for example, can incorporate all functions of a tree. And in its turn, can become a tree. That way perpetuating the specie, it is part of.

From the Egyptian religion of old is understood that there is a process of resurrection. And this remained incorporated in some stories. The story of Seth is such an example. In that story, the narrator describes Seth as an evil man. As he cut his brother's body into 14 parts. Which were later thrown all over Egypt. Isis, the wife of Osiris, travelled at length in desperation to recover the body of her husband. Unfortunately, she could find only 13 parts out of 14. Not knowing what else to do, she went to Toth the patron of sacred knowledge to consult him. Toth knew what the 14 part of Osiris's body refers to, and used his knowledge to bring Osiris back to life.

Obviously, this is a story. And yet, these narratives, in the language of math, had their beginning in the most remote past. And they prove to originate from this sort of knowledge, related mainly to transcendence and resurrection. Which perpetuated for tens of thousands of years. It was close to our time when their meaning was lost. And that due to religious dogmas. Because a religious concept, in which a mighty God is depicted, is easy to accept. Though, a set number which describes a similar or the same idea, it appears less convincing, or speculative. This may have caused in the past a major debate between various cultures, or within the same culture, which might have ended with the defeat of the work on numbers, and, as a result, it was pushed aside from the realm of so-called sacred knowledge. ...If that was a good move, it remains to be seen.

PART 7
THE ENCODED FORMAT
IN THE GRAND GALLERY

It is said that, one day, the pharaoh Khufu reminded the designer to use the sum of one of the two matrices for the height of the pyramid. The sum of the numbers from the first matrix was too small. And the sum of the second matrix was too big. The designer agreed and pondered carefully on that matter. The sum of all the set number from the second matrix is 5849. Or, a pyramid with such a height would not have been possible. The alternative was to either reduce the height one hundred times (58.49 meters), which was considered too small, or to reduce the 14 trinaries of the matrix to binary. So, the designer considered the second alternative and turned all 14 set numbers into binary (8,09,18,18,14, 14,17,18,13,13,14,13,18,09). That sum is 206. As it is the number of bones in a human body.

The builders suggested that the height of the pyramid should be about 146.1 meters—a hint at the Sothic cycle which stretches on a span of 1461 years. But even that was a concern. Since the height of the pyramid had to be used to determine the passing of time. And for that, as presented in the first chapter, the height of the pyramid should be 146.41 meters.

While the designer was discussing with the builders, the pharaoh approached and remained him that the sarcophagus has to be placed at a height that divides the pyramid into two equal parts. And before the designer had time to say a word, the pharaoh reminded him that the design should be based on the encoded format got from the Solar God. Adding something else about sea level.

Before the pharaoh left, the designer tried to assure him that he would be able to solve that matter. However, a pyramid with a height of 206 meters would have the sarcophagus placed at 103 meters above the ground. So, the only alternative was to level the Giza Plateau and apply two forms of measurement. One from sea level and the other from the ground.

As can be seen in the image below, the pyramid was placed 60 meters above sea level. That way, the sarcophagus is 103 meters from sea level, dividing the pyramid in two equal parts.

"The base of the pyramid of Khufu lies about 60 m above sea level, so the tip of the pyramid used to be on 206 m above seal level."

Franz Löhner www.cheops-pyramide.ch

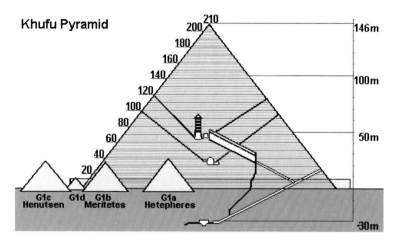

The general view is that the pyramid was erected in the traditional way. But that is not enough to assume that the sarcophagus was carried through the Grand Gallery into the Burial Chamber. Since the height of the passage that links the two, it is not higher than the height of the sarcophagus.

To get at the bottom of this, in the last two hundred years or so, there has been much frenzy work, competing to unveil this ancient mystery. Though neither the way nor the reason the Grand Gallery was built could be answered.

At the beginning of this work, it was claimed that the design of the pyramid is based on a mathematical concept; worked out to describe transcendence. Based on that, it was made up the story of exiting the cycle of life, in which the pharaoh Khufu plays a central role.

Pharaoh Khufu

The above statuette was spotted during an excavation coordinated by William M. F. Petrie in 1903. Contrary to anyone's expectation, the artefact was not found inside the Great Pyramid, known as Khufu's burial place, or at least in the nearby surroundings, but outside the temple of Abydos.

Why did the most powerful man in the ancient world prefer to leave behind just a small statuette that would portray him is, to some extent, a pertinent question. Though we should not be so surprised since the whole concept of the pyramid proves to be out of this world.

In his work, Pyramid of Man, Vincent Brown describes a part of the measurements in the Grand Gallery.

"At the base it is 2.06 meters (6.8 ft) wide, but after 2.29 meters (7.5 ft) the blocks of stone in the walls are Corbelled inwards by 7.6 centimeters (3.0 in) on each side. There are seven of these steps, so, at the top, the Grand Gallery is only 1.04 meters (3.4 ft) wide."

This information inevitably brings to mind the height of the pyramid, the 14 binary from which the height was calculated, and the height of Khufu's statuette. Here we have their correspondent:

1) The height of the pyramid from the sea level is 206 meters.

2) The base of the Grand Gallery is 2.06 meters.

3) The height of the pyramid was calculated from a string of 14 binary.

4) The walls of the Great Gallery are corbelled inside 14 times. (Seven times on each of the two walls).

5) The height of Khufu' statuette is 7.6 centimeters.

6) 'The blocks of stone in the walls are Corbelled inwards by 7.6 centimeters.'

Yet, the designer does not show how the sarcophagus of the owner would pass from the Grand Gallery to the Burial Chamber. Which poses a good question. At the top, the Grand Gallery is 1.04 meters wide. One centimeter smaller than the height of the sarcophagus.

Dividing 1.04 by the length of the unit of measurement

employed for the Great Pyramid, it is obtained the Internal length of the sarcophagus.

1.04 : 0.523 = 1.98

Was then sarcophagus regarded as no more than empty space? Hardly anyone would accept this. Since in the Burial Chamber there is an empty sarcophagus.

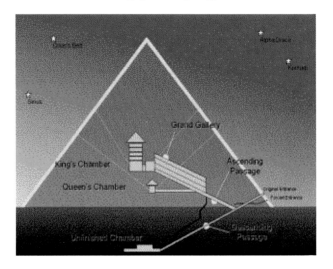

Copyright: IAC Publishing

From the entrance of the pyramid (see the design above), there is a passage that leads to what has become known as the Unfinished Chamber, the Queen's Chamber, and the Grand Gallery.

The Unfinished Chamber was designed first. Or that is what has been assumed. Described as the last resting place for the pharaoh. It is said, though, that the pharaoh had a change of mind and has desired to have the Burial Chamber at a higher level in the pyramid. That room became known as the Queen's Chamber. The legends though tell that soon after the Grand Gallery was finished, the pharaoh Khufu had a new change of mind, and ordered to have his Burial Chamber at an even higher level within the pyramid, ready to have his new wish carried out.

But can any of the above be proven as such? Or is Khufu's statement concerning the design of the pyramid what we should take into account? The pharaoh reminded the designer where the sarcophagus should be placed. Which means that they discussed that mater beforehand. The designer had to present all his calculations on time as the pharaoh to preview the design, see if they were done in accordance with his wish, ask or request some changes. And one of the most delicate things was the shafts. Which puzzled anyone who researched the pyramid. What they were for?

Modern measurements could, in the end, show the length of the shafts from the Burial Chamber towards…the sky.

The Northern shaft is 59,5m and the Southern shaft: 53,55m.

Their length is (59.5 + 53.5) = 113

The measurements are Copyright © 1999 Jean-François Deschamps

KHUFU 's LAST WILL

Why was the sarcophagus placed 103 meters from sea level, and the shafts are 113 meters in length?

PART 8
THE PRIMORDIAL WORD

In The Secret Doctrine, The Synthesis of Science, Religion, and Philosophy Vol II, Anthropogenesis, it is stated that HP Blavatsky tried to demonstrate in her book, The Secret Doctrine, that "man was the primordial word". Quoting again, for the elucidation of that statement, what exactly the author wrote. "The very first word possessed by the Hebrews, whoever they were, to carry the idea, by sound, of a man. The essential of this word was 113 (the numerical value of that word) from the beginning, and carried with it the elements of the cosmical system displayed."

Pondering in frustration, we may wonder what would be the relationship between the first Hebrew word (based on the account presented by HP Blavatsky) and 113. Or why that word was endowed with a numerical value which, as the author implied, is related to a "cosmical system ".

On a few occasions so far, it was maintained that the process of enlightenment the ancients spoke about encompasses 18 stages. In each of them is revealed a sort of information. The Word, which was thought to be the only means used by God in His work, has, as already said, a composite of 23 units of sound. As well it was pointed out that the relation of the two set numbers as 18+23 was used by Hebrew sages to underline the word, God, in the first biblical statement.

In their holographic format these two numbers (see the description below), reveals the encoded meaning of the numeric stanza 113.

```
18< >81
23< >32
=41 >113
```

This would make sense, keeping in mind that the first biblical statement was staged to herald a concept about creation on the power of sound and further it was stated that God created Man in His likeness.

The name God/Elohim in the first biblical statement was underlined with a set of five numbers that count to 41. The result of this operation indicates the same relation:

```
01< >10
12< >21
05< >50
10< >01
13< >31
= 41 > 113
```

41= Elohim/God

113= Man born from (the power of) sound/Man in the image of God.

Interestingly enough is the fact that the biblical statement "I AM THAT I AM", a saying attributed to God, was worked out to describe the same ontological relation between an omnipresent and yet Unseen Being, and 'Man born from sound'.

The numeric representation of I AM THAT I AM is: 14—13—14

In its holographic format reveals the same thing:

14< >41
13< >31
14< >41
=41 >=113

41= "I AM THAT I AM" A saying attributed to God
113= Man in the image of "I AM THAT I AM". Or Man born from the power of sound.

Another example provided by H.P. Blavatsky in her work, The Secret Doctrine, it appears to be much older, and with a clear hint to the hidden meaning of the garden of Paradise. All that, expressed in the language of numbers.

"The theoretical use of crucifixion must have been somehow connected with the personification of this symbol (the structure of the garden of Paradise symbolized by a crucified man)." To which she added "There seems to be deep below deep as to the mysterious workings of these number values -- (the symbolization of the connection of 113: 355, with 20612: 6561, by a crucified man)."

Indian and Tibetan sages claim that the human Soul is much bigger than the body and that it is confined in the body, as the Essenes claimed. And only at the time of liberation the Soul can open its "wings" and "fly" towards a higher realm.

Another old culture, the Sumerian, debated the same things but in a different way. They associated the Soul with the perfect sound. Since, as tradition holds, at the time of enlightenment the Higher Self reveals a certain kind of knowledge about the spring of life, and His voice was said to be the Perfect sound.

The Sumerians described that sound in number (81). And

did associate it with the Soul. So, keeping in mind that at time of liberation the Soul (81) departs from the body, in number that could be described as the square of 81.

81 x 81 = 6561

In the example above, the rapport of the two set numbers, 20612: 6561, was worked out to highlight the process of transcendence. In math that is expressed by π.

20612 : 6561 = 3.1415942

In other words, the structure of the garden of Paradise described by a crucified man had not a negative meaning. Since, as Blavatsky wrote, that was a "theoretical use of crucifixion".

So, it can be inferred that π, which may underline the transcendence of the Self/Soul, was known by ancient men long before the wheel was invented.

The Buddhists, who reflected on the same, came to the obvious conclusion that the Soul is unborn and never dies. Which could help us come to term with the scientific argument

"...Pi existed before the universe came into being and will exist after the universe is gone"

David H Bailey and Jonathan M Borwen

PI: The Next Generation.

What is to be considered, at least as a simple remark, is that in the remote past religion was not what it is today. At then, sages had to prove their concept about creation or uncreated.

The same number encoded as the Man in the Image of God is to be found expressed in various ways at different cultures. The artefact below was discovered in the land of Romania, at Hamangia, and it is about 7000 years old. A UNESCO Heritage.

Taking into account the cognitive position in which the man is seated, it was called The Thinker. The artefact was found in a burial site. And it depicts a man thinking. He sits on a small stool.

The Thinker of Hamangia

At a symposium held at the Romanian Academy in Bucharest, in 1986, the researcher Vasile Droj, brought the attention over the 'synthetic' geometry, codified in the structure of the Thinker.

Later, in November 2005, he published in Migration & Diffusion, Vol 6, a work entitled Key of the Archaic Civilization, in which he debated the same, underlying that the Thinker's "height in centimetres hides the only two whole numbers whose ratio gives the Greek pi with a precision of a millionth"

The Thinker is 113 mm tall, and has the circumference of the circle in which is structured of precisely 355 mm, as seen in the image below.

355 : 113= 3,141592

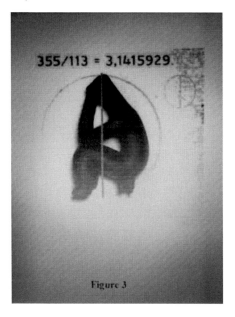

Copyright Vasile Droj

As this artefact was found in a burial site, it is not hard to imagine that it was used to underline the concept of transcendence expressed through the mathematical formula 355/113. This at least would suggest that people in the remote past used to describe the soul as being endowed with the means to transcend, having the power of ascending to a higher dimension after the body enters extinction. All that hidden in an artefact, designed to correspond to a measurement that would incorporate a transcendental number. A symbolical work in the end. But, which, can stand proof of knowledge that we hardly could imagine.

On the same coordinates might be viewed the statuette of pharaoh Khufu. Which it was worked out by using π. That would have suggested somehow that the man was at the time to enter the process of transcendence. Hence the story of exit from the cycle of life, linked to his name.

Interesting is the fact that such exquisite data had begun to diminish once with the beginning of the glacial period and disappeared almost entirely at the end of that natural disaster. That would have pushed human, who hardly could survive, to take refuge in caves. In that context, they might have worked out by way of imagination countless gods, hoping to get help from them.

On the other hand, it might be that all is but cultural reminiscence from a previous culture, that could perpetuate in time for a while. This keeping in mind that the original measurement of the three pyramids on the Giza Plateau was based on ontological data. Which is related to transcendence.

The three pyramids are part of the same design.

For example, the base of the three pyramids should have been

108 meters for the base of the small pyramid
216m for the second pyramid, and
230 m for the big pyramid.
108 +216+ 230 = 554

All measurements, though, were slightly altered. That change was based on calculation.

108.5 m for the small pyramid
215.25 for the second, and
about 230.25 for the big pyramid.
108.5+ 215.25+ 230,25 = 554.

Why these numbers? And what is the logic behind it?

The three pyramids describe a concept. Already discussed, there are said to be 18 stages of enlightenment. In each stage is presented (among other knowledge) the Mystic sound, which is made up of six words.

18 x 6 = 108.

Number 216, in the works of the builders refers to the "God of the Underworld". The one who searches his way out.

Number 23 is the code of ontological data and deals with the exit from the cycle of life.

23 x 10 is 230, the base of the Great Pyramid, which was staged the process of transcendence.

So, the concept related to the three pyramids is expressed in three steps. It begins with revealed knowledge. Then describes the Man trying to work out the meaning of that data. And finally hints at the Man ready to prove his knowledge of transcendence.

If we pay attention to the height of the three pyramids on the Giza Plateau, we can notice something that might need to be carefully considered.

The Great Pyramid is 146.41 meters height.

The pyramid of Khafre is 143.32 meters height. And the pyramid of Menkaure 65.50 meters.

The sum of the heights of these pyramids is 355.

The code of Man in the Image of God is 113.

355 : 113 = 3.1415929

The height of the Great Pyramid from the sea level is 206 meters. Converting 206 meters in cubits yields 393.

From the ground level to the top of the pyramid, there are 280 cubits.

393 - 280 = 113.

113 : 0.523 (the unit of measurement) = 216.

It might mean that the builders of the Great Pyramid played with the idea that, man created in the image of God, was no other but the God of the Underworld.

In a way, it may be said that, since they referred to the God of Underworld as the one who did not possess the knowledge that would enable him to transcend.

Yet, the story of transcendence, in which the pharaoh Khufu plays the central role, challenges that. Inferring that sacred knowledge would enable him to do that. And to explain this, the designer used the set number 414, which, as discussed, it refers to the number of stages of enlightenment and the code of ontological data. (18 x 23= 414), and 198, which refers to transcendence.

414 + 198 = 612, the Solar God (having the power to transcend).

414 - 198 = 216, the God of Underworld (lacking sacred knowledge that would enable him to learn the process of transcendence).

I assume that this teaching was part of the Egyptian culture at the time the Great Pyramid was built. Solar Barge is one of the elements that would support this assumption. Since, as already presented, in the structure of the Solar Barge, made from Lebanon wood, was encoded data about the unseen Barge (meaning hidden knowledge) in which Khufu intended to travel to meet the Solar God.

What else the designer presented in his work makes this story even more interesting.

The internal length of the sarcophagus, related to transcendence (198), the height where the sarcophagus was placed, from the sea level (103), and the length of the shafts, that were worked out to describe the return of the soul to its source, as Man in the Image of God, (113), is the sum that describes in number the sacred knowledge: 414.

198 + 103 + 113 = 414

103 + 113 = 216, the God of Underworld.

198, hints at the power of transcendence.

The technique of encoding these refined forms of measurement is, obviously, based on a plan in which the designer pushed his concept about transcendence to the limit. But that is the result of a considerable understanding of the knowledge he is dealing with. Which for us is no more than a puzzle. It could be guessed what that is about. Though it cannot be said for sure what in reality that stands for.

We know, or batter said, we heard that in the universe all is binary. And that the electron has its 'mirror-reflection' somewhere else. That the magnetism and electricity are the two sides of the same coin. Based on that, it can be said that the two matrices presented here, might hint at something similar.

To illustrate with an example.

The second matrix, is made up of 14 set numbers.

The 'mirror-reflection' of 14 is 41. The name of God worked out in the first biblical statement, is 41.

14 <> 41

All those 14 set-number could be reduced to 801 ("I am Alpha and Omega," a saying attributed to God).

The opposite of 801 is 108 (the number of utterances in the process of enlightenment).

801 <> 108

The number of utterances 108 is, obviously, a key matter in the design of the pyramid.

From the sea level, the altitudes where each of the three chambers- the Subterranean, the Queen and the Burial Chamber- are placed, indicates 30, 81, and 103 meters respectively.

This measurement in its palindromic format yields 108.

30<   >03
81<. >18
103< >301
=214 > 322
322 - 214= 108

This number divided by the length of the Royal Cubit indicates the height of the pyramid from sea level.

108: 05236= 206

A delicate matter like this, hardly anyone would take to heart, since no part of what is presented above was found on any of the known papyri. Or handed down at least as a tail.

So, the reader would have some question to ask. Which is understandable. As a matter of fact, things have been debated most of the time. It is simple to note that even the name of the Solar God has been argued since time immemorial. Some said that is RE. Others believe that is RA. In our time, it is taken as a matter of translation, and debated without much fervor. Though, these things, small they may apparently be, had for a long time now been forgotten. RE refers to the Solar God. And RA to the human being. Both names are abbreviations (as these things were kept mainly as a secret).

What is understood from the work of the designer of the Great Pyramid, is that RE is the one who tries to provide knowledge of transcendence, to enable people to regain what they knew and eventually, evolve. RA is the one who found out that the Soul does not die, but is unable to find out the exit from the cycle of life.

Simply put, the designer uses in his work knowledge from the state of enlightenment. Such knowledge was known, based on the artefacts known to date, in Old Europe, then India and Summer. Hebrew sages prove to have had good knowledge on this. Finally, a sage from Japan, some eight hundred years ago, debated the Mystic sound.

To detail on all these aspects would, inevitably, make this work more complicated. In short, in one of the states of Bardo is the 'story' of RA. The one, who could achieve that would take the road towards enlightenment. But there is a trap. Since the state of Bardo is related to immortality. In the sense that, in that process is understood that the Soul does not die. What as well is understood is that you knew this before. What then is the trap? You don't know then that there is a higher stage, which is related to revealed knowledge related to transcendence, on which the designer of the pyramid structured his work.

These two forms of knowledge, which are entirely different, could create a large number of religions. And there was no winner. The state of Bardo or something similar to it is about human being and immortality. The state of enlightenment is about the universe we live in, a parallel world, and transcendence. As the two matrices are part of the state of enlightenment, the designer used them. But, as we could see, the Greeks and Hebrew prove to have knowledge of that as well. Here is how the number 801, known as the Alpha and Omega, a saying attributed to God, was calculated.

The fourteen set numbers, presented at the beginning of chapter seven and described how the designer used them to determine the height of the pyramid is turned into a matrix.

297 < > 792	356 < > 653	356 < > 653
198 < > 891	359 < > 953	247 < > 742
414 < > 414	198 < > 891	198 < > 891
909 < > 909	913 < > 319	=801 =2286
356 < > 653	247 < > 742	000< >000
=2174 =3659	=2073 =3558	

The result from each of the three columns, in which the matrix was divided, is the same.

3659 - 2174 = 1485
3558 - 2073 =1485
2286 - 801 =1485

This result divided by the length of the Sothic Cycle reveals something special.

1485 (x100) :1461= 101

The Sothic cycle is about time. And we could see that the designer used that as a prime step to finding out a method to determine the number of days in a year. The walls of the Burial Chamber were built from 101 stones. The code of the Solar Barge is 101. In the steppes of Kazakhstan, there is an artefact made of 101 geo-gliphs, which could be entirely seen only from hundreds of km above the Earth.

To get the final result, the above matrix is reduced to binary.

18 < > 81	14 < > 41	14 < > 41
18 < > 81	17 < > 71	13 < > 31
09 <> 90	18 < > 81	18 < > 81
18< > 81	13 < > 31	=45 = 153
14 < > 41	13 < > 31	
= 77 = 374	=75 = 255	

374- 77= 297
255- 75= 180
153 -45 = 108
297 + 180 +108 = 585

Finally, the binaries are reduced to the last digit:

09 < > 90	05 < > 50	05 < > 50
09 < > 90	08 < > 80	04 < > 40
09 < > 90	09 < > 90	09 < > 90
09 < > 90	04 < > 40	=18..... =180
05 < > 50	04 < > 40	
=41..= 410	=30.... =300	

410 - 41= 369
300 - 30 = 270
180 - 18 =162
369 +270 + 162 = 801

PART 9
THE CELESTIAL MAPS

Closer to our time, news broke out that the Great Pyramid had been used as an astronomical observatory, and that was full of all sorts of celestial maps and unusual instruments for measurement. That determined the ruler of Bagdad, Caliph Al Mamoun, who was known as an accomplished astrologer, to break into the pyramid.

Chronicles maintain the year 820, when eager and proud of his adventure, the Caliph requested to have the best architects, engineers, and stonemasons ready for an expedition to Egypt. Once there and facing the pyramid, the Caliph suddenly had a change of mind, hoping to get not only the instruments for measurement and the celestial maps but all the jewelry used to ornate the Burial Chamber, or anything else would cross his way.

Though, instead of joy, the Caliph had to deal soon with the casualties provoked by illness; which was the result of the huge effort.

They tried desperately to break the entrance of the pyramid, though they did not know where that was, as the pharaoh ordered to be sealed off, and it could not be seen from outside.

When finally, they could manage to break one of the walls of the pyramid, they squeezed one by one in. Then, searched each of its corners carefully. What they could find though was no more than a lidless, empty sarcophagus in the Burial Chamber.

Yet, to prove that the exit from such a trap has to be made with the head held high, the Caliph decided to pay for his mistake. But made it in such a way that no one would have had the chance to know it before he explained that later, in a manner of confession, as confirmed by De Salvo, Director of the Great Pyramid of Giza Research Association in his book THE COMPLETE PYRAMID SOURCEBOOK.

"To appease his men, Al Mamoun secretly hid an amount of gold in the pyramid that equaled the just wages of his men. He explained this coincidence on the great wisdom of Allah."

That probably determined Bonnie Gaunt take Caliph for granted, describing him in her book Stonehenge and the Great Pyramid as the first witness who entered the pyramid after it was sealed off, and who concluded that such a sophisticated construction was based on an unusual design.

"Al Mamoun came to the obvious conclusion that the chamber had been built around the granite box and that never contained a mummy nor a lid."

Years later, an Arab legend described the historian Abd-el-Hôkm claiming that the venture of Caliph Al Mamoun was not a failure after all. Implying that "a statue resembling a man was found in the sarcophagus, and in the statue (mummy case) was a body with a breastplate of gold and jewels, bearing written characters which no one understood."

Eastern life - Present and Past by Harriet Martineau (p 224) Lea and Blanchard 1848 Philadelphia

The echo of such a story has reverberated much. It was even said that the lid of the sarcophagus was removed and carried away. Fortunately, we know that such things are no different than reach soil that nourishes weeds. Though, such an unseen force, as the rumour is, can, after all, describe the potential of human imagination exquisitely.

All those who research the pyramid, though, have a different view. Arguing that the passageway from the Burial Chamber to the exit of the pyramid is too narrow. Even for carrying the lid of the sarcophagus thorough it.

It was built that way on purpose. Showing that the sarcophagus could not have been carried from outside through that passageway. And it could not be taken out from there. That suggests that the Burial Chamber was built around the sarcophagus. What then was the reason?

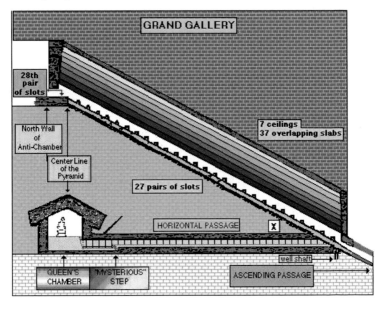

Copyright: Reocities.com project (FIBONACCI site)

The Grand Gallery makes the connection with the Burial Chamber. Yet, the 7 ceilings, the 37 overlapping slabs, the 27 slots- beginning from the entrance of the gallery to the end of the slop 28, in the upper part of the gallery, were endowed with a hidden meaning.

However, in this work, it is not discussed how the Grand Gallery was built. That is the matter for engineers. What is discussed here is the meaning. As this complex is based on a story of transcendence. Which is very complex. Or, if this was done, it means that it was addressed to us. Since the pharaoh did not need this. He requested this. And the work is structured in such a way that it could be decoded.

It is easy to figure out what number 7 stands for since on each part of the gallery there are 7 ceilings, which counts to 14. A hint at the 14 binaries from which is said that the structure of the pyramid was designed.

As well we can have an idea about the number 28. Since the 14 set-numbers were structured in a holographic format, which means a 28 set-numbers.

What about 37 and 27?

The internal length of the sarcophagus is 198.

The sum of all prime numbers from 1 to 37 is 198.

The prime 101 is in position 27.

101 is the number of stones from which the walls of the Burial Chamber were built.

Before trying to see what encoded message had the designer of the pyramid presented here, we need to clarify one aspect of this matter. Since in both instances, related to the numbers 27 and 37, number 1 is used as a prime. A mathematician would inevitably ask why the designer of the pyramid used number 1 in this context as a prime and did not do the same when he calculated the code of the Solar God from prime numbers. The question is pertinent because when the setting of the prime numbers is decided, then it has to be clear if number 1 is taken as a prime or not.

It can be speculated why they did use in one context number one as a prime, and in another instance it was not used. A clear answer I do not have. But what I can say is that the binary system of counting 01 to 09, can be calculated on the first three prime number 01,02,03.

They applied a special method to obtain the counting system. Second. In what the ancients call enlightenment, there are no more than three utterances in a row. In other words, that number is the maximum extension. Like, let's say a three-dimension, in which is said that we live.

However, in that narrative about transcendence, there are two main roles played by Khufu and the Solar God. The later is described as an outsider. He is free. Though he introduced himself as being in no way different than us.

The well-known religious concept, concerning our existence on Earth, infers that we belong to a process of creation. In which the Creator identifies Himself with His own creation. The designer of the pyramid, on the other hand, implies that the so-called Solar God hints at the fact that such knowledge is embedded in our genes. And that he could decode it, and gained freedom. That determined Khufu claim that he would exit the cycle of life in the attempt to meet the Solar God, willing to become one with him. In other words, to gain freedom.

From the encoded format structured in the Grand Gallery it could be understood, that the pharaoh Khufu was not an ordinary ruler. And that his claim about the exit from the cycle of life was based on knowledge.

On the other hand, it is somehow surprising to see that the internal design of the pyramid depicts in an encoded format what in Buddhism is called karma. The first meaning of this concept was related to negative action. Which needs to be annihilated.

In the famous biblical story, there is a different approach to this matter. It is said that at the time the patriarch Abraham turned 99, the Lord appeared to him and said:

'I am God Almighty; walk before me, and be blameless, that I may make my covenant between me and you.' (Gen. 17:1–2).

People used to ask if Abraham was indeed 99 years old at that time. In the remote past, numbers incorporated in religious concepts were calculated. And they, obviously, were endowed with a hidden meaning. The story tells that God appeared in front of Abraham and decided to let him know that from that time on he would be 'blameless'. Alluding that between Him and Abraham, he placed a 'covenant'. Covenant, in number, is 612. Having, therefore, the same code as the Solar God. In other words, it would mean that Abraham could achieve his freedom.

In the Grand Gallery, the concept of freedom/transcendence was worked out by using the same number, 99.

As said, here is not debated the engineering method based on which the Grand Gallery was built. It is discussed the hidden meaning of this work. Which proves to be well thought by people who have knowledge about a world we hardly could imagine.

The number of ceilings, slots, and the overleaping stones counts (07+27++37+ 28) to 99.

Here is their holographic format.

07 < > 70

27 < > 72

37 < > 73
28 < > 82
=99   =297
297- 99=198, meaning transcendence (or freedom).

The four-parts (07,27,28,37) are on each side of the two walls.
7+7 = 14
27+27 =54
37+37= 74
28+28 = 56
In their holographic format:
14 < > 41
54 < > 45
74 < > 47
56 < > 65
=198 =198

A different method to debate the theme of transcendence was used by Hebrew sages. In one of their stories in the language of numbers, is described the relationship between God and His son. Both of them identified with a code number.

The Father (543). He is the One who possesses sacred knowledge. The Son (345) is the one that gets that knowledge.

So, the story depicts them as being in a spiritual rapport.

543 - 345 = 198.

The rapport Father-Son, here, depicts a primary source. Which is transcendental knowledge.

Number 543, which refers to the Father (God), was worked out from three set-numbers: 21, 501, 21.

21 < >12
501 <> 105
<u>21 < > 12</u>
=543 =129
543- 129 = 414

The biblical concept alluded that the Mystic Sound, the 'Word' of God was turned into flesh. But that was just to reinforce, in a way, the first statement referred to creation.

For the builders of the Great Pyramid, as said, creation and transcendence where the two faces of the same coin.

When it comes to the time the Great Pyramid was built, or the time the texts incorporated in the Bible were written down, we assume that that was relatively close to us. With that in mind, we ponder on the meaning of the concepts or stories from those cultures.

Though, when researchers deal with a work engraved on a piece of bone of mammoth, tens of thousands of years ago, then things become quite different. Since between our culture and the history of those people, there is no bridge. The artefact Columbia (see below) was discovered by archaeologist Nicolae Ketraru on the shore of the river Prut, Moldavia, in 1973. On it, there are inscribed 198 dots. The same number we have discussed from the beginning of this work. The design of the artefact is apparently simple. Five strings of dots. Three of them in the upper part that surrounds the 'neck' of the artefact, and two, bigger, encircling them.

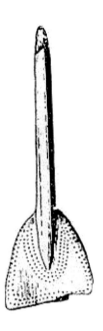

Columbia

Andrei Vartic, one of the researchers of this artefact, wrote in History began at Mitoc, that the five-set of numbers 27,30,24,54,63 counted from left to right or right to left, yields the same sum: 198. To which he added that the numbers 1, 9 and 8 are not part of the five sets. In this way, implying that the primaeval man used the same system of counting we know, and that was intended to be depicted on the artefact. Taking into account the spacecraft shape of the artifact he called it Columbia.

The format of this embroidering found on Columbia could be written as
27< >72
24< >42

```
30<  >03
54<  >45
63<  >36
=198> =198
```

The surface on which those 198 dots were engraved is of no more than 4 centimeters.

The artefact might be viewed as something primitive. Because the dot format could not be described as elaborate writing. Though we have to keep in mind that the Morse language began in the same way. And the Internet uses one binary: 01.

Columbia was worked out from a bone of mammoth, almost 40000 years ago, when the Earth was frozen. And it can be seen clearly that there was design before the writing was done. Much more, that number refers to transcendence. The artefact was probably worn around the neck, like a medallion.

Similar encoding format was depicted on an artefact, which is about 18.000 years old. It was discovered by Ilie Borziac in Cosauiți, Moldavia. This artefact was made from a tubular bone, 10 cm long, polished- having a three-fold shape. The discoverer of such a weird artefact called it 'Portac', a name that in Romanian could be rendered as "a case in which is kept a needle". Because, as Andrei Vartic wrote in his work Portacul lui Borziac, "At the time the artefact was discovered, there was a needle within it, made as well as from a sharp piece of bone." The same author suggested that "the needle was used not only for tailoring but for acupuncture as well."

The artefact called Portac

Design by Ilie Borziac.

In the design above, it can be seen a six set of numbers, disposed on three levels. 63 in all. A number found on many artefacts from the same period. In the lower part of the artefact, there are two set-number of 7 and 9 lines. In the middle part, there are two number-set composed of 16 and 10 lines. And in the upper part of the artefact, there are two number-set of 14 and 7 lines, respectively.

The six number-set are arranged in three layers, flanked by three lines, in an oblique position (in the left part of the artefact). Between the middle and the upper part of the artefact, there is designed a ladder; which indicates a connection between the two levels.

It should be considered the fact that this artefact, from Cosauiți, Moldavia, is 16,000 years older than any known Egyptian papyrus, and the message written on it is in the language of numbers.

Counting the six-number set, disposed in the three layers, we get:

7+9 =16

16+10=26

14+7=21

In their holographic format it yields:

16<>61

26<>62

21<>12

=63 >135

63+135= 198, the same number encoded on Columbia. Or Columbia is about 20.000 years older than the artifact 'Portacul'.

How and why primaeval man put so much accent on this number? In the second matrix, used for the design of the pyramid, the first three-set numbers are 297, 414, 198

All prime numbers from the system of counting are 1,2,3,5,7. The binary format of those numbers, which was used in a remote past, in their holographic format yield 198.

01<>10

02<>20

03<>30

05<>50

07<>70

18 = 180

18+180= 198

The other four set numbers from the system of counting 1 to 9, namely 4,6,8,9 are the numbers that could be divided. In their holographic format, it yields 297.

04<>40

06<>60

```
08<>80
09<>90
27  =270
27+270 =297
```

Number 414 is calculated from the same system of counting by adding the next number, 10, which is the first negative number in the system. Since its opposite is 01. It has this representation:

```
01<09>10
02<18>20
03<27>30
04<36>40
05<45>50
06<54>60
07<63>70
08<72>80
09<81>90
10<09>01
   =414
```

The setting of those matrices presented in this work is based on set numbers that have a hidden meaning. Those in the remote past could not display complex messages on a small artefact. So, the craftsman tried to make use of a specific portal of knowledge, already known, or easy to be decoded. One of the numbers found on artefacts that are about 30.000 years is 23. Of which, the same, we spoke about. It is the code of the Mystic sound.

In the land of Romania were found many artefacts on which this number is represented.

"Most of the pendant's outline is marked with a total of

23 parallel and linear incisions (notches), arranged, by an overwhelming majority, roughly 3 mm apart."

M. Cârciumaru1, E.-C. Niţu, O. Cîrstina , and N. Goutas, Valahia University of Târgovişte, Doctoral School

The sum of all primes from 1 to 23, inclusive, is 101. A number used much in the design of the pyramid. Displayed as an artefact in the steppes of Kazakstan. Seen only from high up in the sky. The code of Solar Barge is 101.

One may consider that all these are no more than coincidences, but the information provided so far shows that there was work on this done by many cultures. And it is not only the fact that they had knowledge about the constant π or prime numbers, but they also used different mathematical methods that have remained unknown.

The question then is if Primeval man was in a close relationship with the one described by the builders of the Great Pyramid as the Solar God. That relationship appears to have stretched on a span of tens of thousands of years. Why then, such relationship came to an end?

PART 10
THE BATTLE OF CHEOPS

From the little historical data concerning the life of Pharaoh Khufu, written or transmitted from one generation to the other, it is hard to have a clear picture about the pharaoh himself. Even scarcer are the things about the time period in which the Great Pyramid was built. It is believed, nonetheless, that before Khufu's reign, the main religion of Egypt was mainly based on a form of worship to a Solar God, even though there was a kind of tolerance or acceptance for a number of other gods.

However, the first encounter about the owner of the Great Pyramid is to be found in Westcar papyrus, believed to have belonged to the Second Intermediate Period (1782-c.1570 BCE) (Joshua Mark. The Westcar Papyrus).

Other sources suggest that the papyrus was written closer to our time. An eloquent example in this sense is "A mythological interpretation of Djedi the Magician of the Westcar Papyrus" by Brendan Crawford, in which is written that.

"The Westcar Papyrus is dated to the 18th to 16th century BC, potentially placing it in the new kingdom where this knowledge is accepted."

In one of the stories from that papyrus, called *Djedi the Magician*, is described that one day the pharaoh Khufu was informed by his younger son about Djedi, a dweller, 110 years old. Who knew where the hidden knowledge, part of the secret teaching of Thoth, the Lord of Knowledge, was kept.

The pharaoh grew eager to find out that mysterious knowledge to design his Burial Chamber and kindly asked his son to fetch the old man.

As soon as the magician was introduced to pharaoh Khufu and asked what did he know about Thoth's secret teaching, the old man offered a kind of testimony by which he managed to infer that he had never been in possession of such exquisite knowledge, and that he merely knows where the rules of that mysterious teaching are kept. Namely, in "a box of flint" in a "room named 'Investigation' in Heliopolis".

To farther avoid any pressure from the pharaoh, in his attempt to get hold of that secret, Djedi intended to make the pharaoh believe that the one entrusted to pass him that mysterious knowledge is "the eldest of the three kings who are in the womb of Reddjedet".

Surprised of such an unusual form of delivery, the pharaoh inquired about Reddjedet. The answer came quickly and carefully chosen:

"she is the wife of a priest of Ra, Lord of Sakhbu, who is pregnant with three sons of Ra".

The above story underlines like in painting, sculpture, music or poetry a few decorative elements which certainly are not the core of the theme, but could give the impression of their great importance. The son of the pharaoh is portrayed as trying to help his father get hold of Thoth' sacred knowledge. The old dweller, Djedi, plays the role of a wise man. The wife of the priest of Ra bears the sons of Ra who are to become kings and would eventually furnish to the pharaoh Khufu what he was looking for.

The storyteller, that way, hints, on the one hand at the fact that the pharaoh was an ordinary ruler, lacking knowledge and, on the other, that the pharaoh was dependent on the power of the priesthood- the one who established the bridge between Ra, as a Solar God, and the pharaoh.

This piece of literary work is, in the end, a historical document. Though it comes in full contrast with what has been discussed in this work so far.

In the old culture of Egypt, Ra was depicted as "an ancient god, but not the oldest of the gods." Yet, "by the Fifth Dynasty, he was a powerful god who was closely associated with the pharaoh." (Ancient Egypt Online)

That rather suggests that the pharaohs could impose their political power more and more, and finally, they were able to surpass the power of the priesthood. In the end, that might have been the case. But the documents, the written stories, once with the passing of time, became, at least in part, the work of the priesthood. As they were the learned ones. And, as it could be seen in that work, written more than one thousand years after the assumed passing of pharaoh Khufu, the Pharaoh was portrayed as a ruler without the necessary knowledge, or dependent on the priesthood.

That sort of ill-intended historical facts echoed even at the time of the Greek historian Herodotus (5th century BC). Who is often quoted. In the Greek language, Khufu was rendered as Cheops.

"Herodotus, who lived in the 5th century before Christ, states that the founder of the Great Pyramid, Cheops, was a prince whose crimes and tyranny rendered his name odious, even to posterity. He closed all the temples and forbade the Egyptians to perform sacrifices; after which he made them all work for him."

(Chapter III The Tomb Theory, p 39) C. Staniland Wake

If indeed the pharaoh Khufu grew up, as legends tell, in a ruling class, and that, as it is said, he was the elder son of a pharaoh, the young Khufu could witness at first hand, how the power of the kingdom at times would fall from the control of a dominant group into the tyranny of another sort of ruler. He would as well have noticed that the power of words, in some instances, would surpass the power of the warriors. Therefore, it is hard to accept that he did not know that the role of the priesthood in the spiritual and daily life of the empire was by far the most important. Since the role of the clergy was not only to enhance the imagination of the subjects about the assumed rewards offered by the deities but to control the way the subjects would obey the ruling class. Much more, he would have been conscious of the fact that by outlawing the ceremonial sacrifices, he would inevitably undermine the will of his own father, who was a supporter of such practices.

By accepting Herodotus description of pharaoh Khufu is not hard. Though, the question of why did the pharaoh Khufu intend to engulf himself in a world of troubles when he could avoid them, should not be ignored. If that was indeed the case, it might mean that, at first, the priesthood supposed that the young king- as Khufu was twenty years when he was crowned- due to his lack of experience, erred in his judgment and expected him to have a change of mind, and let the things flow in the same way as before. Surprisingly, the legends tell that the young man stood his ground.

For such complex things, usually, a king would try beforehand to assure that he has the necessary support. Which generally comes from people who either persist in ensuring the continuity of tyranny or trying to provide the necessary means for a different form of governing.

On the other hand, a prudent king would do this later in life when he is convinced that such a move is possible without creating a huge political turmoil in his kingdom. And of pharaoh Khufu is said that he began this as soon as he was crowned. Or, this turn of events, if they were as described, make one wonder who were those who did support Khufu, and much more, what was his reason in doing that.

Putting all that said, in balance with the concept heralded by pharaoh Khufu, namely that he can exit the cycle of life, would give us some food for thought. And that because a culture with such an advanced kind of knowledge would not bow in front of imaginary gods.

Or, at the time Khufu was crowned, "The gods and goddesses of Ancient Egypt were an integral part of the people's everyday lives.". And "there were over 2,000 deities in the Egyptian pantheon."

Egyptian Gods - The Complete List', Joshua J. Mark,

There was, it can be argued, a real army of deities if that evidence is based on facts. From whom, the subjects of the kingdom expected to have their hopes and aspiration nourished and fulfilled. But if those wishes and prayers remained unanswered? Well, there was an excuse. Which could be presented in all forms of ways. And accepted as accurate. Because, when you live in a culture with almost two thousand deities, and you have to embrace only the knowledge is preached, then you cannot see outside that reality. Except that there is a miracle that would open your eyes. Was then this the reason for which the pharaoh Khufu considered that he has to draw a line in the sand and put an end to all forms of sacrifices and prayers to imaginary gods?

Trying, to show, probably, that there is a higher source of knowledge, out there. Which it was known to all in the past.

If this scenario is somehow close to what has happened then and there, it would mean that Khufu was accompanied by a good number of knowledgeable people, who shared a common goal. It is probably why legends tell that during the construction of the three pyramids of Giza there were not performed sacrifices of any kind. And there was no war.

Why then the priesthood rejected that? Would that delicate matter go against all that belong to the past? More important of all was, probably, tradition. Which could be questioned by the subjects of the kingdom. Since anyone would have had at heart a deity. Or a spontaneous spiritual 'divorce' could not be accepted.

Well, we do not need to say that all sacrifices offered to the gods, were, in reality, a form of income for the priesthood.

This is why the priesthood pondered carefully, and arrived at the conclusion that in reality the pharaoh did not intend to add anything valuable to religion, even if his wish was to reform the old ones with a new one: a religion without sacrifices to gods. And saw themselves in an irrelevant situation.

How then could they respond to this? They might have conjured a way to fight. Though, when a king is crowned the measures taken for his protection would reach a very high level. And that would stay in place for a good deal of time until things would turn to normal. And such an opportunity was considered by Khufu carefully. Pretending of being approachable, showing the wiliness to walk closer to his subjects, and offering now and then 'sacrifices' and drinks to cheer up the kingdom.

But, as it was quoted in the first part of this work, the pharaoh Khufu, depicted in some legends that reached us, lived closer to our time. It might be that another pharaoh, with the same name, lived in prehistoric Egypt. That one spoke of the exit from the cycle of life. How then could we handle this matter?

A story, though complex and interesting, may entirely be unrealistic in its content. A balloon with its external surface fragile. Easy to be blown away by the swiftest wind. Khufu's pyramid, on the contrary, it is the most solid work on Earth. Imposing, but subtle. Making the mind wonder how and why was it built. And, if it is taken into account the main aspects displayed in the story of transcendence, woven in the design of the pyramid, we can notice that they are connected like parts in an opera or a play; structured around a form of knowledge that needs to be decoded. That ontological data through which the Solar God introduces Himself is a real wonder. He appears to be a traveler of some sort, without being bound by anything. Revealing all kinds of hidden knowledge to a designer. Sending encoded messages about parallel universes. Was then he living in one of them?

HIDDEN SYMBOLISM

The French architect Jean-Pierre Houdin spent a large number of years trying to decode the mysterious way Khufu's pyramid was built. Which incited the debate over the modality of construction of the most enigmatic buildings of all times. Above the Burial Chamber there are four rooms, which came to be known as 'the relieving rooms'. Initially was thought that their function was no other but to protect the Burial Chamber from the heavy amount of stone above. The French architect disagreed, Arguing that "The Egyptians did not order granite beams from Aswan for the pleasure of hiding such a quantity of beams inside the bulk: 2.100 tones altogether in the 43 beams distributed over 5 ceilings between level +48.85 and level +60.15 m."

Based on that information it can be worked out the symbolism hidden in the structure of the relieving chambers. And once with it to understand why the pyramid was designed to have an eight-sided feature that could be entirely seen only from space.

The four relieving rooms were designed as an extension of the Burial Chamber. Having the meaning of transcendence. Between the height of the ceiling of the Burial Chamber, situated at 48.85 from the ground, to the last part of the four of the relieving chambers, which is placed at 60.15 meters above the ground, there are 11.3 meters.

60.15 - 48.85 = 11.3

From the Burial Chamber to the North and South spring two shafts, having together a length of 113 meters. Exactly ten times longer than the distance from the ceiling of the Burial Chamber to the last ceiling of the four rooms.

As this may be taken as a mere coincidence, I would like to point out, in this context, something that could elucidate this story.

To describe the concept of transcendence, the designer did not use words, but two matrices of numbers. Which, as we could see, each in part was turned into a hologram. By that hinting at the way a single string of DNA, which is the building block of life, turns itself into an opposite string (creating a hologram). The same method was applied to underline the relation of the Burial Chamber with the relieving rooms.

The Burial Chamber is situated 43 meters above the ground. When the hologram (the opposite) of 43 is calculated, the result is 34.

43<>34

To give us a hint, the designer structured the ceiling of the Burial Chamber from 9 huge stone beams.

43 - 9 = 34.

The four unseen rooms above the Burial Chamber were built from 34 stone beams (the opposite of 43).

34<>43

As the encoding process used in the design of the pyramid varies (all its main parts having applied a different encoding format), it could be doubted that this was based on a concept. The Royal Cubit is one of these aspects. Within its structure, it was encoded the height of the pyramid.

The unit of measurement is divided into 28 parts/fingers. And each finger is 1.87 cm.

1.87<>78.1

1.87 x 78.1 =146 (More precise 146.04)

From the sea level the pyramid was, based on the design, 206m.

From the ground 146 m.

At the time of completion, the pyramid had a capstone with a height of 41 cm. The same symbol used to seal the place where the Solar Barge was entombed.

146 + 41 = 187.

The smallest part, the finger, of the Royal Cubit, is 187.

The height of the pyramid was worked out as a palindrome: 14641.

The four rooms, above the Burial Chamber, were designed as its extension. As it was presented above, the distance from the ceiling of the Burial Chamber to the last ceiling of the four rooms is 11.3 meters.

The speed needed by a spacecraft to depart from the surface of the Earth is 11.3 Km/s.

The height of the capstone is 41 cm.

The speed needed by a body to exit the Solar System is 41 Km/s

"The velocity of escape from the earth at its surface is about 7 mi (11.3 km) per sec, or 25,000 mi per hr; from the moon's surface it is 1.5 mi (2.4 km) per sec; and for a body at the earth's distance from the sun to escape from the sun's gravitation, the velocity must be 26 mi (41 km) per sec."

To calculate the velocity needed by a spacecraft that would depart from the Earth or from the Solar system it has to be known the radius of the body the spacecraft departs. The circumference of the Earth at the equator is 40075 kilometers. And its radius is 6381.36.

40075 divided by 6.28 (meaning 2π) is 6381.36.

The sum of all set-numbers in the second matrix used to design the pyramid (see below) is (2174 + 3659 + 2073 + 3558+ 801 + 2286) 14551.

The internal and external length of sarcophagus, as it was presented so far, were used in all sorts of calculations.

This sum of all set numbers used to design the pyramid of Khufu/Cheops, divided by the length of his sarcophagus. yields the radius of the Earth.

14551: 2.28= 6382.01

The difference between 6381.36, resulted from the division of the circumference of the Earth to 6.28 (2 PI) and 6382.01, resulted from the division of the sum of the set-numbers used to design the pyramid and Khufu' sarcophagus is 0.65 Km.

PART 11
PI AND THE GARDEN OF PARADISE

Theoretical physicists suggest that a universe which has nine dimensions is stable. Therefore, in it, life could be described as perfect. Only that, in that state, a flower would not grow. A human would not be born. It is only when its energy increases and a new dimension is breaking through, then it is when the universe becomes the spring of life.

The builders of the Great Pyramid depicted this in a very specific way. Based, practically, on what the designer offered them from what he, in his turn, got from the Solar God concerning the parallel universes. Which is in sharp contrast with what science proved so far. Namely that we live in a three-dimensional universe.

In physics and mathematics, dimensions are described as the "number of coordinates needed to specify any point within it." As a result, a line is said to have a dimension. A surface of a cylinder or sphere has two dimensions "because two coordinates are needed to specify a point on it." Yet, "The inside of a cube, a cylinder or a sphere is three-dimensional, because three coordinates are needed to locate a point within these spaces."

Previously, it was shown that there is a real similarity between the string of DNA and the matrices used for the design of the pyramid. In the sense that, each number could turn into its opposite. Similar to the permanent process in the building block of DNA.

Keeping in mind that each cell divides in two, and each retains in it all the information from the cell divided from, made science claim that there was a primordial cell from which all the other cells developed.

Would such a thing be described in number?

Our system of counting is 1 to 9. The sum of all these numbers is 45. Surprisingly, number 9, as the last digit in the counting system, holds the sum of all previous eight numbers, plus its numeric value. Therefore 45. To illustrate how this is calculated.

A number is placed to undergo the process of division of a cell. Let's take as an example number 9.

First
A cell divides itself in two.
9 is divided in two.
9 : 2 =4.5

Second.
The cell divided and its divided part retains the same information. The divided number and the number resulted from that division rejoin together.
9 x 4.5 = 40.5

Third.
As each cell obtains the full set of information from all the other cells that preceded it, in number that could be expressed as the sum of the divisions of the number (in our example 9) it was divided from.
4.5 + 40.5 = 45.

This rule could be applied to all numbers. Here there is another example.

Number 26.

26 : 2= 13

26 x 13= 338

338 + 13= 351

Therefore, the sum of all numbers from 1 to 26 is 351.

When it comes to dimension that might be entirely different. Even though, in physics and mathematics, it is specified that the dimensions are reflected by the "minimum number of coordinates needed to specify any point within it."

For hundreds of years, though, the dimensions of the universe have been described as the visible coordinates. A line is said to have a dimension. A surface of a cylinder has two dimensions. And the inside of a sphere is said to be three-dimensional.

How many dimension would then be needed as life to emerge in a universe? Physicist Brian Greene stated that string theory is viable in a universe with "ten dimensions of space and one dimension of time". Therefore 11 dimensions. (String theory: Youtube)

Another renown physicist, Michio Kaku, in speaking about dimensions concluded that, theoretically, a universe needs 11 dimensions. And that what is beyond that is unstable. A universe that reaches the 13 dimensions, for example, would become unstable. Michio Kaku: The Multiverse Has 11 Dimensions.

But, if there are needed 11 dimensions as the universe to be complete where, then, are the missing ones? From 3 to 11…In this work we came across a lot of puzzling things.

And there are many others. Among them, one is about dimensions.

The designer of the Great Pyramid described that in number. And based on that structure showed why they dismantled the Solar Barge and staked its parts in 13 piles. Why all numbers from the matrix of 14 set-numbers was reduced to 801.

Logically, you do not describe a universe of 13 dimensions by pointing at a barge which was dismantled, and its parts stacked in 13 piles. But there was the story of a barge sailing across the sky. And, as we could see, the 'sailing' of that barge was a hint at a Mystic sound said to make a permanent connection between the source of life and us.

Our counting system is 1,2,3,4,5,6,7,8,9

By summing it up we get 1,3,6,10,15,21,28,36,45 (which means 1 plus 2 is 3. 3plus 3 is 6 and so on.) This simple way of adding derives probably from this method.

Number 1.
01: 2= 0.5
01 x 0.5= 0.5
0.5 + 0.5 = 1

Number two.
02 : 2= 1
02 x 1= 2
1+2 = 3

Third.
3 : 2=1.5
3 x 1.5=4.5
1.5+4.5= 6

The summing of the first three numbers is (1+3+6) 10.

The builders of the pyramid argue that a universe of 11 dimensions is parallel with a universe of 12 dimensions. And that they are in harmony. Encoded with the number 801, known as Alpha and Omega.

When a universe becomes old, a new dimension emerges; therefore, the 13 dimensions.

Its code is 1224. Similar to the number of parts the Solar Barge was dismantled into and staked into 13 piles.

Here is the way they displayed that.

(11)..........................(12).............................(13)

01<>10	01<>10	01<>10
02<>20	02<>20	02<>20
03<>30	03<>30	03<>30
04<>40	04<>40	04<>40
05<>50	05<>50	05<>50
06<>60	06<>60	06<>60
07<>70	07<>70	07<>70
08<>80	08<>80	08<>80
09<>90	09<>90	09<>90
10<>01	10<>01	10<>01
11<>11	11<>11	11<>11
....	12<>21	12<>21
....		13<>31

There are counted the numbers on the left in any column and the numbers of the right.

1) 462 - 66= 396

2) 483 - 78= 405
396 + 405 = 801

3) 514 - 91=423
396+405+423 = 1224

801 + 1224 = 2025, which is the square of the system of counting.

That brings to mind the old saying that all is number. In the sense that at the subatomic level things can be described in number. Which would indicate that the universe in which we live was tuned!

Sure, one may argue that this is not based on an Anthropic principle, on which could be scientifically demonstrated that "the universe is as it is because if it was different, we would not be here to observe it". Well, others observed it even better. Our solar system is tuned. And, as it happened, some knew this and did survey the Earth at the time we had no idea that the Earth would rotate around the Sun.

LIST OF WORK CITED

1) Rhind papyri (Alexander Henry Rhind) British Museum.

2)The Great Pyramid Ratio, David Furlong

3)The speed of light, The Physical Measurement Laboratory of NIST.

4) Building the Great Pyramid, Franz Löhner

5) Height Of The Great Pyramid, The Physics Factbook, Perkha Ahmed

6) SKETCH OF HISTORY AND DESIGN OF GREAT PYRAMID, William M. F. Petrie

7) The Art of Ancient Egypt, made available by the Metropolitan Museum of Art, Edith Watts

8) Mystery of Pyramids, Part I, Ian Onvlee

9) A Miracle in Stone: The Great Pyramid of Egypt, Joseph A. Seiss

10) How long is a tropical year, Vigdis Hocken

11) The Sacred Chamber of Osiris, Scott Creighton

12) Pyramid of Man, Vincent Brown.

13 Just Six Numbers: The Deep Forces that Shape the Universe, Lord Martin Rees

14) City of God, Saint Augustine

15) Stanza of Dzyan, Translation by A. A, Bailey

16) The Opening of the Eyes | WND I | Nichiren Buddhism Library

17) The Academy of Jerusalem... Torah from Zion Project, The New Israeli Genesis Exegesis

18) The first Biblical statement, translated from the Greek language by Ivan Panin.

19) 'Proportion and Style in Ancient Egypt' by Gay Robins.

20) Psyche, Erwin Rohde

21) U.S. National Library of Medicine, The structure of a chromosome,

22) Lisa Von Pay and Kevin Norris, the National Science Foundations

23) Truth & Revelation by Moshyia de Broek

24) KHUFU 's LAST WILL, Jean-François Deschamps

25) The Synthesis of Science, Religion, and Philosophy Vol II

26) The Secret Doctrine, HP Blavatsky

27) PI: The Next Generation by David H Bailey and Jonathan M Borwen

28) Migration & Diffusion, Vol 6, Vasile Droj

29) The Great Pyramid of Giza Research Association THE COMPLETE PYRAMID SOURCEBOOK, John De Salvo

30) *Eastern life - Present and Past by Harriet Martineau*

31) History began at Mitoc, Andrei Vartic

32) Portacul lui Basalic, Andrei Vartic

33) Valahia University of Târgovişte, Doctoral School, M. Cârciumaru1, E.-C. Niţu, O. Cîrstina , and N. Goutas

34) The Westcar Papyrus, Joshua Mark.

35) Westcar Papyrus by Brendan Crawford

36) Ancient Egypt Online

37) The Tomb Theory, C. Staniland Wake

38) Egyptian Gods - The Complete List', Joshua J. Mark

39) Escape Velocity, The Columbia Electronic Encyclopedia™ Copyright © 2013, Columbia University Press. Licensed from Columbia University Press. All rights reserved. **www.cc.columbia.edu/cu/cup/**

40) String theory, Brian Greene (Youtube)

41) The Multiverse Has 11 Dimensions, Michio Kaku (YouTube)

Index

PARALLEL UNIVERSES

THE SOMERSE

Cover: East Backwear, near Glastonbury, Christmas 1989

Flooded road, one of the hazards of a winter journey in the old days

The Somerset Levels

Robin and
Romey Williams

EX LIBRIS PRESS

First published in 1992 by

EX LIBRIS PRESS
1 The Shambles
Bradford on Avon
Wiltshire

Typeset in 10 point Palatino

Design and typesetting by Ex Libris Press

Cover printed by Shires Press, Trowbridge
Printed in Great Britain by
Dotesios Ltd., Trowbridge

ISBN 0 948578 38 6

Acknowledgements

We would like to thank our interviewees particularly; Mary Duckett, Edwin Durston, Bill and Freda Ibell, Pat Kerrigan, Michael Richards and Mr. M.F. Wall answered our questions with great patience. Dr. Brian Johnston, of English Nature, and John McGeoch, local bird-watcher extraordinaire, produced documents, information and gave advice. The National Rivers Authority told us of changes in the water industry while Stan Davies of the RSPB sent us up-to-date reports on the Levels. Above all we must thank the people of the moors, our friends and neighbours for over twenty years, who have helped us understand more about this beautiful area.

Contents

Series Introduction

The present series, which it is intended should grow into a list of around fifteen titles, deals with significant and identifiable landscapes of the south-western counties. These contain two National Parks — Exmoor and Dartmoor — and several Areas of Outstanding Natural Beauty.

Our preference is for areas of the West Country which are perhaps less well documented than the National Parks, and for books which offer a complete picture of a particular landscape. We favour, too, an author who is sufficiently well acquainted with his or her chosen landscape to present his story in the round and with an ease in the telling which belies his depth of knowledge. Authors for West Country Landscapes have been chosen with this in mind.

The plan of each book is quite simple: the subject's underlying geology is the starting point. From this basis we are led to an understanding of that landscape's topography, of its flora and fauna and of the particular pattern of human settlement to which it gives rise — natural history followed by human history, in other words. Then we may look more closely at people and traditions, and at the interaction between individuals and the landscape — perhaps as expressed in literature and folklore. Throughout each account, there is constant reference to what may be seen on the ground today.

West country landscapes vary greatly — this is part of their great appeal. Likewise authors vary in their enthusiasms and areas of expertise. All these factors have a bearing on the books which we publish in the West Country Landscapes series. The books are substantial but succinct, well rounded but readable accounts of noteworthy pockets of the West Country, each with its particular characteristics and each penned by individually minded authors.

We are pleased to be associated with the CPRE in the production of the West Country Landscapes series. Any comments and suggestions from readers will be welcomed by the publishers.

Roger Jones, Editor

7

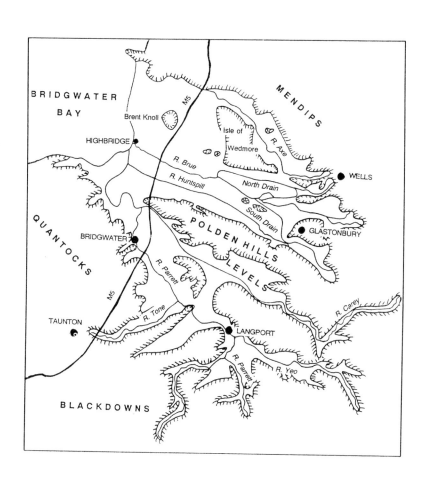

About the Authors

Robin and Romey Williams, and their three daughters, moved to a house sitting just above, and looking over, the Levels some twenty-four years ago. Both remember the excitement of the move and pausing to watch a flight of swans crossing the moors below, the sun lighting their brilliant white feathers, dramatically lit against a dark storm sky.

The most interesting aspect of this move was the ever-changing nature of the scene below. The first winter brought weeks of rain with heavy flooding and there were birds everywhere, great flocks of waders — dunlin, lapwings and snipe — while ducks crossed and re-crossed the sky and there was always something new to catch the eye. Then came the spring and miles of grass supported herds of Friesian cows, milked out on the moors with engines chugging away morning and evening. It was a wonderful time of familiarisation and somehow the magic of the place has never left them over the years, though it has changed and is no longer so rich in wildlife.

Robin was born in Africa but moved back to England when a few weeks old. He has been here ever since, except for some time abroad on National Service and periods of business in the Far and Middle East. He has a degree in agriculture from Cambridge University but now works as a self-employed management consultant, specialising in transport matters in the Single Market. He has written about, and photographed, the moors and Levels for many years now, with articles in such magazines as *Country Life, Bird Watching, Environment Now* and many others. He runs his own photographic library covering Somerset and other British scenery, and British wildlife of all sorts, especially insects.

Romey is a native of Somerset. Although her old home, Weston-super-Mare, is now officially in Avon, she still thinks of it under the old banner. She has spent all but a couple of years of her life in the area, so knows it well. Brock, her dog, keeps her in touch with the countryside, taking her out on the moors for a walk almost every day. She has a variety of local interests and in her spare time writes short stories and articles, of which some have been published.

Willows in the mist

1 Landscape with Water

It is not generally realised that Somerset is hollow, artificially protected over a large part of its area, reclaimed from the sea like parts of East Anglia. Indeed, it is quite difficult to come to terms with this when driving across miles of green fields dotted with cows or sheep. It all looks so solid and permanent. The only clue comes from the glint of water in the ditches surrounding each field.

I was first made aware of this some thirty or more years ago when I visited the Bath and West Show. One of the many exhibits was a relief map of Somerset before drainage had started. It probably covered the period around the Norman Conquest. I looked at it with interest but asked myself where were the places with which I was familiar. A great two-tongued swathe of blue drove into the heart of the county, leaving it U-shaped.

All this area is now contained within the land, the sea held back by walls, the rivers banked above the surrounding land and the whole network of waterways controlled by a series of pumping stations. Over the centuries this landscape has changed from low-lying sea-marsh to brackish wasteland, then to semi-drained land and, finally, to a completely controlled environment, with water-table set artificially. Over the years it has been known by a number of names. Around the bottom of the Brue Valley, down to Burnham-on-Sea, was called Brent Marsh up until the early 1800s. The upper part of the Brue Valley was generally called 'the Moors', because of the peat lying on the surface and its wildness and desolation. South of the Polden hills the name of 'Sedgemoor' has been in use since the Middle Ages.

Sedgemoor District Council administers the bulk of it now and, as a result, today the whole area is known as 'Sedgemoor'. Another name which has come into parlance over the past ten to twenty years is the 'Levels' or, to give the official version, 'The Somerset Moors and Levels'. This has come about mainly through the emerging strength of the conservation movement which became concerned about certain aspects of the draining of the area some ten to fifteen years ago and needed a collective name to convey the spirit of the area. This name has also been officially adopted by the Nature Conservancy Council (NCC), the Ministry of Agriculture Food and Fisheries (MAFF) and the Somerset County Council (SCC), in their planning for the area.

So, Sedgemoor, the Levels or even the Moors — a large and distinct part of the county — needs defining more closely if its history and way of life are to be explored in the depth they deserve.

Geology

The setting for the whole is determined by its underlying structure. The Levels consists of a basin of blue lias which has been scoured by rivers, leaving only a few points protruding from a great plain of alluvial deposits, which were brought down from the hills above in floods. This formed the second largest piece of fen country in England. In the Brue Valley a layer of peat, up to sixteen feet deep, sits on top of those clays. The great expanse of flat moors is split into two by the low rise of the Polden Hills, with various outliers such as the Isle of Wedmore, Brent Knoll, Nyland and the always visible cone of Glastonbury Tor.

Glastonbury Tor is composed of Upper Lias Sand, the Poldens and Isle of Wedmore of Blue Lias and marl, while the Mendip fringe is largely Carboniferous Limestone. But what you see when you look across the great flood plain is clay and peat — in places the clay extends to as much as ninety feet in depth.

In view of modern concerns, it is worth touching upon the subject of radon — that odourless, invisible gas which can cause cancer. This gas arises wherever there is uranium, which is a common constituent of many rocks, particularly the harder ones, such as granite, but is largely disseminated harmlessly into the atmosphere. According to Somerset County Council, the actual area of the Levels itself is not known to contain any significant amounts but there are traces on the Poldens, at nearby Shepton Mallet and in Bridgwater, though not on the Isle of Wedmore. The old quarries at Street have proved to be a source and action has been taken in some areas to remove the gas from individual houses.

Size and Shape

Opinions as to the size of the Levels vary. As usual, it 'depends on what you mean'. I should start by saying that the Nailsea and Portishead Levels, which are in the present County of Avon, and completely separated from the rest, are excluded from consideration in this book.

The Somerset County Council, in their 1983 report, 'Somerset Levels and Moors Plan', refer to the 140,000 acres of 'the flood plains of the Rivers Axe, Brue, Huntspill, King's Sedgemoor Drain, Parrett and their tributaries. The Levels comprise the five to six mile wide coastal clay belt while the Moors are found in the inland river valleys, where there is a thick deposit of peat overlain in places by clay.'

In 1500 it was recorded that the floodable land of Somerset was 70,000 acres, of which just over 20,000 acres had been reclaimed at the time. The area of the Somerset Levels and Moors which is currently declared an Environmentally Sensitive Area (ESA) by the MAFF, is 68,000 acres and is said to include the majority of the Levels. Finally, the NCC refer to the total area of the Levels and Moors as being just over 114,000 acres. So you takes your pick. There is no real agreement. I think I favour the figure of around 70,000 acres spoken about in the days when our ancestors could see the actual effect on their land. It ties in nicely with the area for which payment is being made by the MAFF for preserving this special landscape.

'Our' Moors and Levels start on the coast just below Brean Down, south of Weston-super-Mare, and extend down the coast to the other side of the Parrett and up as far as Steart, butting up against the Quantock Hills where they rise from the floodplain. One arm runs inland, following the line of the River Parrett, by way of Bridgwater, to Langport, and continues up to Ilchester in the very heart of inland Somerset. Indeed the Levels nearly split Somerset into two, ending only a few miles from Dorset. This huge area, the original Sedgemoor, is drained by the tidal Parrett and its tributaries and the King's Sedgemoor Drain, artificially constructed by man and running out to join the Parrett. Sedgemoor is separated from the rest of the Levels by the low lying tongue of the Polden Hills. There has never been any connection between the two systems, except on the narrow coastal strip.

The northern part of the Levels is drained by the Huntspill River, an artificial channel arising from the Parrett and running up to near Glastonbury. The River Brue, which has had its course altered artificially more than once over the ages, runs from a clyse at Highbridge, to Glastonbury and beyond. The third drainage arm is the River Axe, which enters by Brean Down and runs along the edge of the Mendip Hills to near Wells. The Axe valley is separated from the Glastonbury arm of the Levels by a line of hills which culminate in the Isle of Wedmore.

Peat diggings, Brue Valley

The Brue Valley is famous for its peat, which covers large areas to depths of up to fifteen feet or more. Peat used to be dug for burning but has come to be more important in making potting and growing composts or simply for lightening heavy garden soils. Once granted, Planning Permissions cannot be revoked and a great many such were given out earlier this century. So large parts of Somerset will continue to be dug, unless the present campaign to replace with less contro-versial products is successful. Many people are employed in the peat industry and depend on it for jobs in rural areas where farming is using less labour each year. On the other hand, there is no doubt that little of this unique and beautiful countryside remains and many people wish to see some at least preserved. Somerset peat is not completely inert and supports a great variety of plant and animals species which would vanish with its demise.

The Brue Valley is dominated by Glastonbury which lies at its eastern end and broods over the flat, water-bounded land. The town lies beneath Glastonbury Tor, a conical hill with a church tower on its top. The view from the summit is stupendous. The summer solstice is celebrated on the Tor and a variety of beliefs are centred on this prominent hill and its surrounds, including those concerning the great King Arthur. At the other, western, end of the northern Levels another round hill gazes over the moors. Brent Knoll is best-known as a landmark on the M5 on its way down to Exeter and Cornwall. Walking over the moors in the middle of the area, near Wedmore, can be seen Glastonbury Tor on one side, Brent Knoll at the other, while the north is bounded by the Isle of Wedmore. South is the faint outline of the low-lying ridge of the Poldens. The flatness is always relieved by a swell of hills beyond, giving scale and a special feel to the landscape, without detracting from the huge and varying skies.

Viewpoints

One of the most delightful things in life is looking down on coun-tryside from above. It is possible to indulge this passion from many places within the Levels and usually without overmuch exertion, for the area is dotted with strange little hills and bumps which stick up abruptly above the surface of the land, often looking artificial, like Silbury Hill in Wiltshire, though none are believed to be so here. Some are known through their ancient connections, others are lost within the confines of a farm and only known to those who search them out on the map and seek the footpaths which lead to their summits.

One of the best-known is Burrow Mump, set by the village of Burrow Bridge on the road between Taunton and Glastonbury. This round hillock is crowned with a church and has wonderful views of

Sedgemoor. There have been buildings here since Norman times and at one time the church belonged to nearby Athelney Abbey. The church has a long history and has been given to the people of Somerset as a memorial to those who died in the last war; what could be more fitting than this lonely tower gazing out over the waters and green fields of old Somerset. In winter Burrow Mump has an added attraction: Southmoor is deliberately flooded by the local Internal Drainage Board, its trees and gates stick up out of the grey waters to give a surrealistic appearance, attracting great herds of swans and flights of duck at the right time. The flooding is the traditional way of bringing silt onto the land as a natural fertiliser.

Mute swans have become much more numerous
over the Levels in recent years

To the west lies East Lyng where there is a low, almost indiscernible island — the Isle of Athelney. Here it was that Alfred hid from the Danes before finally sallying forth and defeating them decisively. A causeway linked it with Burrow Mump; they were both fortified heavily and hidden in a maze of marsh and overgrowth so that few knew of their existence. Alfred founded an Abbey on the site in thanks for his victory but, after the Dissolution and its destruction, it vanished and no trace remains now.

Another spectacular view can be enjoyed by taking the footpath to the top of Brent Knoll, which lies close to Junction 22 on the M5. Look west from this over the village and to the sea at Bridgwater Bay, east down the Brue valley to Wedmore and Cheddar Gorge, south to the Poldens and north to Weston-super-Mare. You get a real idea of the extent and feel of the Levels from this vantage point.

The ancient hill and settlement of Nyland

A curious mound lies between Cheddar and Wedmore. Traces of medieval buildings have been found at Nyland and a chapel existed there until this century. Signs of burials were found when alterations were being carried out on farm buildings. This island dominates Cheddar and Draycott Moors; there is a small road leading from Draycott to Wedmore which passes its foot and gives access.

Marvellous views are to be had from the footpath which runs around its southern, upper flank. On the road between Wedmore and Wells, the conical island of Panborough stands out from the moor, while a mile or so further on there is another strange little hill which contains the motte and bailey of Fenny Castle, not far from the village of Godney.

There is a tremendous view in both directions from the Poldens, along the ridge-top road between Bridgwater and Glastonbury. Northwards the green and brown of the fields reaches to the blue, far-off heights of Mendip, with the gash of Cheddar Gorge sometimes visible if the light is right. To the east, slender and silver like a monument to technology, the light often catches the radio transmitter mast above Wells. I well remember sitting up by that mast one dark night in 1977, at the Queen's Silver Jubilee celebrations, waiting for the watch fire to appear over to the west and then lighting our own, which was followed by others in quick succession. Looking south from Polden, the land is patchworked in places with plough, and the long silver line of the King's Sedgemoor Drain is prominent. Water catches the eye everywhere, silver glints as the sun reflects off rhynes and ditches while, after long periods of rain, the Levels shine like a huge mirror, the flood waters stretching down into the far corners and along the lines of river and ditch.

Roads

If you wish to see the Levels as a whole, on the grand scale as it were, there are some excellent roads which cross or circumnavigate them. The M5 and the parallel A38 take you from Bristol, through the edges of Mendip and across the western edges to the ancient port of Bridgwater. From there the A39 navigates the ridge of the Poldens, with stupendous views on either side and eventually reaches Glastonbury. The road from Glastonbury to Meare and Wedmore crosses some of the finest parts of the Brue Valley and there are roads off it to peat diggings at Westhay and Shapwick Heath, or to Godney, a slightly elevated piece of ground with one of the oldest settlements in the area. Various roads radiate out from Wedmore, covering the nearby moors, all are fascinating and each reveals varied countryside — some green and open, some willow-bounded and enclosed.

One of the nicest roads for visiting old Sedgemoor is the A361, which runs from Glastonbury to Street, then down and across the moor. It passes over the great King's Sedgemoor Drain with its huge sluices at Greylake, alongside Burrow Mump and the withy beds (willows) at Othery and Stathe, by way of Athelney and eventually to Taunton. Roads cross over from here northwards to Weston-zoyland, past the battlefield at Bussex, to Bridgwater, or south to Langport, a pleasant small town at what used to be the upper navigable limits of the Parrett. It is astonishing to think that sixteen- to twenty-ton barges could penetrate as far as Langport and beyond some four centuries ago. How different the country was then. Now it is served by as pleasant a network of roads as you could find anywhere, winding through villages and hamlets, some of which seem as if they have grown out of the ground and have remained little changed over the years.

Glastonbury

There is no doubt that Glastonbury is the dominant presence in the region. Its sense of authority survives from pre-Reformation days when it owned vast sections of the Levels. This is in spite of the fact that it is a much-diminished place, over-shadowed by the shops and industry of neighbouring Street.

Glastonbury is a surprising town; much of it is built of a hideous red brick which forms the main impression when driving through. The High Street has charm but finds difficulty in supporting its shops, and is succumbing to the pressures of out-of-town shopping centres and the presence of nearby Street. The marvellous and unrivalled ruins of Glastonbury Abbey are hidden behind a garage and car park of unparalleled ugliness and banality. No effort has been made to blend in with the surrounds or to break the outline.

Inside the Abbey grounds, all is forgiven. They are beautifully looked after and there is a tremendous sense of peace and tranquillity. Perhaps the first thing which strikes the visitor is the sheer size of the place. It was and is huge. Before it was destroyed in 1539, it was said to be the longest church in Christendom, north of the Alps. Although a number of the buildings are well-preserved, considering the damage done by the reformers and those who removed stones for their own use over the centuries, much of the structure is indicated only by the lower parts of walls or stones just proud of the grass. The

Abbey is said to have been founded round 600 AD and was at the height of its fame with St. Dunstan as Abbot in the tenth century. There were fires and re-buildings until the present Abbey was built over a period of 350 years from 1184. The astonishing thing is that this huge establishment was built in an all but empty countryside, surrounded by marshes and ever-present water. The most complete part of the Abbey is the Octagonal building of the Abbot's Kitchen, followed by a chapel and remnants of the nave.

Another extremely old but well-preserved building, is that of the Glastonbury Tribunal in the High Street, previous site of the Court House and dating from 1400. This building is a museum and contains many of the finds from the Glastonbury Lake Villages. Towards the outskirts, on the road to the famous Chalice Well (which runs red, so it is said, with blood from the Holy Grail), there is a fourteenth century Tithe Barn, now housing the Somerset Rural Life Museum. This beautifully maintained old building, full of farm implements and other fascinating relics from the past, is well worth visiting.

Wells

The City of Wells is the other great ecclesiastical presence, which goes back in history almost as far as Glastonbury. Unlike the latter, it was not sacked by Henry VIII and kept its power as the bishopric of Bath and Wells. It is a delightful town which has retained its old-world charm, even though it has modernised its shopping facilities and added large new estates of houses which remain largely hidden. Because it has no by-pass you are forced to see much of Wells in any journey which passes through. It becomes an awful bottleneck at busy times and the city has been arguing for years about a possible change of route, but without visible result so far.

The Cathedral, recently cleaned and restored, is set right in the heart of the city. It was built to its present design in 1180. It has magnificent scissor arches inside and a unique clock, constructed in 1390, which has four knights attacking each other every quarter of an hour. The newly-cleaned West Front lies across a beautiful green, seen through an archway as you drive in from the north, while an unusual gateway, the Penniless Porch, greets you by the car-park in the centre. To one side of this is the mellow stone entrance to the Bishop's Palace. The Palace lies inside a moat and is open to the public during the summer. The moat contains a collection of ornamental waterfowl and there is a bell set into the wall which is rung by a swan when it wants food.

Wells is enclosed, busy, intimate, a delightful place to visit, though rather overrun with tourists. Fortunately, it seems able to maintain a life of its own, while meeting their needs.

Bridgwater

I suppose Bridgwater must be included in the Levels, though really only through its location on the River Parrett. It lies principally on the left bank and by tradition and inclination looks towards the Quantocks for its lungs and recreation. However, the town is spreading towards Westonzoyland as its population increases and those inhabitants must certainly be considered to be of the Levels. Bridgwater is essentially an ugly, red brick town, but with a wonderful Georgian heart in King Square. The bricks are the relics of a once thriving brick and tile industry based on the local clay and river silt.

For the visitor the most noticeable thing on entering Bridgwater is the smell. Cellophane has been manufactured here for many years and produces a strong odour of rotten eggs. If you remark on it to a native Bridgwaterian he will reply, "What smell?", or laugh and say he hasn't noticed it for years. The principal feature of the town is the River Parrett, which divides the main shopping street. However, the rise and fall of the tide is over thirty-five feet at the entrance, so there is a considerable difference between the heavily silted waters lapping the banks and the miles of noisome mud exposed at low tide. Further down-river, the old docks have been closed and are now being developed as a marina for those hardy souls who can face yachting in the Bristol Channel, with all its currents and shifting mud banks. Bridgwater remains an important market centre for the area and has a lively annual Sheep Fair.

Bridgwater, Wells and Glastonbury participate in a round of late autumn carnivals which are of the highest standard. Pubs and clubs around the countryside spend all year building wonderful floats, lit by trailer-borne generators. These process through the towns raising money for charity and are well worth the effort of braving the usual autumnal drizzle and crowds.

Langport

The final Sedgemoor township (or is it a large village?) is Langport, ten miles up-stream from Bridgwater and formerly an important port for the centre of Somerset. It is a pretty little place curled along a bend of the river but marred by an unending stream of heavy traffic wending its way between the busy A303, from London, and Taunton. The narrow main street is full of old-fashioned shops with the old ways of decoration and doing business — pleasant and relaxed. Waiting to cross the road, however, can be somewhat traumatic. Langport is well worth visiting and the surrounding countryside and villages are particularly attractive.

Highbridge and Burnham-on-Sea

Highbridge and Burnham-on-Sea, almost inseparable now, so fast have they grown, are very much a part of the area. Sedgemoor District Council and the Lower Brue Drainage Board have their offices there, so much of importance to the area is formulated in these places. They are dormitory and seaside towns, catering for the retired, to visitors during the summer and with a commuter population who whizz along the nearby M5 to Bristol each morning. Little remains to be seen of the old townships which were so much a part of Levels life, but the two places provide access to the area for many people. Burnham has a busy shopping centre and the fresh sea-air makes it a pleasant place to visit.

Wedmore

While this is an upland village, or small town, it lies in the very heart of the Brue valley and its moors and is surrounded by ditches and water and the great flat plains of the Levels. The people who live there — and the population has increased considerably in recent years — still have many connections with the moors. Many families of long-standing, with names going back hundreds of years in the Parish records, have resisted being driven out by rising house-prices and rich newcomers, and live there still. It retains an atmosphere of the moors and is proud of its local connections, its farming and cheese-making. There is some traffic-congestion in the summer but it retains charming and delightful streets with many old-style shops, though they sell the latest fashions and food. The church is superb and there are some ancient pubs, recommendation on its own. It is difficult to believe, however, that Wedmore was once a busy port discharging sea-going vessels.

The Land and its Uses

For all the towns and villages which fringe them, the Levels and Moors are by no means thickly populated They are windswept in autumn and spring, rainlashed in winter and lush and hot in summer. The underpinnings of the soil are unstable and, by its very nature, the land is always subject to some flood, for it is all below sea-level at some part of each day. It only takes a mixture of events — heavy rain in the hills, spring tides and gales piling up the waters in the Severn Sea — to cause the swollen rivers to spill their banks and inundate the fields on either side. Raised areas, islands in local parlance, exist in many parts, but they have to be reached by roads across the lower areas. Those that can be built upon, have been so in the past.

Reed mace on old peat diggings

The Levels is essentially an agricultural region and looks likely to remain so, even if the squeeze on farming continues, as it threatens to do. There have been many changes over its history, but it seems the area will remain one of permanent grassland, and will follow a long tradition of providing low-cost, high-quality grass for great herds of dairy cattle. About eight per cent of the area has been drained and ploughed. There is every hope and indication that this will not increase further and may well disappear in the fullness of time, leaving a traditional landscape of cows, grass, water-bounded fields and pollard willows.

The structure of the modern Levels is much the same everywhere. The fields are open, of permanent grass, and ringed with ditches which are maintained by the farmer. These lead into rhynes which are looked after by the local Internal Drainage Board (IDB) which, in turn, feed into drains or rivers which themselves are a part of the responsibility of the National Rivers Authority (NRA). This latter is an independent body charged with flood-prevention, preservation of water quality and the environment, together with conservation. It also has a number of other duties and responsibilities. The NRA took over from various local Water Authorities as a result of the 1989 Water Act. It operates the various pumping stations, controls most of the sea-walls and generally ensures we do not drown in our beds.

This sight of water in the Levels is all-pervasive and cannot be ignored. If you walk across the fields you are bound to come across a ditch or rhyne; you cannot pass and have to return the way you came. Access to the moors is by way of droves. Many of these have now become full-blown roads, others remain as they were planned. They were constructed originally when the various moors were enclosed and drained, starting around 1790. The people who planned this arranged for access to the fields without going through another owner's property. The green lanes were set aside as being common to all the riparian owners of the fields they served. It was their common duty to maintain them and to keep them open, and so it has been to this day. In general, they have become places where the public can also walk the moors without hindrance, though few are actually rights of way.

This network of droves is the jewel in the crown of living on the Levels. There are few places in this country where it is possible to walk for hours away from the metalled roads. They were originally just pieces of field with a ditch on each side and bridges to take cattle over cross-rhynes. No surfacing was planned as such but, over the years, and particularly with the coming of the tractor, they have been stoned and filled where needed. Some are rutted and muddy but others retain their green appearance and a horse may be galloped along them. But it should not be forgotten that they are a part of the farming system, not a place where the public have a right to be. The farmer's tolerance allows us access to walk and enjoy this beautiful countryside.

Some parts are wide open, without a tree in sight. This is not the natural state of the countryside. It was a tradition to edge the ditches with willows and alders which marked the roads in times of flood and provided stakes, hurdles, garden poles and spars for thatching. As the demand for these fell and the trees overgrew and split, many were allowed to die. The old tradition of planting willows along ditches to strengthen the banks has been overtaken by another practice — to clear the banks for mechanical cleaning of the ditches. When I see a bare field with no shelter I wonder if this is sensible husbandry — surely cattle do better with some shelter to get out of the wind or the sun? Certainly the trampled ground under shelter trees seems to bear this out. In other parts farmers have maintained the trees and they add to the landscape. Long lines of pollard willows edging the fields have a special beauty of their own, varying in all the different weather faced on the Levels, from delicate shapes pencilled in the mist, to hard silhouettes against the setting sun.

It is a strange place to live, even if your house lies on one of the surrounding uplands, for it is always damp and humid. The actual rainfall over much of the area is low — not much above that of East Anglia — but the ground is a sponge, holding water and surrounded by water. The clouds precipitate on the surrounding hills, the Quantocks and Mendips having particularly high rainfall, and the streams and rivers run down to the Levels where they slowly meander, evaporating in the hot summer sunshine. I know the Brue Valley best, as I live looking over Tealham Moor, and it is not uncommon to be longing for rain on the garden, yet watching the clouds rolling over Glastonbury Tor in the distance, or seeing Mendip black beyond our sunshine. On a summer day, with the sun beating down, you

Sunset on winter floods

can feel the weight of moisture rising up from the surface of the ditches and from all over the field surfaces. In autumn this is displayed visually as the cold evenings come in. The mists rise up, first from the ditches, then run across the surface of the grass, hanging a foot or so above the ground. Cattle move across the fields with their heads and backs only appearing above the white shroud. It is a time of great beauty and also of mystery. It is no wonder that the legends of Arthur arise from this area — one can imagine the horses splashing across the causeways with only the head and shoulders of the riders visible in the moonlight above the mists.

For sufferers from sinus the heavy mid-summer air can be an oppression which is difficult to bear, bringing with it headaches, depression and extreme lassitude. Spring also can be a particularly difficult time to get moving. Yet the place has a reputation for long life. In the old days people suffered from arthritis and rheumatism, were often twisted and knobbed, bent double, but lived a great many years. This particularly affected those who lived out on the moors before the great pumping stations controlled the water-table.

Most houses were set on slightly raised ground, yet even there the waters rose enough in winter to force them to live upstairs, cooking, sleeping and living, while the lower storey was lapping with water. No wonder they suffered from the damp. Their business lay out on the moors, cutting reeds, ditching and looking after cattle on the remote moorland pastures in summer. Most have gone now. They moved to the upper grounds and abandoned their houses as soon as they could afford it, though some of the children brought up in such surrounds still speak of the peace and beauty as something very special. It is possible to find the remains of many farms, cottages and settlements by the edges of droves. The secret is to look for a pile of nettles and brambles, with the odd fruit tree leaning over nearby. This is all that remains of where a family used to be, in living memory, in circumstances not that far removed from peasants in the Third World today.

In summer the weather is splendid; there is noticeably less rainfall than in surrounding areas, and often blue skies and long periods of sunshine. Sometimes this leads to long periods of heat-haze, when the surrounding higher edges dry to a dusty brown, though the Levels retain their colours as the water-table is raised in summer. The older pastures do not have that fresh green look in summer which you might expect. This is because the herbage is not pure grass, but a wonderful mixture of many species which give it its excellent feed value. Many fields go red-brown in high summer and look as if they are dry. In fact they are red with sorrel and other herbs, sometimes dotted with yellow flags even in the centre, though most of these beautiful irises line the banks of the rhynes. Many fields are unsprayed and have been fertilised only with silt or cow-manure over the years. They start the spring with a flush of celandines and dandelions, followed by the brilliant yellow of king-cups, usually by the ditches but all over in certain fields. The next phase is a pale lilac flush as the lady's smock takes over. Then come marsh orchids, though nowadays these are mostly confined to the edges of the water. Co-incident with the cuckoo flowers are great swathes of Queen Anne's Lace along the droves, swaying white in the wind. Midsummer brings the heavy scent of meadowsweet and the similar, but scentless, meadow rue, making the fields a rich and tangled mass of cream flowers and long stems.

The hedges on the surrounds are hard-white with blackthorn in March while, at the end of May, all the roads are edged with great billowing masses of cream as the hawthorn comes into full flower, with its scent filling the air. The green of the ditches is richly varied, from the pale of Canadian pondweed to the sharper colour of rushes and the dark greens of various flower stems. In spring and summer it looks as though all life is billowing out and nothing can stop reproduction as a function. Lushness is the perfect word to describe the feel of the place.

Agricultural Change

Up until the start of the 1980s there was only one direction for agriculture — onwards and upwards. After the experiences of two world wars, when we had been squeezed by submarine blockades and lived on restricted rations, increasing agricultural production became an obsession. It took precedence over virtually everything else. Farmers became a protected species, receiving subsidies to plant things and subsidies to remove them. There was a dash for agricultural efficiency and 'improving' the land at any cost. As a consequence of this, our farmers became the most efficient in Europe, producing huge yields of cereals, quantities of milk and large numbers of animals. Planning permission was not needed for agricultural buildings, subsidies were available for draining any piece of marshy land and it became commonplace to plough up even such national treasures as Exmoor.

There was nothing any of us could do except enjoy the cheap food which resulted, though it is often forgotten that this was combined with high taxation. Britain joined the EEC and things became even worse. Enormous sums were spent in supporting further agricultural production until it was realised that there were intervention stores filling with unsold, heavily subsidised food. The situation could not go on for ever and in the early 1980s the first reactions were felt. By then there were milk lakes, wine lakes, wheat mountains, butter mountains and many others — in stores which were costing money to run, filled with products which had cost money to produce and had been heavily subsidised by the tax-payer through EEC funds.

Milk quotas were introduced, based on allowing people only ninety per cent of the previous year's production. There was a huge shake-up in the area, long famous for its milk. Farmers retired, others sold their quotas to rival farms. Milking herds became bigger and, after a time, profits recovered again. But by then beef herds were on the increase to replace the cattle lost to the new order.

At the same time the conservation movement was starting to flex its muscles, tentatively at first, but with increasing confidence over the years. Initially, there was a vague feeling of unease at the way in which the country was changing; fields were becoming larger, hedgerows disappearing, ponds being drained, marshes altered and cultivated. Wildlife was disappearing at an alarming rate. The countryside was becoming more like a factory and less accessible to ordinary people. The new leisure revolution gave people the time, the money and the mobility to get out into the countryside and see what was going on and they did not like what they found.

At first this was only a feeling but soon hard facts followed which showed a catastrophic change taking place, and the rate of change was accelerating. It became clear that many old pastures were vanishing, that certain flower, insect and bird species were on the verge of extinction and that the shape, feel and smell of the countryside was being transformed. The varied, colourful and beautiful English countryside was becoming a uniform waste of monoculture — in one part all yellow rape seed, in another the same green ryegrass. Elsewhere, enormous fields of wheat stretched to the horizon. This was not the England people remembered or wished to enjoy.

The Government decided to take action through its agency, the Nature Conservancy Council, which had been establishing a long list of Sites of Special Scientific Interest (SSSI). These were individual fields or areas where something worth preserving lived, whether it be insects, flowers, mammals or birds. In 1981 the Wildlife and Countryside Act introduced measures to protect these SSSIs. The owner was required to contact the NCC if he wished to make any changes which might affect their status. He might also be required to take some positive action in the other direction, to improve the chances of survival of those species. In either case, the landowner could come to an agreement with the NCC and receive compensation for loss of profit, so that he would not lose from his support for wildlife and the country would gain. Although full of problems to start with, the system has settled in nicely now and is generally regarded as an improvement, enabling care and thought to be put into conservation without damaging people's living.

In 1984 the EEC decided, by way of the MAFF, 'to introduce a new scheme that would help to protect some of the most beautiful parts of the country from the damage and loss that can come from agricultural change.' This was revolutionary thinking indeed and an admission that the problems noticed by the public were not just imagination. Ten areas were selected for this special treatment and virtually the whole of the Somerset Levels and Moors was one of them.

Lapwings on the floods, Tealham Moor

What a change from an unrecognised piece of countryside a few years before, known only to those who lived close by, to one which warranted this treatment. The Somerset Levels Environmentally Sensitive Area (ESA) was introduced in November 1986 and, by 1991, over fifty per cent of the usable land had been taken up by farmers under the scheme.

The ESA is a remarkable concept and one which has the chance of completely altering the way we look at the countryside and reducing change to a manageable pace. Under this scheme, which is of profound importance to the Levels, farmers are entitled to payment as a right. It is entirely up to them whether they participate or not but the take-up is a remarkable tribute to the careful drawing up of the objectives, rules and payment levels.

The first scheme, just coming to the end of its life, involved two levels of payment. The first required the farmer to continue his work in a traditional manner. It placed restrictions on the amount of fertiliser used, forbade new under-drainage, required the ground to be grassland and trees to be maintained. The second tier placed greater restrictions on the farmer by further reducing his stocking and fertiliser rates and prohibited sheep on the land in the winter. The first tier paid £33 per acre and the second £48. Many farmers favoured the first, for it was little change from their usual practice. A new scheme is due in 1992, with four levels of payment available, designed to preserve the landscape more effectively still.

Since so much of the land is also SSSI, it has been possible to maintain traditional farming practices to a considerable degree without affecting farming profits. In times of difficulty, with decreasing general subsidies and falling prices, this has been welcomed by many farmers who have long regretted the gradual passing of a way of life. One change is that all further individual drainage of the area has been stopped. No more land is being ploughed and some is reverting to permanent grass.

The most visible change in the countryside lies with the numbers and types of farm animals to be seen out on the fields. Ten years ago, in summer, the fields would have been covered with black and white Friesian dairy cows, with the occasional Hereford bull running with them to produce beef followers. Sheep were rarely seen and other colours of cattle, apart from the soft browns of Jerseys and Guernseys, were unusual. During summer the cattle were milked out on the fields in bales. These are little tin sheds mounted on runners and wheels which are towed from field to field and contain milking parlours with engine-driven milking clusters. Twenty years ago, some moors would have ten or twenty such bales in sight, with the engines popping away in the distance in the early morning.

Times have changed. There are far fewer bales. Many herds are based around permanent parlours on the hill ground, with the moors reserved for beef herds, silage or hay. The most startling change of all is the arrival of great flocks of sheep. Without chemical drenches to control liver fluke and other diseases, it would be impossible for them to live on such wet pastures, which are perfect host to the snail which is a part of the fluke cycle. Sheep have proved profitable and there has been a boom in keeping them, fattening hill-bred sheep on the Levels or breeding lambs directly out there. This has made up for depressed beef prices and a lesser requirement for milking cows as the country faces its second reduction in milk quotas. Even the colour of the herds has changed. Foreign bulls, Holsteins, Charolais and others, have brought strange white and parti-coloured cattle to add to the ever-present Friesians.

Cows and reeds, Westhay Heath

Over the years, agricultural pressures have led to ever increasing applications of fertiliser to maintain output and profitability. With fertiliser prices expected to rise in real terms, this will become a less attractive option in the future. The Levels have an opportunity to come into their own again as one of the major milk-producing areas, through their natural fertility. Recent tests by the NCC and others have shown that natural, unimproved, lightly or unfertilised wetland grass produces yields approaching the best in the country — provided the water-table is held high. This has the advantage of being produced at low cost compared with those who have to fertilise heavily to achieve adequate yields. Winter silting, through flooding, improves this yield further. Clearly more research is needed, but every indication is that the traditionally farmed Levels, kept as wetlands, have an excellent future. If this is so, it will meet the needs of farmer, conservationist and the public.

If the Levels had been ploughed, and there was every sign of this happening before the Wildlife and Countryside Act of 1981, then they would have become like the Fens, high-yielding deserts without boundaries, enormous fields stretching into the distance and farmed by relatively few people. The villages, heavily dependent on farming, would have vanished and an empty, unattractive countryside would have resulted, with tons more unwanted produce pouring into store. At least that prospect seems to have been averted, though there are other problems, as will be seen later.

The Levels remain a clearly-defined entity, of special beauty and character. Will they be able to remain as such or will the pressures of business, of profit and modern living, force them into the mould of conformity, so they become just another green desert?

Wells Cathedral, with its intricately carved north front

2 History — Secular and Monastic

For all their emptiness and unhealthy climate in times gone by, the moors and levels of Somerset have a rich history and are at the very core of the development of the English nation. Great waves of conquest have battered at the doors of the county and foundered among these marshes, impenetrable except to those who were born nearby. They have acted as both the nightmare and the saviour of the region, providing a constant source of food and succour against their enemies when they wished to melt out of sight.

From Prehistory to the Kingdom of Wessex

Around 4,500 BC, the development of sand-dunes on what is now the west coast of Somerset, prevented salt-water flooding the inland marshes; gradually this transformed the interior into a huge swamp, with great expanses of open water, reed-fringed edges and islands of higher ground. The first known traces of humans occurred at this time and are marked by the presence of a great many flint tools left around their camp-sites in the drier area and on the islands. All trace of this wandering hunter culture disappears by 4,000 BC but, by 3,000 BC, settlers were well established in Somerset. Bronze age relics have been found at Ilchester, Glastonbury and Cannington, dating from around 2,000 BC.

The peat of the Brue Valley has preserved artefacts within it particularly well, so more is known about the early history of that area than other parts of the Levels. Sharp-eyed peat-diggers and others have unearthed a series of significant finds since the early 1800s. The most important of these have been based around trackways leading into the swamps and soft ground of the interior. The oldest is the Sweet Track, named after the digger who first spotted it in 1970.

The trackway dates back to 4,000 BC. and was a raised walkway between patches of firmer ground. On Walton Heath, near Street, a section of track made of hurdles dates from around 3,500 BC. This construction spread the load and virtually floated on the surface of the soft ground. In 3,000 BC a platform of brushwood, held in place by stakes, was built off an island of firm ground at Westhay to give a hard edge from which other trackways radiated.

Chronologically, the next track is the Abbot's Way, found in 1835 at Westhay Heath, running between Westhay and the raised island of Burtle. This dates from 2,500 BC and is one and a half miles long. The name is a misnomer as, when it was first discovered, it was believed to have linked medieval Burtle Priory with Glastonbury Abbey buildings at Meare. However, the trackway pre-dates these by over 3,500 years at the least. A further major track was discovered in the 1930s, dating from 1,400 BC. This ran from Meare Heath towards Shapwick, over a raised bog for more than a mile, and was solidly constructed of oak.

At nearby Edington Burtle a box of bronze ornaments and tools was found buried in the peat and well preserved. These have been dated at around 1,600 BC. A dugout canoe was found near Shapwick, dated after 1,000 BC, so a great deal has been discovered about life in those far-off days, though confined to this corner of the Brue valley, near the edge of the Polden Hills.

From the period starting at 1,000 BC, water-levels varied as heavier, then lighter, rainfall became the norm. In 250 BC, perhaps earlier, two villages were built right in the marshes. The first of these 'Lake' villages, near Glastonbury, was discovered by Arthur Bulleid in 1892. It is a fascinating story, as he had been earlier involved in examining Lake villages in Switzerland and had thought there must be others in existence. Conditions on the Levels seemed similar and so he started to search and continued his examination over several years. Eventually he came across signs at Godney, where he conducted extensive excavations. The site of the village occupied over three acres on an artificial island made from wood, clay and wattle. It is believed that between five and seven groups or families, amounting to around one hundred people, lived there, and that the settlement lasted until 50 AD, when rising water defeated the efforts of the inhabitants to keep pace with raising the level of the foundations. It appears to have been a civilised place, containing thatched huts with more than one room, hearths and clay floors. The whole was protected by a wooden palisade.

A further village was discovered at nearby Meare by the hard-working Bulleid. Eventually it turned out to be two closely-located, but separate, settlements. They were of a quite different nature to that at Godney, with less substantial underpinnings and no palisade, while the huts did not appear to be permanent. It is believed these were seasonal gathering places for hunters or fishermen. A number of middens were found on the sites and the scientists discovered a great deal about the people, their domestic animals and the wildlife. It is sobering to realise that pelicans, boars and sea-eagles were common on the Levels in that age.

By 400 BC climatic changes had killed the plants feeding the bogs and stopped further formation of peat. The peat beds were then left intact until we started digging them so vigorously this century.

Between 43 and 410 AD, Britain was occupied by the Romans and became a province of the Empire. There was a Roman camp on Brent Knoll, alongside what is now the M5, looking over the northern arm of the Levels and, no doubt, keeping guard over the comings and goings of the local inhabitants on their way up river or into the depths of the marshes. At the other end of the Levels, though above them on higher ground, the Cangi were defeated by the Second Legion, near Wookey, in 49 AD. Heath House, on the edge of the Isle of Wedmore, was a military camp at this time, identified as such by skeletons found in 1883.

Gildas, the historian, wrote about rising sea-levels and the arrival of the Saxons in 547. He is said to have lived for some while on the inhospitable island of Steepholm, between Weston-super-Mare and Cardiff. Those West Saxons won a great victory at Old Sarum in 552 and then spread across the West Country. Ceawlin was recorded as King of Wessex in 556 but his kingdom did not extend beyond North Somerset. The Levels remained untamed and free and, no doubt, completely inhospitable to outsiders.

The Battle of Penselwood opened up the far West Country to the Saxon invaders in 658. Cenwealh, King of Wessex, founded the bishopric of Winchester around 650, of which Somerset was part. The Saxon tribe from which the men of Wessex sprang was called the 'sumorsoetas' — Somerset and Somerton, long the capital, spring from that. By 680 the men of Wessex had reached the edges of Devon.

The Church was the dominant force over the area for hundreds of years, exerting its influence through the agencies of the great monasteries and Abbeys and the Cathedral-church at Wells. These bodies taught the people of the area, employed them, helped them worship and drained the moors to provide grazing for their cattle. For much of the time they were more important than the King and certainly as rich. To talk about the history of the Levels is to be involved in the ecclesiastical affairs of the time. Glastonbury Abbey in its heyday was nearly 600 feet long and famous for its design and carvings. Wells Cathedral is amongst the most magnificent of all cathedrals. The other Abbeys, Muchelney and Athelney, were also splendid buildings, though less well known nowadays.

Glastonbury

The story starts with the earliest days of Christianity. Legend says that Joseph of Arimathea travelled from the Holy Land and reached Glastonbury in AD 63. He walked over Wearyall Hill in Glastonbury and planted the thorn stick he carried with him. It blossomed on Christmas Day and has done so ever since, conforming with the old calendar which puts Christmas some days after the present date. Joseph is supposed to have met a Celtic King there who gave him XII Hides of land upon which he erected a church. Reference to these XII Hides has re-occurred throughout history, while the tree is a fact. Celia Fiennes visited Glastonbury in 1698 and noted the presence of the Holy Thorn. The original was cut down finally in the seventeenth century, though defying earlier efforts by a Puritan in Elizabethan days. His axe is reputed to have bounced off cutting the man, and eventually he was blinded by a chip from the tree. Fortunately many cuttings had been taken and their descendants may be bought locally to this day.

Glastonbury has always been seen as a Holy place. The story of those early days is cloaked in mystery and misted by time. What references there are come from much later, from a time when people romanticised and embellished stories as they were handed on by word of mouth. It is difficult to know whether one should be cynical, or accept that there is always a grain of truth in such passionately held beliefs.

It is said that, after Joseph, there were always groups of twelve hermits living there, representing the twelve apostles. A wattle and daub church was built on the spot, of which traces have been found and, so it is said, St. Patrick came there in the first quarter of the fifth century. The story holds that St. Patrick was born near Glastonbury and returned from Ireland to be the first Abbot, starting the great tradition which led to the growth of the greatest and most famous of all Abbeys in the land. He persuaded those hermits living there to become the first monks.

St. Patrick was followed by many other men who went on to become great and famous, some even saints. In 563, St. David of the Scots was supposed to have visited Glastonbury. After that there is silence and little is known for two hundred or more years until King Cenwealh of the West Saxons gave Godney, Meare and Nyland to the Monks of Glastonbury in 660. This event signifies the coming of the Saxons into the West Country and a new tradition. The battle of Penselwood was won by Cenwealh in 658, after which he took over all Somerset as far as the Parrett. Glastonbury was treated by these Saxons with great reverence. King Centwine gained control of the Isle of Wedmore in 682, naming it 'Vadomaer' after one of the Saxon leaders, Vado the Famous. He then became a Christian and granted the Isle to Wilfred, Bishop of York, who transferred his rights to the Abbey of Glastonbury. However, the next King would not confirm these rights and claimed the Isle as royal property, one of a number of such disputes.

King Ine, one of the greatest and most Christian of kings, built and dedicated the first Saxon church at Glastonbury in 704. He went on to increase the Abbey's holdings and gave it ten hides of land at Brent, one at Bleadon and ten at Sowey. Later, he persuaded the Pope to take Glastonbury directly under his patronage, a moment of great significance in the standing of the Abbey.

Glastonbury was in the hands of the Danes for a short time in 878, before they were defeated and converted to Christianity at the Peace of Wedmore. But during this time they pillaged and utterly destroyed it, so for a long while it was no longer of any importance as a church, though remaining a seat of learning. King Alfred encouraged

Glastonbury but never put the energies into it for which he was famous; these went instead to the founding and promotion of Athelney Abbey.

Glastonbury Abbey revived its importance under the great and saintly Dunstan. St. Dunstan, who lived from 925 to 988, was born at Glastonbury and became Abbot in 942, then went on to become Archbishop of Canterbury. During his time three kings were buried at Glastonbury — Edmund, who made him Abbot, Edgar, who made him Archbishop of Canterbury, and Edmund Ironside. During his tenure St. Dunstan lengthened Ine's church and added a tower, as well as erecting various monastery buildings. King Edwy gave part of his Manor at Wedmore to increase the wealth of the Abbey in 950. During the eleventh century, Abbot Thurstan began a new church. Then, in 1030, King Canute came to Glastonbury to declare respect for the privileges and rights of the Abbey. This occurred after he had united Danes and Saxons into one nation again.

With each great event Glastonbury increased its stature and power in the outside world. It is difficult to imagine now how important this quiet place must have been in that time. By 1100, under the new Norman masters, Glastonbury Abbey owned forty-one manors and 442 Hides of land. One tenth of the population of Somerset was said to live on Abbey lands and it was the richest and most important establishment of its time.

Around this time a Norman, Abbot Turstin, was appointed by William the Conqueror. He seems to have been a difficult man, with ideas foreign to those prevailing at the time, and had to call in soldiers to deal with his 'turbulent' monks. But apparently he was so unreasonable that eventually the King took the part of the monks and exiled the Abbot.

Fire gutted the Abbey in 1184. This started the major construction work of building the 'great' church, by Ralph Fitzstephen, under the patronage of Henry II. It was finally dedicated in 1303, though never fully completed. His Lady Chapel opened in 1186 and was famous for its inside decorations of panels painted with stars, planets and moons. In the early fifteenth century, Abbot Nicholas Frome finished the Chapter House and other great works, including new Bishop's quarters and a wall around the abbey precincts, as well as erecting that remarkable building, the Abbot's Kitchen, which stands to this day. Later that century further work virtually completed the buildings, including some vaulting under the central tower and magnificent flying buttresses at the end of the Choir.

The great event of 1190 was the 'discovery' of Arthur's Tomb, during the abbacy of Henry of Sully. This will always remain a controversial event, leaving people to wonder whether it was a genuine belief or the first example of a public relations coup designed to raise the fortunes of the Abbey!

In 1192 the bishoprics of Bath and Glastonbury were combined under Savaric. Then in 1219, Pope Honorius III declared, 'The union of Bath and Glastonbury is to be dissolved. The Abbey is to be under its own Abbot, freely elected in the usual way.' In 1275, the Chapel of St Michael on the Tor collapsed (an early example of jerry-building?) and was rebuilt completely in the first half of the fourteenth century.

The last Abbot was appointed by Cardinal Wolsey in 1524. Richard Whiting was a quiet and compliant man who had a reputation for scholarliness and true Christian compassion. Somehow he got caught up in the politics of his day and suffered the final blow. In spite of signing the Act of Supremacy for King Henry VIII, he was accused of treason. This was dropped, but eventually he was convicted of robbery. On 15th November 1539 he and two of his monks were put on hurdles at the foot of the Tor, dragged up to the top and hanged, drawn and quartered, his remains being displayed on the great gate of Glastonbury Abbey, in Wells, Bridgwater, Ilchester and Bath. So ended the history of one of the most remarkable establishments in Britain.

One of the glories of the Abbey was the library. The great scholar, John Leland, was sent by Henry VIII to visit Glastonbury in 1533, as a part of his journeys through Somerset which he recorded in great detail in his diaries. In these he wrote that he was completely inspired by the first sight of this magnificent collection: 'a burning desire to read and learn inflamed me afresh'. He spent days examining the books, 'with the greatest interest'. An earlier catalogue, in 1248, recorded nearly five hundred titles, though this is believed to understate considerably the total number held there. Some were of remarkable antiquity and value. One was said to be a Gospel dating from the second century. The great King Ine is recorded as having contributed to the books at the Abbey while St Dunstan commissioned and wrote books and added greatly to the reputation for scholarship of Glastonbury. The fire of 1184, which led to the start of the Great church, must have destroyed many volumes but some were certainly saved, as the later catalogue showed.

Not everyone was allowed to enter this world. Leland had access through a letter from the King, others needed special permission from the Abbot. In spite of this recorded pleasure, and reports sent to the King, virtually none of the library of thousands of books survived the general destruction wreaked by those who broke down the Abbey. It is incredible to think that such examples of the great and glorious history of English scholarship should have been allowed to be destroyed, as they were all over the kingdom at that time. Indeed it is difficult to reconcile these orgies of destruction, both then, and later in Oliver Cromwell's time, with the declared aims and intents of well-educated rulers, the gentlemen of the time. A recent book on Glastonbury, by James Carley, likened the time of the Dissolution to rule by a police state. This seems to be the only explanation — implementation of a theme by local thugs who were completely out of control.

After the Dissolution of the Abbey in that same year, what remained of Glastonbury Abbey passed briefly into the hands of the Duke of Somerset in 1547, who then introduced a colony of weavers from the Netherlands. He only lasted until 1550, before being executed for treason. Plans were raised for starting a new foundation of monks but this died with Mary Tudor and thereafter the place remained in private hands until 1908 when the ruins were taken over by the Church of England. Much of the building was used to make foundations for the road from Glastonbury to Wells.

In 1751, Matthew Chancellor was said to have been cured of asthma by drinking from the Chalice spring three Sundays running. As a result a Pump Room was built in the next year, when there were ten thousand visitors. In the seventeenth century the ruins briefly went back to their original purpose when the Kitchen was hired by the Quakers as a Meeting House.

Muchelney Abbey

One of the other great ruined Abbeys on the Levels is that of Muchelney, situated, not above, but surrounded by the moors. The Abbey is a part of the moorland scene, encircled by ditch-lined fields, with flat land extending to the horizon. I remember well the first time I saw the Abbey, spotlit by brilliant sunshine against a black background of storm clouds. It looked commanding, mysterious, just right in its location. Muchelney has lain in a state of ruin for the past four hundred years or so, since voluntarily closed down by its monks. It is large, with the bases of its walls preserved against bright-green lawns, but one part is nearly complete: the Abbot's House and its Cloister Walk. This is still open to the public daily in the summer and has wonderful ceilings, fireplaces and windows which are worth travelling a long way to see. It is surrounded by a working farm, as used to be the practice for these self-supporting abbeys in their heyday.

Muchelney Abbey, the Bishop's House

The Abbey was started under a Charter given by King Ine between 676 and 705. It was a famous area for eel fishing and, in 1086, the estate of Muchelney paid taxes of six thousand eels a year, a considerable amount. The original Abbey was rebuilt under Abbot William Wyke around 1500 and it is recorded that, between 1511 and 1538, Muchelney leased out two hundred acres of pasture to pay for further building work. The final moment came in 1538, just forestalling the Dissolution, when Muchelney Abbey was dissolved voluntarily under mountains of debt. So it was incompetent business management rather than Kingly oppression which deprived us of another great church establishment and building though, if it had survived another few months, the result would have been just the same.

Athelney Abbey

The third great Abbey, of which no trace exists, was Athelney, founded by King Alfred in 878, in honour and thanks for his great victory over the Danes. Because of its origin and the importance of this spot, it is ironic, as well as sad, that this of all the Abbeys should have vanished totally.

Alfred was one of the very greatest of our Kings, one who shaped the future of the nation more surely than almost any other. He deserves to be remembered in the form of his great work, the Abbey, not a strange-looking obelisk erected a couple of hundred years ago.

In Alfred's day Athelney was surrounded by impenetrable marshes and only those who knew its secret ways were able to land. It was linked by some form of causeway to nearby Burrow Mump. Only a couple of acres of Athelney was said to be usable at the time. The original Abbey was built on piers sunk in the ground and remained in this form until 1320, when it was restored. We have little information about its size, form or way of life. It was destroyed so thoroughly on the Dissolution that no trace of it remains. The island is now important for withy growing and has a timeless air of its own. It is difficult to associate its rural peace with some of the greatest events in English history and the passionate interest of one of England's greatest kings.

Wells

Wells has long been important as a great centre of Christianity in the west, but never had the same impact on the Levels as Glastonbury. Possibly this is because of its position, hidden from the flat lands by foothills, whereas Glastonbury is visible over most of the northern moors. In spite of the seniority of the Bishop of Bath and Wells, the Abbey remained the place where Christianity was seen to have taken root. No King Arthur strides the pages of Wells history, so it loses out also on the romantic front. Nevertheless it is a great centre, but one shared with upland Mendip, not wholly of the Levels.

The story of Wells Cathedral starts once again with the great King Ine. He founded the bishopric of Sherborne, which included Somersetshire in its fief. St. Andrew's Church at Wells was said to have been built in 705 on the advice of St. Aldhelm, the Bishop of Sherborne. The Bishopric of Wells was separated out from that of Sherborne in 909 and Athelm was the first Bishop. After a great deal of intrigue and roguery, the Bishopric assumed the title of Bishop of Bath and Wells in 1244. This gave ascendancy over the Chapter Cathedral of Wells and the Abbey at Bath. After the Dissolution the bishop was elected only from Wells, and was enthroned in Wells Cathedral, but the title remains.

The first church was enlarged in the twelfth century. A cathedral school was established at Wells in 1185, and continues to this day, while the great cathedral was completed in 1190. This quickly fell into ruins — someone's calculations must have gone badly wrong. It was rebuilt in its present form in the last quarter of the twelfth century by Bishop Reginald de Bohun and continued by Joceline Trotman of Wells, whose brother built Lincoln Cathedral. The Cathedral Church of Saint Andrew was consecrated in 1239 and took over two hundred years to complete, although it features complete harmony in design, a considerable tribute to its original planner. Various bishops continued to add further portions over the years, beautifying, strengthening and improving, but always preserving that wonderful sense of a single entity, which is its glory.

The Cathedral and its people were not classed as monastic so, although some damage was suffered in the Reformation, it continued its existence, being re-confirmed in its ancient rights and customs by Queen Elizabeth in a Charter granted in 1592. Clearly the Bishop of

Bath and Wells was better suited to political wheeling and dealing than the unfortunate Abbot Whiting.

Wells has always had its connections with the Levels. In 1062 a Royal Charter from Edward the Confessor granted the church at Wells land in Wedmore and, through the Queen, land at Mudgley and Mark. In 1065, by way of another Charter, this was increased to, 'not only all that the bishop and his predecessors have obtained of the king and his predecessors, or by purchase, but whatever the church under his rule is seen to possess ...... In the place called Weddmor a possession of four hides.' They remained in the same ownership until 1547, though they passed from the Bishop to the Deans of Wells in 1136, when they were referred to as 'Wedmoreland'. A Bishop's Manor House was built at Blackford early in the fourteenth century but was demolished later in the century as being 'too splendid and unnecessary'.

Thomas Cromwell was appointed Bishop of Wells and Lord of the Manors of Wedmore and Mudgley in 1537. He must have been busy plotting the destruction of all he saw before him while in this position, as it was he who carried out the Dissolution and suppression of the monasteries—one of the greatest acts of vandalism in the world, carried out by a gangster/courtier who eventually suffered the same fate as those he overthrew. The value of monastic property in Somerset was estimated at £7,500 in 1535, in the form of no less than twenty-three monasteries, so his target was substantial.

King Ine

King Ine reigned from 688 to 726 and was one of the great and saintly influences of his time. Indeed he could be described as one of our truly great kings, although he reigned only over Wessex. He was a Saxon warrior and scholar of renown, a deep-thinking man who devoted much of his time to affairs of the church and encouraged the spread and sustenance of Christianity in every way possible. He founded the Bishopric of Sherborne, which included Somersetshire, and backed the Abbey at Glastonbury with gifts of land, his protection and a new church. Ine is particularly renowned for the code of laws he drew up for Wessex in 693. For the first time these gave definite rights to British subjects, including the right to hold property. Land was split into 'hundreds' for administrative purposes, each consisting of one hundred hides. A hide was sufficient land to support a family and varied in size from place to place, according to the fertility of the soil and local conditions — a very practical measure.

The King travelled to Rome twice, an enormous effort in those days. The first time he went to secure the future of his favourite Glastonbury, by persuading the Pope to take it under his protection. After his return he re-examined his work, decided he had done all he could for his people, by way of education and the rule of law, together with a secure Church, gave up his crown and went to Rome with his wife. They are said to have led a life of devotion and great simplicity there.

Wessex survived between conquerors after that, a dark time of Danish invasion and counterstrike, but maintained its identity. The Golden Dragon flag of Wessex appeared for the first recorded occasion in battle in 752. In the ninth century Egbert ruled the whole land at last.

Alfred the Great

Perhaps our greatest and most remarkable king made his name in Somerset, on the Levels, and promulgated much of his finest work within its boundaries. If the county were to be associated with only one man, Alfred must be he. He was born in 849 and died in 901, a short enough life but sufficient to change the face of England for ever. Alfred was not born a man of Somerset; he came from Berkshire, the son of Ethelwulf and brother to King Ethelred of Wessex, whom he succeeded in 871. He was educated in Rome when young but came home to fight the Danes.

His critical year came in 878, when all seemed to be going against him. He was forced to hide in the near-impenetrable wilderness of the Isle of Athelney. Only locals knew their way through the maze of waterways to the hard ground within. 'Islands' in the old sense were often only pieces of ground raised slightly above the water-table. Somehow he managed to retain lines of communication out of this fortress in the middle of the marshes and gathered forces from Wiltshire, Somerset and Hampshire to meet the Danes at a place called Ethandun. There are many arguments about the location of this battle, translated commonly as Edington. There is an Edington on the Poldens and this would make sense in light of subsequent moves, but many prefer the Edington of Wiltshire.

Whatever the place, it was a great victory for Alfred and changed the course of history. Guthrum the Dane, and his followers, were taken to Aller, near Athelney, and baptised. From there they were conveyed to the Royal Palace at Wedmore, for the ceremony of loosing the Chrism, or baptismal robe. We even know a bit about some of the lesser personalities involved — Eolderman Aethelnoth of Wedmore helped at the peace-making ceremony in his village. Guthrum's baptismal name was Athelstan. He died in 890, still a Christian. This victory was a famous moment and of the greatest significance in our history. Prior to the battle most of England was dominated by the Danes; afterwards the country was split into two and the process of absorbing these warriors into the general fabric of society began. The north-east was assigned to the Danes under the Danelagh and they pledged never again to attack Wessex. Alfred ruled the county south of a line from the Thames to Chester. The King declared thanks for his victory, and for the sanctuary given in his times of exile, by founding an Abbey at Athelney.

Alfred was a great and wise king who introduced much that was beneficial to his people, including further codification of the laws, so that people knew where they stood. He had an insatiable appetite for books and for learning, as well as education for his subjects. He translated a number of books which were for the general good and was said to have devoted half his income to scholarship. In 1693 a most remarkable find was made at North Newton Park, near Athelney. A magnificent jewel was picked up, made of gold and enamel. It formed the top to a staff and was inscribed in Saxon, *Aelfred mec heht gewyrcan*, i.e. 'Alfred had me made.' In 1801, Colonel Slade erected a monument to Alfred on Athelney, which stands to this day, being the only trace left of those great times in that sleepy spot in rural Somerset.

S.H.Harvey, the famous Vicar of Wedmore, who took such an interest in its antiquities and published the four volumes of the 'Wedmore Chronicle', excavated the supposed site of Alfred's Palace in 1880. He discovered no trace of the Palace, but did find a medieval building, dated about 1100, which was probably the house of the Lord Dean of Wells. An old man told the Reverend Harvey that it belonged to a man who was 'not a king but just like a king.' In 1547 Mudgley

Vicar's Close, medieval street in Wells

passed from the care of Wells to the Lord Protector, the Duke of Somerset — a perfect description. Memories can be long in country districts. It is now believed that the actual Palace was on the site of the present Manor House.

Domesday

Duke William of Normandy landed in Sussex in 1066 and defeated Harold at Hastings, changing the course of our nation's history for ever. It is not generally realised that the final spark of revolt against the Normans came in Somerset, at Montacute in 1068. After that it was a slow process of humiliation, then integration, with the Normans orchestrating all the moves and heading the major estates which controlled the land.

One of the first things the Duke decided was to carry out a survey to find out exactly what he had conquered. The result was the great Domesday Book of 1085, one of the most amazing undertakings imaginable. It covered the majority of the country, including the whole of Somerset. In the survey a great deal of land was not taken into account, but this was because it was deemed worthless. For instance, 179,000 acres in Somerset were unaccounted for. This was the marshy moorland, which was totally unproductive at the time.

Some astonishing facts came out of this extremely detailed analysis, which must have cost a fortune to carry out so meticulously. For instance, vineyards were recorded at North Curry, Glastonbury, Meare and Panborough. Domesday figures showed a population of 519 burgesses in Somerset towns and 12,858 un-free people in the countryside, together with 50,000 sheep. The principal towns and boroughs included Bath, Ilchester, Milborne Port, Bruton, Langport, Axbridge, Taunton, Frome, Milverton and, possibly, Yeovil and Watchet. Taunton had a population of three hundred people, Bath one thousand and Ilchester five hundred, then came Milborne Port, Langport and Axbridge. Nowadays Langport is a sleepy little place on the Levels and Milborne Port only a handful of houses, in those times they occupied places of significance in the county.

The records show the famous XII Hides of land held tax-free by Glastonbury Church, around which centres so much of the history of the Abbey. A fascinating insight into people and the worth of holdings at the time comes from a mention of Bishop Giso's Manor of Wedmore. His manor was valued at £17. There were four serfs, thirteen villeins, fourteen bordars and eighteen cottars (landless peasants) living there. So these great estates were large in area and worth mentioning in such a survey, yet there were few people. It must indeed have been an empty place.

The Middle Ages

No major historical events impinged on life in the Levels during the Middle Ages, apart from the plague in the middle of the fourteenth century and its effect on population. Wars went on and people served their time in them but Somerset did not figure particularly.

Significant events were local. Bridgwater Castle was completed by Lord William Brewer in 1210, together with a bridge over the River Parrett — most important locally. Of purely local interest, a Reeve's Feast was instituted at North Curry in 1215 and survived until 1868. Those present could drink as much ale as they pleased while two candles were burning; the sort of festival event which few would forget who had taken part. Of the highest significance, the river was canalised near Street Bridge in 1290 and a cutting made to supply a mill at Northover. This changed the northward flow to Bleadney to a new flow to Meare, forming an expanded Meare Pool which, because of its carp fishery, became one of the most important possessions of Glastonbury Abbey.

In the early fifteenth century Bridgwater imported 400 tons of wine a year from Bordeaux and was ranked as the twelfth port in the country, even though it was an exceedingly difficult place to navigate, with fast running tides and shifting sandbanks. Without engines to help there must have been some real problems. Sir Walter Raleigh, in a report to the Queen on the vulnerability of ports to Spanish invasion, discounted Bridgwater as a threat for this reason.

The Civil War

The Civil War was fought as ferociously over Somerset as any other part of England but is perhaps remembered here best for one of the region's great sons who took such a prominent part in it all. Robert Blake, Lord Admiral of England and soldier, was born in Bridgwater in 1599, grandson of a Mayor of that town. He was elected MP for Bridgwater and took up the Parliamentary cause against the king. In

1653 he was made Lord Admiral and defeated the previously all-conquering Dutch Admiral van Tromp at Dover. He was buried in Westminster Abbey in 1657 but, in the flurry of recriminations and revenge at the time of the Restoration, was exhumed and moved. His statue looks over the main street of the town to this day to remind us of past events.

The Civil War started in 1642, with Parliament looking for change from King Charles I. It is a story of pride, prejudice, ill-judgment, and missed opportunities. Loyalties were deeply divided, family against family and even families against themselves. Somerset was especially important to both sides, situated as it was between the King's stronghold at Oxford and the fiercely Royalist Cornwall. In 1644 Taunton was besieged by the Royalists and was held successfully by Robert Blake in his first career as a soldier. He repeated this process again in 1645, when a series of crucial battles was fought for the control of towns and villages on the Levels. The New Model Army beat a stronger Cavalier contingent at Langport in July, in what was called the Long Sutton 'mercy' by Cromwell, the last major battle of the war. Bridgwater Castle, a great and apparently secure Royalist stronghold, was captured by the Roundheads earlier that same year, leaving Parliament in full control of the county and virtually finishing the war.

While there were loyalties fiercely felt on both sides, it seems that the ordinary people suffered from the passage of either army, with their animals and grain being taken to support the soldiers. Some Royalists had a particularly bad reputation for general mayhem, while the Parliamentarians also caused problems in dividing out church property for the poor, not always appreciated by the good folk who had supported that church for so long. The end must have been a mighty relief to those who simply wished to get on with their lives. The aristocrats and big families of Somerset gained or suffered according to their agility, loyalties or ability to keep out of sight at the right moment. Fortunes were made and lost as a result.

The Restoration was heralded by promises of religious toleration, but eventually Parliament passed laws saying that there should be no public worship outside the Church of England. There followed periods of unpleasantness when people were asked to inform on neighbours about their church-going habits, though apparently without much success in this area. Freedoms came and went and generally it was a period when people felt oppressed and unsettled. This led on naturally to Somerset's next great event, where it was centre stage for the whole country to observe.

The Sedgemoor Rebellion

In England people worried about the accession of James II to the throne when his brother, Charles II, died. He was not a popular person. He was openly Catholic and known to be against any form of religious freedom, which was anathema to those who had fought to preserve liberties in the Civil War. James, Duke of Monmouth, was a dashing young man, much-favoured by those who were against James and, more important, the illegitimate son of Charles II. Even while Charles was alive, clear lines of loyalty were being drawn up. Then Monmouth made a bad error of judgment and undertook a visit to the West Country in 1680 and to other parts of England a couple of years later. He was promised military aid by local Whigs (Whig was the name of the party of those who wished to maintain the Protestant succession, Tories were those who favoured the king, whatever his religious belief.) There was talk of assassinations of the King and the Duke of York, which came to Charles's ear. Monmouth was exiled to the Low Countries, from where he heard of the King's death and the accession of James II.

By 1685 the Duke believed he had sufficient support to make a bid for the throne of England and landed at Lyme Regis in Dorset on 11th June that year. He came with three ships, but only just over eighty men in his 'army', relying on raising men from his supporters in the West Country.

He gained support, but it was said that the actual fighting force never exceeded eight thousand men. The campaign only lasted three weeks, but has left its mark in Somerset to this day. As I said before, memories are long in the country and the savagery of the suppression of the Rebellion is talked about still and many places reflect it in local names.

After declaring against the King, the growing band marched to Ilminster, Taunton — where he was proclaimed King Monmouth — Bridgwater, Glastonbury, Shepton Mallet and on to the gates of Bristol. They faced nothing but a few local skirmishes during this time and were feted all the way. But around Bristol, and later Bath, the people became aware of four thousand troops assembling under Lord Feversham and the welcome died. After that it was all downhill. The army was now in retreat, though it had done little real fighting. Monmouth believed an army of ten thousand was waiting for him further to the west, so he marched back to Bridgwater, via Wells and Glastonbury, where he found his new army did not exist. By now it was a depressed band of aristocrats at the head of the army, though the majority were labourers, shop-keepers and yeomanry who retained their fierce beliefs and loyalty. Against them they had the cream of the English army, including the Life Guards and a Division commanded by the great Churchill, later the all-conquering Duke of Marlborough.

On 5th July 1685, Monmouth looked down from the church tower in Bridgwater and saw an opportunity to defeat the King's army, who were camped on the moors out at Westonzoyland. Feversham appeared ill-prepared for attack. The troops were not dug in and there were only a few cavalry patrols out on the moors. It must have been a period where the marshes were at their rare firm stage, when animals could roam the surface. It seemed a perfect opportunity for a night attack. And who knows what might have happened if they had succeeded, which they so nearly did. Would our history have been quite different?

Six thousand of his men were led by Monmouth across the moor that night. Just short of the Bussex Rhyne, a great ditch behind which the Royal forces were camped, a shot was fired. It is quite possible that this was fired accidentally by one of Monmouth's men; but it was enough to alert the enemy. And something else went wrong with the plan: it appears that the local guide had lost his way in the ever-present night-time mist and was not sure of the location of the rhyne. Monmouth's cavalry were never able to attack the camp as had been planned. The battle gradually swung over in favour of the Royalists. Monmouth's progress has not become known as the 'Pitchfork Rebellion' for nothing: weapons were lacking. There were only three big guns and the cavalry was badly led. By daylight it became a rout. The rebels were slaughtered on the battlefield, with over seven hundred dead, against only twenty-seven of the King's men. More were summarily hanged by the victorious troops.

*Westonzoyland Church, where rebels were
held after the Monmouth Rebellion*

The prisoners were marched off the battlefield and crowded into Westonzoyland Church. Locals are said to have buried over thirteen hundred corpses in great pits out on the moors. The rebellion was at an end but many had escaped, including Monmouth himself. This gallant young man behaved in a less than gallant manner, fleeing his troops at a relatively early stage, when he saw the battle was lost. He was caught and, in spite of begging for mercy and offering to buy his way out, was executed on Tower Hill.

The ordinary people suffered repression and sometimes appalling fates, firstly under the notorious Colonel Kirk and his so-called 'lambs'. They were left to tidy up after the battle and hanged people without trial wherever they found them. Then came Judge Jeffries, sent down by the King to clear up this 'festering sore'. It is known that he presided over local trials at Dorchester, Ilchester and Taunton and others outside the county. As a result 233 people were hanged, drawn and quartered. Of these, six men were hanged at Wells and six at Axbridge. Although there is no record of this, it has long been believed in Wedmore that Judge Jeffries stayed in the village, held court at the market-house in the Borough and that a man was hanged from the market cross. The local doctor was known to have treated wounded people from the battle in secret. Hanging was not the only punishment; eight hundred people were transported to the West Indies. Thus the impact on the West Country and its population was considerable and memories are long in these parts. Several generations later a direct descendant of Judge Jeffries felt it impossible to drive through Somerset in safety.

On a different note, the 13th Regiment of Foot was formed to guard prisoners taken at Sedgemoor. Later it fought with Marlborough in Holland, and became the 1st Somersetshire Regiment at Wells in 1782 — glorious ends from inglorious beginnings.

Declaration of Indulgence

Somerset, through Ken, Bishop of Bath and Wells, was next involved in one of the most significant events in English history. In 1667, and then again in 1688, James II issued a Declaration of Indulgence suspending all laws against Roman Catholics and Dissidents. On the second occasion the King ordered that this should be read out in all churches throughout the land. A number of Bishops, including Ken, refused and were put on trial, being accused of uttering a libel through a petition they put to the King. After a long trial they were acquitted and the nation reacted with great joy.

The significance is not so much the event — a nation reacting against the re-introduction of Catholicism — as the fact that this was the last time a King made an attempt to set aside a Parliamentary Act. This led in turn directly to William of Orange being invited over, with his wife Mary—Charles II's nephew married to King James's daughter — to assume the throne.

Times of Change

The earliest traces of a public conscience may be seen in the early eighteenth century. This appeared locally, rather than at a national level, and it is interesting to see this emerging in the towns and villages associated with the Levels. For instance, it is known that a free school existed in Wedmore in 1707. In 1789 Hannah More, a friend of William

Wilberforce, the campaigner against slavery, started her first school at Cheddar. Her influence and schools later spread across the moors to Wedmore, in spite of the opposition of the church. Further illustration of change comes also from other records found at Wedmore. In 1734 a meeting of the Wedmore Vestry considered erection of a poorhouse. That same body agreed in 1764 to pay Richard Glanville eight guineas 'for the surgery work of the poor as is not able to pay for themselves' — an early example of the National Health Service.

A number of famous people were born and reared out on the moors at this time. Two famous seafarers were born at Butleigh in 1724 and 1726. The first, Viscount Hood, was the Admiral who captured Toulon and Portugal in the Napoleonic wars, while his brother, Lord Bridport, commanded the Channel Fleet and defeated the French off L'Orient. In 1795 John Billingsley of Shepton Mallet published the remarkable *Survey of Agriculture of the County of Somerset Drawn up in 1795*, which gave a complete picture of the time, down to the smallest detail. For instance, it noted that 1/2d to 2/- per rope was paid for ditching on a particular moor. He was responsible for the enclosure of much of Mendip and also applied his talents to draining Sedgemoor. To complete the tale, he helped found the Bath & West Show.

Langport was the birth-place of a man who became famous throughout the country: Walter Bagehot was known as an extremely influential editor of *The Economist*, but he was also a merchant banker with Stuckey's Bank which in those days printed its own bank notes and helped to finance a number of west country firms.

The last quarter of the eighteenth century saw a burst of activity in draining the last of the low-lying marshlands of the Moors and Levels. A great many parts were enclosed and drained at public expense, this then being charged out to the riparian owners. People have said this was a great period of injustice in England, when people were forced to sell their new enclosed lands because they could not pay for the drainage and laying out of the droves, but I think this is a misunderstanding. Much good came from the changes. It was inevitable they took place as the county became more populated. Instead of just subsisting, the smaller owner started to receive wages to work regularly on his richer neighbour's land. The yeoman became more settled in his holding, and more able to afford the capital expenditure which became a necessity in improving output to feed the growing population. Enclosure had its injustices, certainly, but it was a part of the evolution of the country, and unavoidable.

How productive these moors became is illustrated by a remark made by William Quekett of Langport in 1800: 'In the summer months the moors appear covered with snow. This is caused by the immense flocks of geese which are fed there chiefly for the sake of the feathers and quills.' This era of innovation and agricultural improvement also threw up another industry: the first large-scale willow planting in England took place at West Sedgemoor in 1825. Willows are still grown in the same manner round Athelney and Borough Bridge to this very day, and baskets, chairs and other products are woven nearby by descendants of those original growers.

The Age of Engineering

It is difficult to know when the real Industrial Revolution began. The Spinning Jenny came in 1770 and shortly afterwards steam was used to drive machinery in the cotton trade, but this did not really affect the Levels. Instead, industrial technology was used to transform and drain the Levels to promote farming or the movement of goods through the area. The main theme of drainage is covered in a later chapter, but that was not the only tale.

In 1827 the Taunton to Bridgwater Canal was opened, followed shortly by the Glastonbury Canal, which ran for a generation before physical problems finally defeated it. The weight of water in the canal was not sufficient to keep the soft peat from welling up in the middle as a result of the pressure exerted by the spoil on the banks. The cost of continual dredging was too much to sustain this new route from Glastonbury to the sea.

The canals were to be the great saviour of the county, opening up tracts to large-scale transportation at a time when roads were totally dependent on the state of the weather for their utility. It is difficult for us to realise just how closed the country was in those days. For instance, the road between Cheddar and Glastonbury just did not exist at the beginning of the nineteenth century. Floods and swollen rivers made any route for carts impassable for much of the year. Waterborne transport on rivers and canals was different; boats could move almost constantly. Unfortunately the canals were only a

Willows and a rhyne

temporary expedient. They proved too slow when the next great communication system opened up — the railways. In 1841, the first trains ran on Brunel's Bristol and Exeter Railway from Bristol, via Highbridge, to Bridgwater. Even so the Taunton to Chard Canal opened the following year but it never realised its potential. In 1847, the Taunton-Bridgwater Canal carried a record 79,000 tons, mostly Welsh coal, after which the railways gradually took over.

The first train ran between Highbridge and Glastonbury in 1854. In 1857, the line was extended from Highbridge to Burnham, to link with a regular steamer from Cardiff. This service ran until 1888. In 1890 a branch line was opened between Bridgwater and Edington Burtle, providing a link between Bridgwater and Glastonbury. This railway revolution lasted in its turn until the early 1960s when motor transport took over much of their local role.

Villages were still self-contained in those days, though factories proliferated. Between 1840 and 1860, the population of Wedmore, at more than 4,000, was at its peak. It contained a brewery, brick works, tannery, two windmills, two blacksmiths, two wheelwrights, two saddlers, a cooperage, shoemaker, a tailor and a barber, a clock-maker and a large emporium much visited by people from the surrounding area. The first census, in 1801, showed a population of 2,122. In 1901, 2,741; in 1971, 2,400.

1850 saw the start of emigration on a large scale. Already farms were losing labour to the cities. These were difficult times and the New World offered opportunities. Often the poorest went first and it is possible to find the remains of empty cottages all over the moors, dating from these times. With enclosure and drainage, people seized the opportunity to build out on the moors under antique laws which allowed them freehold if they could build a cottage and light a fire inside twenty-four hours. Life was not good. Many people who live on the Levels today tell tales of their parents and grandparents out on the new-drained ground, perhaps on an area slightly raised above the rest. In winter they had to move upstairs when the flood water invaded the ground floor. Boats were tied up outside the window, for those who could afford them. Water from the ditches and marshes was used for washing. Drinking water had to be fetched from hillside springs. No wonder they left it all when the opportunity arose, either to go up on the hills or to emigrate to a place with a better future.

It is reported that many villages halved their populations in the mid-nineteenth century, with free passages being offered to Australia, though the overall effect on population was very much less than this.

The Twentieth Century

There have been too many developments affecting the Levels and its population to step back and categorise them in a book like this. The development of drainage is best left to the appropriate place for further explanation and discussion. Suffice it to say that the most spectacular advances in this way have taken place in the last forty years, threatening the whole existence of the area as a special and separate entity.

As canals reached their commercial finish in the last century, so did local railways in this. In the 1960s most of the branch lines were closed down under the infamous reign of Dr Beeching. With it Somerset lost the 'Slow and Dirty' (Somerset and Dorset Line) which wound its way across the very heartland of the moors, taking many people to shop and others to sell their produce in market.

The biggest change has been for people outside the area to recognise its special nature and significance. This has always been a secret place, with many parts only reached by roads or tracks which are on the way from nowhere to nowhere; now that so many people have cars it has been opened up. This has brought problems and advantages. If the Somerset Levels is to be saved from becoming just another piece of featureless countryside, it will be because it has become better known. Its downfall could be because too many people visit it and transform its character. This is a dilemma now faced by a great many parts of Britain.

Glastonbury Abbey, fountainhead of Christianity in the west

3   *Glastonbury and a Dream of Arthur*

At the very core of life in the Levels lies the legend of Arthur. It has inspired men over the ages, been the centre of the revival of fortunes of the great Abbey of Glastonbury in the Middle Ages and of the tourist industry in the present time. Some people say that no such legend could exist without some grains of truth, others that it is based on absolute fact, while others again say it was a total invention of publicity-mad monks. You takes your choice, as they say.

I like to believe there is something behind it all, just as I have a romantic hungering to believe that Drake's Drum is waiting down below for that crucial moment in British history when Drake is needed again. The promise of Arthur is very similar, that one day, in our darkest hour, he will emerge from where he sleeps in the Fortunate Isles and ride forth to our rescue.

What I am certain of is that the area would be very different without Arthur in the background, influencing church, people and the tales that are told. Other places claim Arthur — Tintagel, Wales, Brittany, Winchester — but none have a more direct claim to legend, with points of clear identification for the main events of his life and his death — or is it an endless, waiting sleep?

The tale has its background in the earliest stories about Glastonbury. When Joseph arrived at Wearyall Hill, not only did he plant the thorn, but he also buried the Holy Grail, which was said to contain drops of the blood which fell from Christ at the crucifixion. To this day there is a spring in Glastonbury from which the water flows blood-red. Chalice Well is visited by thousands of people every year who half-hope, half-believe that this colour demonstrates the presence of the Grail far below. The story of the chalice is a vital part of the development of the Arthurian story. The search for the Holy

Grail dominated the activities of the Round Table.

There are various dates associated with Arthur, all of which tie in to actual events in history. Writings in the ninth century gave these, together with the name, 'the great leader, Arthur, defeated the invading English at Badon Hill in Wiltshire in 502'. The final date is that of the death of Arthur at Camlan in 539, coinciding with a last desperate attempt to stem the influx of the great Saxon hordes. Modern excavations show that Cadbury Hill was fortified in the year 500, with a large wooden hall in the centre. Could this be Camelot, site of Arthur's headquarters?

Arthur is variously held to be a British chief, a last official of the Roman Empire, left behind to stem the barbarian Saxon hordes when the last of the Romans pulled out in 410, or the High King of the region, sitting in tribute over local Kings. Whatever his rank or origin, he is shown as the final hope for Britain, holding out against the continental hordes pouring into the country, anxious to have a share of the pickings. Britain was on the brink of the Dark Ages and Arthur its only hope. The legend, however it grew over the ages, is likely to be right in these initial assumptions. Such a figure did exist, fought the newcomers, was successful for a while and was killed in his final triumph. Then the land vanished into darkness for a period.

However, the famous historian, Gildas, born in the same year as the first great battle, makes no mention of Arthur. In 1125, William of Malmesbury wrote a treatise, 'On the Antiquity of the Church of Glastonbury', with no reference to Arthur, Joseph of Arimathea or the Glastonbury legends but, in 1170, Alain de Lille wrote about the people of Brittany and their implicit belief in the fact that Arthur the Briton still lived. He went on to say that this followed the prophecy of Merlin that there would be doubt about the King's death. So the story was alive and well at that time.

In 1177, Henry II was told by some Welsh Princes about Arthur and his burial in Glastonbury and seven years later suggested to the Glastonbury monks that they should search for the remains of the King. He said an old British singer (teller of tales) had prophesied that the remains would be found in Glastonbury in a hollowed oak, sixteen feet below the ground. The Abbot of Glastonbury started searching for the remains and in 1190 succeeded in his quest. This description was given by a historian of the time:

At a depth of seven feet was a huge broad stone, whereon a leaden cross was fastened: on that part that lay downwards, in rude and barbarous letters, this inscription was written upon that side of the stone that was towards the stone: *Here lies buried King Arthur in Avon Isle.* Digging nine feet deeper, his body was discovered in the trunk of a tree, the bone of great bigness, and his skull perceived ten wounds, the last very great and plainly seen. His Queen Guinivere, a lady of passing beauty, lay by him, whose tresses of hair, in colour like gold, seemed perfect and whole until it was touched, but then showed itself to be dust.

The leaden cross found with the stone was said by Giraldus Cambrensis to have been inscribed: *Hic jacet sepultus inclitus Rex Arthurus cum Wenneveria uxore sua secunda in insula Avallonia.* The cross was copied and measured by Leland in 1540 and stayed in the hands of a Wells family until the eighteenth century. Then it disappeared.

The remains were placed in a tomb of black marble which was again opened a hundred years later in the presence of Edward I. The bodies were re-buried in front of the high altar and the skulls placed outside. In 1278, Edward I, spending Easter at Glastonbury, ordered the re-opening of the tomb and inspected the relics.

The tomb is said to have been destroyed at the Dissolution, surprisingly, since it had been looked upon as an important piece of history by all England. Perhaps this shows how out of control were those who actually carried out the work of destruction at the monasteries. A plaque above a rim of stone marks the place now where the grave used to be, inscribed:

Site of King Arthur's tomb. In the year 1191 the bodies of King Arthur and his queen were said to have been found on the south side of the Lady Chapel. On 19th April 1278 their remains were removed in the presence of King Edward I and Queen Eleanor to a black marble tomb on this site. This tomb survived until the dissolution of the Abbey in 1539.

Recently I read a most fascinating book, *The Legendary XII Hides of Glastonbury*, by Ray Gibbs, a moorland farmer in the Brue Valley. In it he provides a translation taken from the monk, John of Glastonbury, in 1380. It talks about a 'Prophecy of Melkin' written in the fifth Century, which referred to the coming of Joseph and the 'cruets', later translated into the Holy Grail:

> *The Isle of Avalon, ...*
> *there, has fallen asleep.*
> *Amid these Joseph in 'Marmor'*
> *of Arimathea by name,*
> *has found perpetual sleep.*
> *And he lies in a two forked line,*
> *next the south corner of an oratory*
> *fashioned of wattles,*
> *for the adoring of a mighty virgin,*
> *by the aforesaid sphere-betokened*
> *dwellers in that place, thirteen in all.*
> *For Joseph has with him*
> *in his sarcophagus,*
> *two cruets, white and silver,*
> *filled with blood and sweat*
> *of the prophet Jesus.*
> *When his sarcophagus*
> *shall be found entire, intact*
> *in time to come, it shall be seen,*
> *and shall be open unto all the world*
> *from then on neither water, nor the dew of heaven*
> *shall fail the dwellers in that ancient isle ....*

In the twelfth century Geoffrey of Monmouth published the first of the fantasies about Arthur, with considerable embellishments on the original tales. This was the first mention of the full 'Glastonbury legend'. In scholarly circles Geoffrey has a reputation for writing his own history when the story did not seem sufficiently exciting. However, there are common elements to the story of Arthur, forming a thread through everything that has been written since the beginning. Since then, further embellishments have been added, culminating in the medieval knightly romance, *Morte D'Arthur*, by Sir Thomas Malory, published by Caxton in the fourteenth century. This book has been the inspiration for most of the romances which have followed and the bulk of the more fanciful legends developed for the tourist industry over the years.

Fenny Castle, ancient fort on the River Sheppey

The basic original story is that Arthur was born of an illegal liaison between a King and the wife of another King, and was raised away from the court, unaware of his destiny and origin. Somewhere in the background, always a part of the story and running through it like a thread, is the story of the great sorcerer, Merlin. He arranged for a magic sword, Caliburn, or Excalibur in later versions, to be held in a block of stone inscribed, *Whoso pulleth out this sword of this stone, is rightwise king born of all England.* At the pre-destined moment Arthur plucks out this sword and assumes his rightful place, advised by the powerful Merlin. He is faced by the incoming hordes and must fight twelve battles before Britain is saved and united. His half-sister,

Morgause, ensnares the unknowing Arthur one night and conceives his child. The resultant son, Mordred, is to be his downfall.

Arthur marries Guinivere, a lady of great beauty, who is kidnapped by King Melwas and taken to Ynis Witrin, the Isle of Glass — Glastonbury — from where she is rescued by either Arthur or one of his followers. Later versions show this to be Lancelot, his chief knight. Melwas is defeated in single combat, but spared, to become a devoted follower again. Glastonbury comes under the direct control of Arthur and is situated near his main base — later called Camelot.

Merlin realises his time has come and hands over his powers to a girl, Nimu, who becomes the Lady of the Lake. Mordred joins Arthur, rises in favour, aided by the magic of Morgause, and is recognised as his son. Arthur goes to the Continent to protect his interests and leaves Mordred as regent. He is falsely reported dead by Mordred, who has himself crowned King and either marries Guinivere or tries to marry her — versions differ. Arthur returns, confronts Mordred at Camlan and, all tales agree, is prepared to compromise and avoid fighting his son. The battle starts by accident when one of his people is bitten by an adder and draws his sword to kill it. This is the very signal agreed to start fighting in the event of treachery.

Arthur spears Mordred who, in a last moment of strength, pushes himself along the spear and wounds Arthur on the head, mortally. The field is left in the hands of Arthur's men. The last battle is won, and lost.

Arthur has his followers carry him down to the shores of a lake, where his sword is sent wheeling out, to be caught by a hand and drawn down beneath the waters. Then a boat arrives, with three queens in it, together with the Lady of the Lake. He is rowed off into the darkness to Avalon, to be cured of his wounds. There he is said to be sleeping, waiting for the call.

Later embellishments add the story of the search for the Holy Grail, of Lancelot, Gawaine and Galahad, the perfect knights, and the Round Table. The Britons turn from sturdy tribesmen to medieval armoured knights and the whole becomes a fantasy, but with all the original elements still contained within it. Arthur's stronghold, Camelot, with Avalon, is a centre-piece of the story.

In the late nineteenth century Tennyson produced his epic poem,

'Idylls of the King', celebrating the story:

> *To the island-valley of Avilion,*
> *Where falls not hail, or rain, or any snow,*
> *Nor ever wind blows loudly; but it lies*
> *Deep-meadowed, happy, fair with orchard-lawns,*
> *And bowery hollows crown'd with summer sea,*
> *Where I will heal me of my grievous wound.*

More recently many others have followed, with T.H.White's *Sword in the Stone* and Mary Stewart's four novels, starting with *The Crystal Cave*, being the best known. T.H.White refers to a recurring theme, Arthur being 'the once and future king', taken from verses written around 1425 and telling of Arthur's return in the hour of need. The legend simply will not lie down and die and it still meets a need to believe which lies somewhere deep inside many people. The final romance has yet to be written.

Glastonbury and the Levels remain at the heart of all this. On a misty autumn morning it does not seem too fanciful to look across the moors and imagine the clink of bits and creak of saddles as a band of soldiers and their ladies wend their way along some ancient trackway — *Tirra-lirra by the river, sang Sir Lancelot.*

Willows and a rhyne, the quintessential Levels

4   The Draining of the Wastes

It is impossible to say when drainage of the Levels or surrounds really started. Sea-levels stabilised around the fourth or fifth century AD, when sea-floods brought the final deposition of silt into the area. Before that date the peat deposits had already finished their growth and were in extent much as today. The church and community of Glastonbury was founded around the same time. The world was starting to take shape as we know it and the march towards modern times had begun in a recognisable way. The first drainage probably started at this time, as the population increased and needed to clear more land for cultivation, or for their animals to graze.

The great marshes of inland Somerset — the Levels of today — were a boon as well as a barrier. They may have brought disease and discomfort but were also a means of movement inland and a harvest of ducks and other creatures. For instance, it is known that the River Axe was navigable to Bleadney, where there was a port, in the eighth century. This enabled sea-borne goods to be brought to within three miles of Wells at the time the first church was being built there by Saint Aldhelm, Bishop of Sherborne. So water-borne transport was well advanced and, no doubt, help was given to the flow and depth of rivers to ensure continuity and reliability of navigation, but little else was done.

The Middle Ages
By 1085, the Domesday Book recorded that clearance and drainage of the slightly raised grounds were well on their way. Although the moors at Wedmore were described as useless, there were seventy acres of meadows nearby. In 1129, the Abbot of Glastonbury was recorded as inspecting enclosed land at Lympsham. So already the

monks were nibbling away at the edges of damp ground, though not tackling the really marshy waste grounds. From the Iron Age until the thirteenth century the Levels were considered as marsh and to be avoided by all means. The monks would probably have considered those who made a living from wildfowling and trapping marsh animals as the equivalent to aboriginal indians, quite beyond their understanding. For it was the community of monks which saw the potential for clearance, enclosure and, eventually, drainage. They were the great landlords of the area, richer than all except the greatest of the noblemen and with the intellectual capacity to plan and design great schemes, for the communities attracted some of the greatest scholars of their time.

Efforts continued to improve water-borne traffic, a process which went on into the Middle Ages and beyond. In 1200, Richard the Lionheart approved the construction of a wharf at Rackley, near Axbridge. The first efforts to control flooding on the Parrett were recorded at the same date. The banks were built up in critical areas and the process has continued to the present day, always increasing the carrying capacity further but bringing other problems in its wake. To make more effective use of the land, it was necessary to keep sea-water out. The first sea-walls were built and clyses (the local name for a sluice) constructed to let water out but prevent high tides entering the system.

This started the whole process of control which was the prelude to actual drainage. It also gradually changed the marshes and wastes of the Levels from saline sea-marsh to fresh-water lagoons and bogs, a vital prelude to agricultural reclamation. All this is first recorded round 1200. Some may well have taken place beforehand, but written evidence does not exist. When the Normans arrived they were meticulous in recording what they found, and events as they took place, culminating in the great work of Domesday.

In 1234, 722 acres were enclosed by walls and reclaimed at Sowey, the low-lying island near Westonzoyland which was a centre of effort and expansion over many periods. But the next big date comes one year on, when the Statute of Merton recognised the rights of the Lord of the Manor to enclose the waste or common ground, provided he left sufficient pasture for his free tenants. This opened the way for a great many schemes and the face of the countryside started to change. Prior to that time it was almost impossible for sufficient unencumbered land to be gathered together to make worthwhile the expenditure of capital, in the form of labour and materials, on improving the wastes. After this date the landlords could promote their most ambitious schemes, while the free tenants had their rights protected. Nothing was mentioned about the un-free, for they had no rights. But, because of the need for willing labour, they too would have benefited from the opening up of new grounds.

Enclosures were planned and carried out. Rhynes were dug across the ground to speed the outflow of water, while boundary ditches helped drain as well as enclose. The pattern of drainage was being set for the future. Rhynes are the wider ditches which carry the waters away from fields into the river systems. Today these are controlled by the Internal Drainage Boards, while the river systems come under the National Rivers Authority. In those times there was no distinction, the whole lot being planned and carried out by the great religious landlords. Where drainage or water-flow crossed boundaries there would have been liaison, the one with another.

This initial drainage was confined to the clay belt. Peat land was generally excluded from any consideration of drainage for centuries to come. The engineering problems of soft peat, which flowed back to fill pits or ditches dug in it, was to take many centuries to solve satisfactorily. The peat soils of the raised bogs of the central Brue valley were considered particularly acid and useless. Up to the end of the eighteenth century the levels of the peat bogs went up and down by as much as six feet between dry summers and wet winters.

The first reclamation on the Levels was said to have taken place to the east of Glastonbury. The main monasteries of Glastonbury, Athelney and Muchelney were responsible for the drainage that occurred at this period.

Taming the Rivers

While there was a continual process of enclosing and opening up the land on the edges of the marshes and the more stable wastes themselves, the main thrust for improvement was aimed at improving transport and inland navigation. This had its effect on the land surrounding these areas which led to a gradual opening up of parts of the Levels. In the thirteenth century the River Tone was tamed and land around it reclaimed by the Dean of Wells and Abbot of Athelney. Sea-going ships could reach up the Axe to Wells, and then Glastonbury, by way of Meare Pool. The country was a mass of new waterways, which included re-engineered existing rivers and ingenious solutions to improving navigation. The flow of some rivers was actually reversed during this work. Whatever else they may have been, there were some great engineers among the people of the Abbeys and Wells Cathedral. It could be described as the golden age of water-manipulation and is difficult to comprehend from where we stand. All this was done by sheer hard physical labour with few manual aids.

One of the great engineering feats was the construction of the Pilrow Cut and the changing of Ferlyngmere to become the huge Meare Pool of the Middle Ages. This opened up the sea-route from Glastonbury, via Mark, to join the River Axe. The Pilrow Cut, from the Brue near Tealham Moor to the Axe at Biddisham, was completed in 1316 and was tidal for its length. The Brue, Hartlake and Sheppey rivers once flowed north through the Panborough/Bleadney gap. They were diverted to Meare Pool, which was enlarged considerably. In the time of Henry VIII the pool was five miles in circumference and one and a half miles long. The complete works for the whole system were not finished until after 1500. These were truly gigantic efforts which would be difficult to imagine, even with modern equipment, and become quite breathtaking when considered in the light of the technology which existed at the time.

The present outlet of the Brue at Highbridge was known to have existed in 1324, but it may not then have been connected to the rest of the Brue Valley. At the end of all these works it was possible to bring sea-going vessels up the River Axe and then either along the north side of the Isle of Wedmore to near Wells or, via the Pilrow Cut, south of Wedmore direct to Glastonbury and Street. Vessels could also travel from Bleadney, at the end closest to Wells, direct to Glastonbury by a rather convoluted route through Meare Pool. It was an astonishing transformation of the countryside and opened up Glastonbury and Wells to the outside world. It was recorded that seats for the Abbey were brought by sea from Bristol to Glastonbury in 1500.

The remains of this once important river-way still exist, but it is

Winter flooding on Tealham Moor

impossible to imagine it in its heyday from these. A tiny ditch may be followed, from the present North Drain Pumping Station on the River Brue, along a field boundary to join a wide section following the main Wedmore-Burnham road through Mark. At a sharp corner, by the White Horse pub, it turns north and peters out in a maze of minor drainage ditches. It is difficult to imagine this remote and empty countryside ringing to the sound of people poling or towing barges up-river.

A great deal else has changed over the years. It is said that the main street of Wedmore, the Borough, was a wharf off the River Axe in the fourteenth century. The waters of the River Lurbourne flowed into it from the higher ground at Sand and Blackford. The name is commemorated in the lane called the Lerburne, which runs down to the moor below, ending just above the present course of the Axe. The problem in understanding all this is trying to imagine that the water-levels were then higher and that many rivers, rhynes and drains have had their courses altered considerably over the years. Men have

*Cottages lining the remains of the Pilrow Cut,
formerly navigable by sea-going barges*

played God with water on the Levels for more years than can be comprehended. It is a man-made landscape in every sense of the word, where people have turned conventional wisdom on its head, reversing the flow of rivers and dealing with problems where gravity apparently ran counter to a solution.

By 1500, one third of the floodable land in Somerset had been reclaimed; what remained was the moorland wastes north and south of the Poldens. These represented 23,000 out of 70,000 acres said to be at risk of inundation at the time. The remainder was hard-core marsh, a tangle of reeds, rushes and undergrowth seamed with channels and water lying close to the surface. It was recorded at the time that 12,000 acres of King's Sedgemoor was only usable for grazing for two to three months each year.

After the Dissolution

The Dissolution of the Monasteries, in 1530, must have thrown the region into chaos, as much of the drainage work on the moors and surrounding land was carried out through the Abbeys. However, it is interesting to note that the Abbot of Athelney was summoned for neglecting ditches in 1443, implying there were already overlying authorities who controlled this aspect.

Although the sea-walls continued to be developed and strengthened over the years, Acts of God still took their toll. In 1607 the whole of the Vale of Avalon flooded, twelve feet deep, when a sea-wall gave way at Burnham. The floods extended twenty miles inland and five miles in width. Thirty villages were submerged, while Glastonbury was completely surrounded by water.

The Parrett was navigable from the sea up as far as Langport in 1600; fifteen- to twenty-ton barges were in regular use. It is difficult to realise this when you look at the muddy river now. It must have demanded considerable skills in navigation with the huge tidal ranges involved. Within a few years of this, King James I disclosed plans to drain and enclose much of Sedgemoor, but nothing had happened by his death in 1625. In 1638 it was reported that nearly 2,600 acres of Tealham and Tadham Moors lay un-reclaimed and continued as such until near the end of the eighteenth century. Just over 30,500 acres of the Levels remained undrained in 1638. The great Vermuyden, responsible for much of Fenland drainage, was involved in further extensive drainage plans in 1655, but sold out after many delaying tactics from the opposition.

There was another great storm in 1703, bringing inland chaos when waves broke four feet over the sea-walls. In 1712 Meare Poole disappeared from the map, after it was finally drained.

The Great Enclosures

But the really intensive draining of the last of the marshes began in earnest around 1770, continuing in the first quarter of the nineteenth century. Sedgemoor was drained at this time, together with the untamed peatland of the Brue valley. A great surge of agricultural vigour spread across the land, coinciding with a complete change in the working structure of the country. The Industrial Revolution took people from the land and housed them in the great cities. There they had to be fed, instead of growing their own food at home. Farms mechanised and there was a desperate need for more farmland to meet ever-increasing demands for food.

Not everyone approved of this rush for drainage. The cost was high and had to be met by those who owned land or pastured cattle in the area. In 1771 there was considerable opposition at Bridgwater to a Bill for 'draining, dividing and inclosing King's Sedgemoor', but this could only halt the rush of progress temporarily. Although the Sedgemoor Bill was defeated, by 1791 an Act for Draining of King's Sedgemoor was passed. Huge engineering works diverted the River Cary from the Parrett into the King's Sedgemoor Drain and to the sea, by way of a clyse at Dunball. The enormous new drain was fifteen feet deep, fifty-five feet wide at the top and only ten feet wide at the bottom. This Drain cost £15,000, but the associated ditches and rhynes, cut to drain the surrounding fields, cost a further £28,000 — enormous sums in those days.

Modern Times

Between 1785 and 1791, much of the lowest portion of the peat moors in the Brue Valley was enclosed under a series of special Acts. By 1795 John Billingsley wrote in his *Agriculture of the County of Somerset*:

> Brent Marsh, the land to west of Poldens down to Bridgwater ...... Areas enclosed in last 20 years, Wedmore and Meare 4,400 acres, Nyland 350 acres, Blackford 900 acres, Mark 2,000 acres, Shapwick 100 acres, Westhay 1,700 acres.

The 1801 Brue Drainage Act allowed the river to be straightened and a new clyse with a lower sill was constructed at Highbridge. New Rhyne, later to be widened into the North Drain, and the South Drain, were cut with outfalls into the River Brue; the resultant flow was not sufficient, but it still had beneficial effects. Before that, thousands of sheep were recorded as having rotted in the Parish of Mark each year. Controlled flooding was then introduced to raise the land by silting. In 1802 the Axe Drainage Act effectively ended the inland cargo capability of the river, when floodgates were installed at Bleadon, halting sea-going traffic to Wells via the wharfs at Rooksbridge and

Greylake Sluice, on the King's Sedgemoor Drain

Rackley.

An Act was passed in 1795 to authorise a canal from Langport to Ilchester, bypassing the bridge at Langport, giving barge access to the very edge of the Levels. The sea-wall was again breached at Huntspill in 1799 and filled the Vale of Avalon with salt water. This remained in the Axe valley for five months of that winter and must have soured the grass for years to come. But all was not gloom. Reports showed that although only one coastal grazier was worth £1,000 earlier that century, by 1800 it had risen to over fifty, ten of them valued at more than £100,000 — truly enormous sums. By 1810 the land surrounding the Axe had been brought under control by extensive works. It was reported as being some of the richest land in the kingdom, with extremely modern dairy farming. But in 1811, sea-floods again reached Glastonbury; the sea-walls were not up to their job yet.

By 1816, West Sedgemoor was looking something like its present appearance, with rhynes, bounded with willows, as boundary marks.

The rhynes were eight feet wide at the top, four feet at the bottom and five feet deep, acting as cattle barriers as well as drains. The first commercial willow-growing in Britain took place on Sedgemoor in 1827, with beds being cut annually in a very similar manner to present-day practice. The resultant withy shoots were used for weaving baskets and other objects.

Work was started in 1829 on a canal linking Glastonbury, by way of the South Drain and the lower reaches of the Brue, to a tidal lock at Highbridge. Finished in 1833, it was never a success, suffering from the peat rising continually in the centre of the channel. By 1854 the railways had duplicated the route and it closed. The opening of the Bristol to Exeter railway line really started the process. The Somerset and Dorset Line, 'the Slow and Dirty', which ran over the moors, was much loved locally until its closure in 1954. In the 1840s, the Taunton to Bridgwater Canal, later extended to Chard, carried great quantities of Welsh coal until it too was defeated by rail competition.

The Pumping Stations

One of the most significant events in the history of the Levels took place with the introduction of the first steam pumping station on Westonzoyland Moor in 1830, followed by one on Southlake Moor fifteen years later. Both were inadequate and over-costly but they showed the way to the future. Flood waters could then be lifted from low-lying areas and pumped into rivers, canals and drains inside raised banks on their way to the sea. Land could be ploughed which had previously been too wet to grow arable crops. But without artificial fertilisers this proved over-optimistic and much reverted to permanent pasture. By 1860 a second generation of much more effective steam pumps was starting to show just what could be achieved. One of these machines is still in existence at Westonzoyland and is open to the public. It is fired up and demonstrated regularly.

Another most significant date came in 1870, when full commercial peat-working started. At that time the product was used extensively for fuel or for bedding livestock. By 1900 the industry had started developing a new use, still in operation to this date. From then on the peat was being used increasingly for making special growing composts, though this did not really take off until after the Second World War. Sixteen thousand tonnes were dug in 1954; this rose to 63,000 tonnes in 1966 and 195,000 tonnes in 1985. By 1991, environmental considerations were putting pressure on the continuation of the industry. Alternative products are being sought with some urgency before all the original unspoiled peat landscape is lost for ever.

In 1872 another great flood burst into Somerset, covering 70,000 acres and, a year later ague, a mild form of malaria, was reported as being of concern in the Brue Valley in early spring. Further bad flooding occurred in 1880 when rabbits were reported to be taking refuge on house-roofs. In 1900 it was said that the drainage situation was no better than it had been a century previously. Periodic flooding was serious and seemed to produce no more than 'more reports and words'. In 1902 the Bridgwater-Bristol road flooded. In 1917 there was further bad flooding at Meare and Shapwick, when the Brue burst its bank after nine inches of rain had fallen in twenty hours. This was fresh-water flooding and much more acceptable than salt. Up to 1930 it was normal for the pumps to be able to cope with winter precipitation. Excess water was allowed to spill over into safe areas such as Aller Moor. Many farmers welcomed the silt as natural fertiliser.

As long as sea-levels remain as now, or higher, in combination with huge ranging tides, inland flooding will continue from time to time. This arises when there is insufficient time to let the river water empty through the sluices when, for instance, winds are high, piling water into the Channel at times of spring tides. These fresh-water floods are inconvenient, even dangerous at times, but they do not ruin the ground. However in 1919, 70,000 acres were again inundated with salt water, poisoning the land. The south bank of the River Tone was breached in 1930, flooding 10,000 acres from November to February. Athelney, Curload and Stathe had to be evacuated. Since then a steady range of improvements have been made to cut down the flooding to manageable proportions and to try to avoid sea-water flooding at any cost.

The 1877 Somersetshire Drainage Act, though much modified and now added to by the 1989 Water Act, still controls the activities of the Internal Drainage Boards. Prior to that, individuals had been responsible for 'policing' drainage activities. It was felt they were susceptible to outside influences and should be replaced by Boards responsible for the drainage of specific areas. Decisions would be taken collectively and the costs apportioned amongst the users and owners, according to a formula. The Somerset Rivers Catchment Board was constituted in 1930 to cover the whole region and between 1939 and 1943 made considerable improvements to the King's Sedgemoor Drain. It was widened to thirty-six feet at the bottom and eighty feet at the top, to give a catchment of 50,000 acres and direct drainage for 9,000 acres. In 1970 a new channel was cut between the King's Sedgemoor Drain and the River Parrett and there was further widening of the Drain.

Another important piece of drainage took place during the Second World War. The Puriton munitions factory needed 3.5 million gallons of water per day as a guaranteed supply, so a channel was dug between the Parrett estuary and Gold Corner. The new drain was called the Huntspill River and was made five miles long, with sluices at each end to impound the water, in the form of a long, thin reservoir. The engineers were unable to sustain the planned depth of twenty-four feet, as the weight of spoil on the banks forced up the bed in the centre. Eventually sixteen feet was determined as being practical, but pumps were necessary to keep the planned quantities flowing. The diesel engines at Gold Corner Pumping Station could move 250 million gallons in twenty-four hours. Surrounding areas were transformed and became dry in winter. Many other pumping stations were converted to diesel at this time and were capable of dealing with almost any conditions.

The next major new construction was a pumping station, and enlargement of New Rhyne to become the North Drain, on Tealham Moor in 1950. This enabled the waters flooding the lowest part of the peat-moors to be lifted into the Brue whatever the state of flood. The next stage, gradually installed in all the pumping stations, was automatic pumping by electric motor. This occurred in 1987 in the North Drain. Other stations were converted earlier, many between 1969 and 1970. Prior to that, pumping only took place when there were men on duty in the stations. In the later years, as costs of labour rose, there were restrictions on overtime, except when flooding was taking place, so pumping did not occur at weekends or overnight. Automatic pumps, with sensors installed to switch on and off at predetermined heights, did away with the need for people to be present. The pumping became much more intense and efficient.

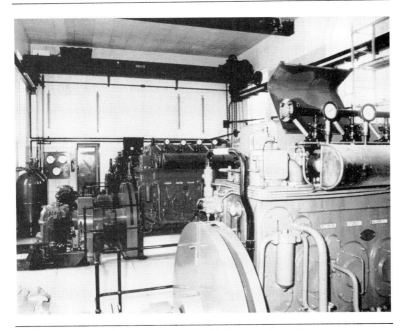

North Drain Pumping Station on River Brue

The Nineties and Beyond

We are all deeply concerned about greenhouse gases and rising sea-levels. It is interesting to see what effect these might have on such a low-lying area as the Levels. At present the mean high water springs are equal to, or above, the height of the clay belt at all points along the coast, almost ten feet above the present-day level of the inland moors and fifteen feet above the lowest moors in the Brue valley, but flooding is held off by seawalls. Only the Parrett and its tributaries are still open to the tide which, under exceptional circumstances, can penetrate as far upstream as Langport. The rest is insulated from the sea by walls and one-way clyses. If we talk about increased heights of, say, six inches, a considerable amount in real terms, this will have little effect on the general sea-defences, which can be steadily increased to accommodate it.

The real effect is felt in estuaries and rivers open to the sea. These are subject to surges, as the increased water flows into the funnel, and a six inch rise can be translated into feet as it goes up river. This

Digger, tamer of the floods, framing Burrow Mump

is where the main extra flood-defence work would have to be undertaken or, perhaps, we might see the final closure of the Parrett, with a clyse at Bridgwater, keeping surges to a minimum. It is not generally known that the Parrett has its own small version of the Severn Bore rushing up river at each tide. This is a practical demonstration of the effect of surges in confined banks, where tidal range is high.

The Levels have progressed through a number of stages as the years passed by; from raw marsh to natural water, fisheries and wildfowl, moving to part-flooded grazing, open only for a few months each year, to semi-drained meadows with a good grazing season, and to flood-free permanent pasture with the potential for high-yielding arable fenland.

It is this final stage that has been largely omitted; though some pasture has been ploughed, it remains well under ten per cent of the usable land and is likely to diminish in the future. It is likely that agricultural yields will continue to be curtailed for the future and there is no longer the need to pull every available piece of ground into production at the expense of all else. We have come to recognise that our country is shrinking and there are some special parts which should be preserved for us all to enjoy. Fortunately the Somerset Levels comes into this category.

In the early 1980s a new phase of agricultural life arrived, with the passing and implementation of the Wildlife and Countryside Act. For the first time brakes were put on agriculture, as Britain and Europe realised that agricultural over-production could ruin them. Various schemes were introduced to pay farmers to work parts of their farms by traditional methods. In theory, these stopped the further development of the Levels, maintaining them as traditional grasslands. Among other effects this also meant that the continuing artificial lowering of the water-table was stopped. The Water Board, and its successor the National Rivers Authority, agreed to leave the winter and summer water-levels, at the pumping stations, as they were in the early 1980s.

Since then minor changes in pump-settings, and automation of river-level readings, have given more control over the water-table and understanding of its effects. For all this, the Levels have continued to dry out, a condition favoured by that minority of farmers with deep-drained systems but much deplored by most of those with traditional fields and methods of farming, as well as those interested in the wildlife of the area.

The wealth of the Levels: part of the great milk herds

5   A Place of Villages and Farms

Although towns and cities such as Glastonbury and Wells have been described earlier as dominating the Levels, this is only true from a historical point of view and through the influence they now have as shopping centres. The Levels are truly rural in outlook and influence. Farming dominates the views, the conversation and the outlook. It is a place of green fields stretching to the horizons, set beneath low hills which frame the view and, above all, it is a place of villages.

Because the Levels are dry in summer the villages are smiling places, wreathed in sun. They bask in the heat and their gardens flourish. Driving past, you gain the impression that the walls store the sun and let it out again slowly, so there is an extra aura of warmth surrounding them. Some are commuter villages but many are of a slower pace, not always inhabited by the original families, but at least by those who stay for a goodly part of their life. Like most places they have their difficulties, as well as their advantages. There are problems for children in that there are few entertainments, little transport, and their school friends often live some distance away. The village shops and, even more important, the sub-post offices, are under pressure from a mobile community. People go to Taunton, to Bridgwater or Street, for their big weekly shop. The village store either has to specialise in exotica, as in the bigger community, enlarge its stock greatly or desperately try to reduce prices to meet the competition. The other solution is to open at all the anti-social hours so as to catch those who have forgotten to shop elsewhere, or tempt them to change their habits because of the sheer convenience. If they are not over-borrowed it is possible to survive; those who are under-capitalised find it near-impossible.

The Post Office is the hub of any village and helps keep it alive.

Without one, people have to travel to collect their allowances, pensions and stamps. A Post Office, run by the right person, holds the village together, usually combining the job with that of the village shop. A board outside, proclaiming someone's birthday and a window with leaflets for the 'Best Kept Village' competition, betokens the sort of place with such a heart. They do far more than just keep the village going; they make sure that old people are given time, societies are publicised and that new people meet some of the older inhabitants. The postmen and women who spread out from the village are a vital lifeline and friends to many outlying and potentially lonely people. They know everyone and report in if there is no sign of a person in the morning. The milkman fills the same role and between them should ensure that accident or illness is brought to the attention of the right people. There is a thin line between nosiness and helpful friendliness, but most country people prefer that the effort is made. It is what makes living in a village so worthwhile.

In discussing the villages of the area it is easiest to deal with them in three distinct batches — coastal, the Brue valley and Sedgemoor. These really do not overlap and have very different characters. This is not a travel guide, with detailed descriptions of each village; rather, I hope to give a feel for the character of the area and how it is changing, by looking at groups of villages with common character or background.

The Coastal Belt

This sounds an indefinite description but has some real meaning nowadays. The coastal villages have been cut off from the rest by the long line of the M5. While the motorway was being constructed it formed a physical barrier, now you are conscious always of crossing it, whether by bridge or underpass. The villages on the other side were always of a different type to the rest, the new road has emphasised this difference.

It is curious the way a road forms a barrier, reducing a moor to a narrow pocket, even though in reality it is a part of a larger area the other side of the road. This is certainly so close to Bridgwater, where otherwise you might think of it as being a part of the Levels. The land becomes suburban farm, rather than a part of that curiously difficult to define moorland which depends on sweep and an indefinable feel for its existence.

The land between Brean Down and Bridgwater comes into the general scope of coastal plain. It does not really feel the same as the rest of the Levels. For a start, many of the fields are edged with wide, low hedges as well as ditches. These are quite distinctive, cut down to a sharp edge, not much above ground level when seen from outside, but sufficient to make a real, stock-proof barrier. The curious thing about this land, especially in the middle part, round the little roadside cottages of Wick, set hard against the lane like a near-continuous wall, is that the fields are not level. They are bumpy, slightly hillocked and wave into the distance. This is in contrast to the main part of the Levels, where the land is quite flat but for the regular lines of surface furrows, designed to clear the initial flush of water into the ditches.

Lympsham is seen from the main Weston road but has much more to offer when penetrating the side lanes. There is a magnificent church and a number of beautiful old houses, set in fine gardens, and it is the picture of what an English village should be. Further south, the village of Brent Knoll surrounds the western part of this prominent hill. While the church is set up on the slope, with a few old houses round it, and a new estate nearby, the majority are close to moor level. It is difficult to see whether they are raised on the edges of the hill-slope by a few feet or close to the natural level of the moors. They certainly look as if they might have been near flood-level in older days. Clearly it has been a substantial place for a long time. Many of the houses are large and old, some being really beautiful in their long-established gardens. Some pubs and shops make it a good place in which to live. The church is famous for its carved pew-ends and is set in a most delightful churchyard. There are paths to the summit of the Knoll and wonderful views across the Levels in all directions.

On the other side of Bridgwater there is a further small part of the Levels. I must confess I find it difficult to rate it with the rest, it is so separated and of a different character, but it is a fascinating part and, I have no doubt, will have sufficient stories and characters to make it worth a tale on its own. There is a subtle variation between sea-marshes and our Levels. This part has more the feel of reclaimed land won from the salt-marsh. It smells of the sea and has the sounds of the sea, with the wild calls of curlew, redshank and other waders.

There is a long edge of sea marsh to this part and some people are fishers making their living from the Bristol Channel, rather than the land, though sheep range the saltings and the fields are dotted with the black and white of many Friesians. Combwich is an ancient port, now silted and used only by a few hardy yachtsmen. The Channel has a rise and fall of nearly forty feet at this point and the huge currents sweep craft along at great speed: knowledge of the area is vital for sailors pitting themselves against the sea. Combwich is growing but still has a heart which makes you feel a part of our island race. You expect men to walk down the street in roll-collared guernseys and turn into rose-covered cottages. There is still a smell of tar and there are up-turned boats by the sea edge. But the river is heavily banked and spends most of its muddy life way below eye-level.

The road wends its way along the edge of the flat-lands to Stockland Bristol, with some beautiful cottages and an impressive collection of coaches waiting to take tourists around the country. From there it turns north-east towards the very tip of the land, Steart and then to Fenny Island. Steart Island itself lies offshore in a sea of mud for most of the time. The sea shelves extremely gradually here and is very dangerous for this reason, as it is said to flow faster than a galloping horse. You need local knowledge if you are to venture offshore for the shellfish which abound, for the mud is treacherous, in parts hard and safe, and in others deep clay which sucks the foot under. The local fisherfolk who live traditionally off this harvest do so by pushing mud sleds to reach fishing nets strung across strategic points far offshore. They deserve the living they make.

The Brue and Axe Valleys

This is the area of the great peat moors, north of the Poldens, and differing in character and agriculture from Sedgemoor. Perhaps the heartland of the Poldens is the best place to start, looking northwards but very much on the Brue side of the hills. A succession of villages, touching each other in parts, and growing into each other everywhere, lines the ridge — dormitories for Bridgwater, with new houses in-filling every space which becomes available. Puriton, with its massive munitions factory, dominates the western end and Catcott the other.

Riverside farm at Godney

These villages have some beautiful old hearts to them with a number of solid, comfortable country houses. Agriculture was the reason for these settlements on the dry ground above the Levels, where farm-houses could be built and cattle over-wintered. Now most have been taken over by people working in industry, though an agricultural machinery merchant, Gwillam's of Edington, who produced most of the milking bales in use in the area, still operates in the centre.

Further along, but off the hill and down on the very edge of the moors, lies Shapwick, an attractive village with an old centre and new houses well mixed in, dominated by a large and splendid church. The heart of the peat diggings lies north of the village, on the road to Westhay and Meare, in a wild and beautiful country with a particular feel of its own, and delicate, slender birch trees behind lush meadows. Years ago these meadows would be pink with orchids in spring, but nowadays this wonderful sight has quite disappeared.

Westhay and Meare lie off the road between Glastonbury and Wedmore and have lost much of their character in recent years, with considerable new building and filling-in of orchards and gardens. Of particular note are the church and medieval Manor House in Meare, as well as the perfectly maintained Abbot's Fish House, dating from monkish times and set on the edge of the former Meare Pool or Ferlyngmere. The Manor House is now a farm and is a perfectly unadorned, unaltered building in plain stone, appearing, I would imagine, as it always has, as well as performing the same farming functions. It stands alongside the singularly beautiful church with its line of pollard limes.

Venturing beyond and north of Meare takes you to the secret parts of Godney and Westhay moors. Godney is a tiny village built along the banks of the Sheppey River, the houses raised up above the countryside. Until recent times, when a spate of modernisation has taken place, it always seemed to me to be a part of the Levels which can have changed little in the last hundred years and more. It had an air of being in a time warp, and the countryside around it is nearly always empty. Nearby Polsham, and Fenny Castle with its hill-fort, are also of the moors, but being modernised rapidly. The villages on the long ribbon development between Wedmore and Wells are not of the moorland. They have a feel of the hills and are separate. There are local bets as to how long it will be before Wells is joined to Wedmore along this road.

Mark runs along its own causeway above the moors, towards the coastal belt. It is the most amazingly long village with little depth away from the causeway. At one stage it had three post offices, which says something. The heart, if such exists, is around the church and alongside a wide rhyne which is all that really remains of the Pilrow Cut, the sea-going link with Glastonbury and Wells in the Middle Ages. Huntspill and Bason Bridge used to be real moorland hamlets, best known for the milk factory which employed so many people before its closure. Now they have an air of dereliction and have become associated more with the industrial estates of nearby Highbridge, to which they are poor brothers. Some of the outlying moorland houses are set back behind rhynes, with bridges joining them to the roads, and form a most particular type of moorland community. From here the road runs on towards the Poldens past the great pumping station at Gold Corner, to Wedmore or directly to Woolavington. There are some delightful willow-shaded fields which look as if you would be unlikely ever to see anyone else within them. Two of the routes cross the Brue at points often extremely busy with fishermen. Fishing is popular in the area and people regularly visit from as far away as Birmingham. In the appropriate season men stay all day, sheltering from blizzard or sun under green umbrellas, their wives often sleeping in a nearby car.

On the northern part of the moors, above Wedmore and following the line of the Axe, the villages are hill settlements. Even the lowest have to be on some slight rise in the ground to have survived the great floods which were so much a part of the area. Stone and Chapel Allerton are pretty little places with some ancient cottages. They have a reputation for being particularly happy villages in which to live. Cocklake sits both on the hill and down on Monk Moor, below Wedmore. A lonely moorland road crosses the Axe here and splits on either side of the great bump of Nyland. I talked to someone who lived there and was told it should more properly be called Nyland Tump. This dominates the landscape below the lowering mass of Mendip running along the horizon. One side is wooded and a buzzard can often be seen wheeling endlessly up in the thermals above it. The cattle look like black and white toys on the side of the hill. On the northern side there is a little grouping of farms which makes quite a settlement. Nyland has always played an important part in the area, as a part of manorial grounds.

The villages along the south-western slopes of Mendip are very much a part of the hill rather than the moors. Their main activity in the old days was growing strawberries on the southern slopes, until foreign imports eroded their advantages. The strawberries are still said to taste better than anything you buy from abroad. Cheddar and Draycott were the centre of this trade, served by its own railway line — now defunct and a part of a cycle path.

Sedgemoor

Although the whole of the Levels is sometimes referred to by this name, it still really applies only to that part south of the Poldens and, even more particularly, to King's Sedgemoor and West Sedgemoor. The word has an air of dash and glamour to it, perhaps arising from its historical connections with Monmouth and the Pitchfork Rebellion.

Where better to start than within sight of Alfred's Isle of Athelney. The road from Street splits off for Taunton at the little upland village of Ashill, winds its way down from the low hills and dumps itself on the wide flat expanse of the King's Sedgemoor. It is a fast, often straight road, bringing the first glimpse of those great horizons and the gleam of water in ditches. You cross Greylake Bridge, with the huge sluices controlling the level of the King's Sedgemoor Drain beside it, and over a couple of other closely-linked drains, before rising up to Othery — a long, narrow village of no great distinction other than having a garage which specialises in selling those country-dwellers favourites, secondhand Volvo estate cars. As you leave the village the road narrows and is steeply-banked to the left. In winter, Southlake Moor, the land over the other side of that bank, is often flooded. The local farmers have voted for many years to flood the moors in winter, so as to silt the ground, and this produces a wonderful summer sward, as well as a truly spectacular winter scene.

However, the flooding is best viewed from Burrow Mump, as it is known locally though, for some reason, the Ordnance Survey insists on calling it Burrow Mount. This extraordinarily artificial-looking island stands up above the moor and is crowned with an ancient church. The National Trust provides a small car-park and it is a must for any visitor. The views from the top are spectacular, showing the form and detail of Sedgemoor as is difficult to understand from elsewhere.

Burrow Bridge is a delightful little village with plenty of character still, particularly in the centre and along the banks of the Parrett, which is crossed by the road. In high summer the roses trail the walls of the houses and it seems a reflection of all the summers you have ever seen, the washed walls hot, the gardens lush and the interiors cool — as all good cottages should be. On one side of the bridge stands the pub, while the Mump and church lie along the line of the bridge and behind the pub. The river is heavily banked and flows well above the land on either side at high tide, though it is a fast and muddy stream which does not encourage boating or other waterborne sports.

Just beyond this bridge a side road leads along Athelney, through Curload and on to Stoke St Gregory. This little road runs alongside the River Tone, and there is a marvellous view from Stanmoor Bridge, up to Burrow Bridge and the Mump, with its church dominating the

River Parrett, near Burrowbridge

countryside. The river runs down to the moors on one side, while the Mump is reflected in the water the other way. The route along Athelney is fascinating, whether walking the river on the northern bank, or driving along the southern where the houses are all high above the road on the raised banks of the river. This is the centre of the willow-growing area, impossible to ignore, with fields full of growing willow-wands and bundles stacked in the yards of farms opening tantalisingly to one side or the other.

Stoke St. Gregory is a large, well-spread village sitting above the lower levels of famous West Sedgemoor. It is raised up slightly with parts on different levels giving it an air of an old-fashioned garden — you are turning corners constantly and finding yourself in a quite different setting. The church, with its octagonal tower, stands in the very centre, next to a shop and opposite a pub, and there is an air of peace about it all. West Sedgemoor is a low-lying level which, over the years, has been the centre of much controversy, first with plans to drain it, then becoming the centre of a row about newly announced plans for Sites of Special Scientific Interest (SSSI), strongly resisted by local farmers in the early 1980s. It is a beautiful, tranquil area, on which there is a large RSPB reserve, famous for its wintering and breeding birds.

At the other end of this moor there is a most beautiful village. North Curry has many classical buildings, a market cross and an enclosed green laid out like a town square. It looks a prosperous, well maintained place, where commuter meets countryman, with the emphasis on the latter. It certainly does not look as if the commuters have prettified it or taken it over completely. Throughout this area, and into the nearby Isle of Athelney, there is a feeling of countryman and countryside surviving. The cottages have grown into the surrounding ground, those on the river edge are part of the bank and their gardens are the old-fashioned sort, with an assortment of colours blending into each other and vegetable patches set among them, both equally important. It is a happy-feeling part of the world, comfortable and ordered, well-tuned to the pace of life in a rural setting.

The long arms of the Levels penetrate far inland and some of the most secretive and delightful parts are towards the edges. Long Load and Long Sutton, villages on nearby main roads are, as their names imply, settlements along the line of the road, raised up above the surrounding floods in the old days. Many of their houses are of that wonderful mellow golden Ham Stone for which nearby Montacute is famous. Even on grey days they have a warm, welcoming feel to them. Many are thatched and the roofs are surmounted by straw birds at the peaks. This area is wonderful to behold on a bright winter's day, with long runnels of water on the near fields and great sheets filling the lower-lying ground.

South of Long Load, a meandering road takes you to Muchelney, past open fields and ditch-edged pastures to a part where it crosses a most lovely stream at Muchelney Hams. If you want to find a perfect rural scene this must be it. The water laps the grass, without banks, so the stream flows apparently level with the field, willows hang over on one side and a farmyard is set back on the other. It is a scene of perfect tranquillity. Muchelney itself is a tiny village with some gems of houses in it, including a medieval priest's house. The centre is dominated by the church which has a wonderful, and still brilliantly-coloured, painted ceiling, where the angels wear Elizabethan court dress.

Next door to this masterpiece lie the remains of the Abbey, the second oldest religious establishment in Somerset, founded by King Ine around 700. Muchelney was one of the great abbeys which controlled and dominated the area for so long, though falling finally not to King Henry and his servants but a mountain of debts brought on by bad management. There is a surprising amount of the buildings still left, though there are also long rows of stones on the ground to show where the main walls stood. The Abbey is set next to a working farm, of which at one time it was a part. It has been beautifully restored by English Heritage and is really worth a visit. The Abbey-church has virtually disappeared. It was large, nearly 250 feet long inside, and set on this island in the marshes. Even today it is sometimes cut off by floods. This must have given it a marvellous feeling of being a sanctuary from the outside world. What remains is a remarkably well-preserved Abbot's House, with upstairs and downstairs rooms, a wooden barrel ceiling in part and the lower half of a cloistered walk which must have been quite superb in its tracery of arches. There are carved fireplaces, stained glass panes and many carvings pre-

Cottages in Muchelney village

97

served from other parts of the Abbey. Parts of the walls show traces of curious painted decorations. Each time I go to Muchelney my sense of enjoyment and well-being increases. It has a serene atmosphere.

The Abbey is raised slightly above the surrounding Levels and may be cut-off in winter, when the floods fill the nearby fields and the great herds of Bewick's swans fly in from Siberia. Muchelney is isolated in the real sense. It is on a by-road and surrounded by farmlands, willows and ditches. It is another place with a feeling of great tranquillity.

The next leap takes us back across Sedgemoor to where the famous battle took place. One of the finest roads to reach this is by way of Burrow Bridge, following the course of the Parrett as it winds along beneath its high, raised banks, though you miss thriving Middlezoy by doing so. The river bank is dotted with farms, some with imposing period houses of great size. Cider orchards run back from the edge. They appear shut-off from the outside world, self-contained and secretive. Away from the river bank this is a part more cultivated than much of the Levels but retains that characteristic feel. It is open country, some ploughed, some grass and farmed hard. Weston-zoyland has grown to meet the needs of an increasing population in the nearby Bridgwater area and is a mix of ugly new houses and some delightful old properties.

The road from the Parrett runs along a causeway to the south of the village, with the cottages set on a long line high up on the bank, which raises them up to look across the Levels. While there are signs to indicate where the battlefield was, the Bussex rhyne, scene of the confusion which led to the ultimate slaughter, is no longer there. The church is one where men were hanged from the tower and there are marks on the walls said to have been made by the rebels sharpening their swords before battle. You are unlikely to have much of a feel for the day here. It is the most civilised (or is it de-natured?) of the villages in the area. Better by far to walk deep into the open countryside and imagine what it must have been like that early morning. If you can do this when the mist is rising from the ditches I fancy you will shiver and thank the powers you were not there on that awful day.

Before you reach this centre-point of history it is worth a detour to visit Middlezoy, firmly set on the ancient isle of Sowey. This is a comfortable little place, with a recognisable village heart set around a fine old pub, the George, remarkable now for an extensive and interesting collection of real ales on draught. It gives the impression of still being a country village, not having lost its heart to the commuter population. There are Somerset accents still and old men in work-stained boots in the corner of the bar. It is comforting to find this place surviving and thriving, yet with new businesses in evidence. A village should be a growing and evolving place if it is to survive. The secret lies in how to do this without losing the feel and atmosphere built over the centuries.

What is somewhat surprising to anyone brought up with tales of Sedgemoor rhynes and marshes, is to find this is an undulating countryside, the land rising and falling quite noticeably. The true Levels lie further over, before Othery and on to Chedzoy and beyond. This is a cultivated part, with ploughground, improved pasture and all the signs of modern-style agriculture.

The main road runs unremarkably towards Bridgwater for a while. Take the turning marked Chedzoy and then on over the King's Sedgemoor Drain to Parchey and Sutton Mallet. The Chedzoy sign comes well before the village, seeming only to encompass a couple of large farms, then the cluster of houses starts along the twisting line of the road, eventually ending in a thatched cottage of considerable charm. Many of the larger buildings are of indeterminate age and doubtful beauty. There is no stone close-by, so they have been built of Bridgwater brick, which is a particularly harsh and uncompromising red that does not seem to mellow with age.

Beyond Parchey is a most delightful corner of old cottages, overhanging willows and swans on green rhynes. The Drain is extremely wide at this point and often lined with fishermen undergoing some competition. It can be incredibly tranquil as evening falls and the breeze drops, leaving trees reflected against clear patches of light in the water. Sutton Mallet is a tiny and charming village with a most unexpected and photogenic small church at its very heart. There is a whole string of small villages and hamlets which runs along the southern, sun-warmed slopes of the Poldens towards Street, many down on the lowest contour. All repay further exploration in an unhurried manner. Fruit is grown at Stawell and may be picked by the public in season.

I hope I may have given a feel of this special land and its villages, but there is no substitute for going to look for yourself.

Although farming employs fewer people than it once did, it is still predominant, by virtue of the green countryside surrounding the villages. Farms used to be labour-intensive, now most are highly mechanised, whatever branch of farming they undertake. Many farms employ just the farmer and his wife, the children leaving to work elsewhere when the time arises. A dairy farm, still an important sector even in these times of reduced milk quotas, demands total attention from its owners and operators. Someone has to be out milking early each morning, Sundays and Bank Holidays included, and must attend to the same business in the afternoon. There is no let-up in the routine. Some, who can afford it, employ a relief-milker to give them a regular break, but most just do not have holidays and have not done so for many years. The profit on a small farm is not sufficient to allow for such a luxury, although the actual living may be reasonable because of home-grown food and other advantages of being self-employed.

Dairy farming brings in a regular milk cheque and so is still regarded as a reliable means of making a living. Beef cattle and sheep are less demanding, though both have their moments, particularly sheep, but you have to wait for your money, until the cattle have been fattened or raised, or the lambs are ready for market. As a result, a lot of working capital is required. At the end of a couple of years' wait for a steer to mature the market may fall, so the money obtained barely meets the costs of production, to which must be added the interest. You have to be good at guessing the markets in the future, and shrewd in your use of money, if you are to remain a farmer through the varying conditions brought about by government over the years. Many smaller farmers enjoy the way of life and would not change it for anything else, even though their earnings rank with the lowest wages in the country.

'Holidays! I never take they!' If they own the farm, the only way to a pension may be to sell on retirement, which puts their successors immediately into the hands of the Banks. On the other hand, agricultural land has risen enormously in value over the past fifty or sixty years, particularly on the Levels, where much ground which used to be counted useless waste is now valuable pasture.

In recent years the biggest problems in farming have been faced by those who have been encouraged to modernise, drain, buy new machinery, all of which require heavy capital outlay. Bank borrowings have killed many a farm. Although this has happened here, many of the Levels' farmers have wisely stuck to their native skills and those methods best suited to a wetland permanent pasture. At the stage where this might have changed, through the possible drainage of the Levels on a big scale, the government stopped further ploughing and drainage, through the SSSI scheme, which applied to much of the Levels. This was then followed by a further scheme, that of the Environmentally Sensitive Area (ESA) which paid farmers as a right if they volunteered to maintain a low-intensity style of farming suited to the area, which was the preference of many of them anyway. No so-called improvements are entertained under this scheme and no extra money need be spent on capital intensive schemes such as arise with ploughing, root crops and grain.

The call for capital locally has tended to be for normal replacements of tractors, silage making machinery, for hay or replacement animals and so has not hit so hard as elsewhere, when interest rates rose steeply in the early 1990s. For all that it is not a time for farmers to be happy. The pressure of high interest rates has hit the ultra-modern, high-efficiency farm on drained land worst. Such a farm has been dependent on high capital expenditure. But even the traditional grassland farmer is affected. High interest rates touch everyone down the chain, increase costs and reduce demand. The traditional farmer, with low-tech processes, has always been able to take a hitch in his belt, live off the land, and not replace equipment for another year or so, but eventually even he begins to feel the twin squeezes of government and EEC policies. Those who have the fall-back of the ESA scheme must feel much reassured compared with other parts of the country which do not have this.

Willow Growing

Other activities take place on the Levels. There are a number of exotic crops not generally found elsewhere. Willows have been grown in Somerset on a commercial basis since 1825. In 1957 there were 1,500 acres, concentrated around the Isle of Athelney. Since then there has been a steady decline as imports bite and people look to different needs for their shopping and in the house. In 1970 the figure had fallen to 500 acres. In 1991 the acreage was believed to be between 400 and 500 acres so the decline continues, though much slowed. The willows are grown close together in fields and cut to the ground each year. These stumps then grow long, slender, straight rods, up to six feet or more in a season. When they are cut they are either boiled or stripped, depending on the colour finally required, and dried. The final product is used to make chairs, stools, baskets, tables and a variety of other objects which, to the connoisseur, have that indefinable life and feel, far superior to plastic woven into the same shapes. In many withy fields you used to see cider-apple trees grown, so that once the withies had reached the end of their useful life after, say, twenty years, a splendid orchard remained.

Willows lining the river at Godney

Teazel Growing

An even more specialised crop is the growing of teazels. The makers of fine worsteds and similar very high quality cloth have never found a steel or other substitute which combs and cleans the cloth as efficiently as a frame fitted with teazels of a certain variety. The little hooks on the seed head comb without damaging the fibres and could have been designed precisely for the job. This trade is said to have been confined to the valley of the River Isle, around Fivehead, for a couple of centuries. Again, teazel growers are faced with competition from abroad and the changing requirements of the cloth-manufacturers, though in 1991 there were somewhere between twenty and thirty acres of teazels being grown, with a return per acre higher than cereals. I have been told there is good potential for expansion, for the crop is very much in demand. It suits the heavy clay soils around Fivehead well and the quality is superior to French or Spanish teazels, which dry out too much in the hotter summers. However, it is faced with a new pest — deer have a distinct liking for the prickly plant and have increased in numbers in recent years. There is only one buyer of teazels in Britain, who comes from a family firm in Yorkshire, but he also believes there is a good and expandable future for this unusual crop.

Peat

The great crop of the region, if that is the right term, is peat. This is confined to the Vale of Avalon, along the line of the Brue, edging the low line of the Polden Hills. The peat was based on raised moss deposits in the valley. It is a major industry in Somerset and the county is facing upheavals at present as a result of the tremendous publicity being given to stopping its production and conserving the area as a special habitat for wild life, wild flowers and plants. A great many people in the Brue valley depend on peat for their living and are deeply worried about the future in an area where industry is never likely to flood in.

In 1989 there were some thirty producers, varying in size from a few acres to holdings of over a thousand acres. By 1985 the total production amounted to nearly 200,000 tonnes and the industry employed the equivalent of 250 full-time jobs, though many more people are affected, as they work part-time. In January 1988 there were just over three thousand acres with planning permission for peat extraction and over five hundred operating without permission — though this is not such a condemnation as it seems. Some of these diggings go back before planning permission was required. Peat digging is broadly divided into three main areas in the Brue Valley, a northern zone on Westhay Moor and southern, between Shapwick and Meare, with a third in the Sharpham area. In 1989 it was estimated that potential reserves of around nine million cubic feet of material existed — equivalent to 3.8 million tonnes of peat or forty-five years' production at 1985 figures.

Peat has been cut for fuel and animal bedding for much of history. Most farms had corners of fields traditionally cut by hand for peat. One neighbour of ours remembers spending many hours when he was a lad some forty-five years ago, cutting the tangle of irises and other herbage which grew on the patch where peat had been cut, in an effort to bring it back to grazing. Now it is virtually impossible to see where that had been. The only sign is that the corner of the field is the first to hold water when it rains heavily. At the start of this century, peat began to be used horticulturally and the amount cut each year began to rise, though limited by hand cutting. After the Second World War production again rose steeply, as commercial firms started to mechanise output.

A most spectacular method of production is still commonly used all over the area. Trenches are cut by a special slow-moving machine. It cuts blocks and stacks them to one side for drying. Alternate rows of blocks, trenches and uncut pieces, form a geometrical pattern of chocolate peat, gleaming water and the delicate green of reeds growing between. It has almost become a symbol of the Brue countryside.

Cider Apples

The final crop which must be mentioned, seen as a symbol for Somerset as a whole, is that of the cider apple. A few years ago I might have written that it was a vanishing crop and way of life. This is no longer true, though the form of the orchards has changed somewhat. In Britain we have a special feel for links with our past. The ancient cider orchard certainly fits this category. There is something timeless and beautiful about an old, twisted apple-tree, with lichen growing on its trunk and branches. Cider was a part of a man's wages when he worked on a farm — as most people did a couple of hundred years ago. The labourer was given his cider in quantities measured in gallons, rather than pints, for he sweated hard in physical labour such as hay-making, though this drink was said to be from a less strong second pressing.

In Somerset this tradition survived until quite recently and cider was a way of life. Many years ago I used to go around farms dealing with various agricultural products. Wherever I went on the Quantocks, or down on the Levels, we would talk about our business, then relax for a few minutes — life was not so hurried twenty-five or more years ago. I would be asked if I would like a drop of cider. It was impossible to refuse, so one was led deep into the gloom of a shed to where the barrels stood on staging. An encrusted mug would be produced — no germs could survive local cider — and drops of a golden, often cloudy, liquid would trickle in. Conversation definitely livened up after that. The secret was to sip, so as to keep the one mug going, for the next farm would inevitably repeat the process.

In those days a great many varieties of apple were grown to make the appropriate blend which suited their particular palate. Varieties, such as Kingston Black, were planted as standard trees and grew to considerable size. This was to allow the grass beneath to be grazed by cattle and sheep without damaging the trees. There were various customs associated with cider-apple growing, some of which still survive in some parts, including the ceremony of wassailing.

For a while it seemed as if the new commercial ciders would use fewer British apples, preferring instead to buy in known varieties of apple pulp from the Continent. Then a determined programme of orchard replacement was started, with varieties suited to their needs, and orchards designed where mechanical methods could be employed for picking. The acreage of new cider orchards continues to rise. At the same time, farmhouse cider has come back into fashion after all but vanishing. I must confess that some of the cider I drank in my farm visiting days was diabolical — acid, sometimes vinegary and definitely not out to suit the town visitor. But now a more discriminating producer has arisen and a number of presses have reopened locally. Cider is produced in different degrees of sweetness and it is possible to have it mixed to suit your palate. A free glass or so while deciding this is a part of the process, and very enjoyable too. The only problem with farmhouse cider is that it starts oxidising and changing its taste the moment it is drawn from the cool, air-free conditions of the big barrel in which it is made, so it should be drunk quickly. Great tales are told of its potency but this is not true of the cleaner, more hygienic modern brew. It is strong, but not noticeably more so than a pint of beer. Thank goodness we have come to terms with cider again. It is a superb drink and as Somerset as the Levels themselves. There is also hope that some of the old orchards will be preserved, while seeing the growth of the modern trees.

6 *People of Sedgemoor*

Many people live on the Levels or make their living in connection with the landscape. Who among these should represent the area, its characteristic lifestyle, spirit and humour? The People who comment here reflect the best of the traditional way of doing things and remark on their fears for the future. Let them speak for themselves

Cheesemaker

Mary Duckett was born in the village of Mark, about four miles from her present home in the hamlet of Heath House. Her family was not wealthy but her father was diligent and clever; in fact, he was the third person in the village to own a car — a high-backed Wolseley.

The family owned about thirty cows and, according to the way the price of cheese and milk went up or down, they made Cheddar in the summer when there was more milk about, and Caerphilly in the winter — as it did not dry out like Cheddar. However, there might be gaps of anything up to two years when no cheese was made. This was mainly her mother's work, with some helpers. His main interest was as a dealer. He went to the Tuesday market in Highbridge, where he had a store under the Town Hall. All the local farmers brought their cheeses — mainly Caerphilly — and the dealers would go round the stalls, testing them by hand, some by using a cheese borer, rather like an apple corer, which was inserted into the side. A portion was then tasted before the sliver was put back.

"Did they do this to all of them?" I wondered, thinking how cross the farmers must have been to have holes in their prized cheeses. "How could they sell them after that?"

Mary smiled. "No, they only tested a few. They were very good

Mary Duckett

at judging by feel and sight. But you never washed a cheese borer, you know — only wiped it clean. My father bought in most of his cheeses at market and we would pack them up there and then, eight cheeses to a crate, put them on a hand cart and wheel them to the station, which was just off the Market Place. Most went to Wales, some to London and a few to Scotland. Caerphilly was particularly popular with the miners because it kept moist underground and, being salty, made up for what they lost when working."

Mary left school at sixteen. Perhaps she might have chosen to work somewhere else but, at the age of nine, her sister had been diagnosed as suffering from Still's Disease. Mary decided to stay at home and help. This was when her cheese making career began. The milk used for this was done by hand — no washing of the teats — out in the fields in the summer and indoors in winter. About four of them would go out by horse and cart, each milking six or seven cows at a time. This was preferable to being indoors where, though your particular cow might be tied firmly by the neck, there were other hind quarters very close around you and cows can administer a pretty nasty kick. The milk they sold went to the Cheddar Valley Factory, the churns being collected by lorry from a stand by the farm gate.

Cheese making, in a round copper vat holding eighty gallons, was long and tedious in those days. When it came to the scald stage, they had to dip off the whey into a seven gallon, two-handed warmer and stand it in a furnace of hot water, then pour it back into the curd. They continued doing this until the required temperature was reached, which must have meant a great deal of to-ing and fro-ing with heavy vessels. Sometimes they asked the Agricultural College at Cannington to send them an Instructress for a week to teach the art of cheese-making to a group of eight to ten young people in the area. This was great fun as they worked two to a ten gallon tub and, as well as enjoying the company, also acquired a lot of useful knowledge.

Mary married Roland Duckett in 1942 and came to live at Walnut Tree Farm. Ten days after returning from honeymoon one of their twenty-eight cows was diagnosed as having foot and mouth. All were destroyed, together with twenty sheep. They were left with two horses and two dogs. What a way to start married life!

Roland's sister, Ethel, had been the main cheese-maker up till then, and, although she moved out of the farmhouse with her mother, continued this work every day until she herself married. Mary was very fully occupied with producing two boys and a girl in the early years, so had little time to help much and they managed with living-in help. However, after a couple of unsatisfactory girls, Mary decided that enough was enough. "I don't think they really trusted me with the cheese up till then," she said, "But I decided I could do it and I started again. We still had some help for a time."

Being war time, with all the problems of rationing, milk was in short supply, so they could only make cheese for eleven months of the year. Caerphilly, being a quick ripening cheese, was not allowed, so it had to be Cheddar, which was stored for six weeks before being graded and collected by the Milk Marketing Board. Regulations were very strict, but the family was allowed to keep one large cheese a month for themselves. One gallon of milk makes approximately one pound of Cheddar, and even more in the autumn when the milk is richer. Autumn cheese tastes much better, Mary reckons.

It was still a long process, though, with a very early start to light the fire in the steam boiler. What a disaster when it went out, delaying the cheese making and upsetting the whole day. Cheddar is slow to make — Mary recalled one night when they were vatting it at 10pm, because the "acidity was so slow". During the summer they pumped water by hand from a well to cool the milk, as it was ten degrees lower than tap water.

What a relief when electricity was installed after the War, although one memorable day the steam raiser had a blow-out and oily soot covered everything, including a large basket of washing waiting to be hung on the line. That took some clearing up.

In the early 1950s it became possible to return to making their favourite, Caerphilly, once again. Now they had to find their own market, so they started by contacting some of Mary's father's old customers. In one instance this entailed loading the pick-up van and travelling across by the Aust Ferry to South Wales, where they delivered the cheese to the wholesalers, for the princely sum of one shilling a pound. This was then sold on to the customers for two shillings a pound! That did not last very long and soon dealers started coming to the farm. Nowadays they travel some distance — from Sussex, Dorset, London. And every month Mary parcelled up two small Wedmore Cheeses (Caerphilly with Chives) to send to John

Arlott in the Channel Isles. If they were delayed he soon got in touch!

These dealers have also asked for some variety and now, apart from the chives, caraway seed, cumin and garlic are added, with appropriate names and wrapping. Some goes through a complicated smoking process, and it is even possible to produce a Brie-type cheese using a soft Caerphilly which is kept for six weeks. Needless to say, with the Listeria scare, hygiene is extremely important and inspectors arrive to make spot checks at intervals.

Although the cheese making, including Cheddar, does not take so long as in her childhood, Mary is on hand about 7.15 am, dressed in white apron and boots, ready to start her stint in the dairy. The culture/starter has already been added to the overnight milk at 6.00 am before it is warmed to seventy degrees. It is then warmed a further ten degrees and left for one to two hours. The morning milk comes in, is added and brought up to ninety degrees. It can be seen that temperature is vital and must be accurate. The thermometer has been known to go wrong so a second one is on hand for a double check.

Rennet is then added to the three hundred gallons which goes into each day's cheese making and the mix is stirred in a particular way. If the bottom of the mixture is disturbed at this stage it will separate and cannot be re-formed. The eye of the expert sees that bubbles are beginning to appear and stay, which is the start of the thickening process. Now is the time to go away for half an hour and have a well earned breakfast.

On returning, they are confronted by a solid junket, which is cut with the curd knife before being stirred gently. Then it is scalded, followed by more stirring until it firms up, when the whey is drawn off, with the curd going to the bottom of the vat. When they kept them, the whey used to be fed to their own pigs, but is now taken by tanker to the fields each day for the young cattle. Otherwise, disposal could be a problem, because whey cannot be put down drains, due to the smell, or spread on the ground, where it burns the grass.

There is still further cutting and spreading of the curd before adding salt. Then it is put into moulds and pressed for about an hour. After that it is out of the moulds again to be rubbed in salt while the cloths are rinsed in salty water, and back into the presses until the following morning. The last stage leaves the cheeses floating in strong brine for twenty-four hours before storage.

"And — the final job each day, which I must not forget to tell you about, is the washing up. This can take quite a time and must be done properly." And I have seen this for myself, having called at the farm around that time in the morning to buy a nice large piece of Caerphilly and some of their butter and clotted cream, both of which are made from the separated whey. The cloths are fluttering out on the clothes line and a milky stream runs away down the channel near the back door. On cold winter mornings I look at their hands, which have been in some form of liquid on and off for the past two or three hours and are now engaged in scrubbing utensils, and I wonder how their skin copes.

"We're not in the dairy at the moment," Mary added "because it is being done up. The boys have decided that they are going to get an automatic stirrer. I'm not too sure about it — there's nothing to beat the trained touch — but it should save time. I have to admit that most of the changes we've made over the years have been for the better. I suppose we could grow bigger and produce more, but that can lead to problems with finding extra labour. We have bought more quotas to provide extra milk, and there certainly is a demand for cheese, but we don't want to make a rod for our own backs."

Almost as an afterthought, she casually mentioned that, unknown to them, one of their dealers had entered their Caerphilly in a Wine and Cheese Exhibition in London and it had come first in Great Britain. A French cheese had won the overall international prize, but who cares about that? One of 'our' local cheeses had swept the board up in the city: I felt really proud. Cheese making requires great skill, taking into consideration time, temperature, acidity and weather — even the different fields in which the cows graze.

"Experience is a great help," Mary said quietly. I should certainly think it is — and who better to know than one who has perfected the art over the last sixty years.

Countryman

Edwin Durston lives in a fine old cottage at Catcott, where he has been most of his life. He retired in 1988 after a lifetime in farming, seeing the old cottages which surrounded him knocked down and replaced with new, his spinster neighbours, relics of the slaughter of the First War, replaced by people who commute into Bridgwater or elsewhere.

Mr Durston is the son of a farmer and worked for him until he died in 1962, when the holding was split up between the family. The total holding was eighty acres and they milked thirty cows at the time. From there, he went to work for his cousin until retirement, letting the grass on the fields he owned. He started working with milking cows, then moved to a beef herd with his cousin.

He led a carefree life when young, though with little money to spare. Before the war, people took up farming to survive, not to make money. There were no jobs available in the 1930s and anything seemed worthwhile.

Water was always a problem:

"You watched your own supplies in the summer. In 1921 there was a terrible drought and the whole village ended up getting their water from one spring at the end of the lane. Normally you managed to make it eke out. The coming of the mains supply in 1936 was much welcomed. Nowadays we don't seem to know what to do about water. You have forty-eight hours of rain and its all gone within a day. The ditches and rhynes have all been widened so they let it out like a bath emptying, leaving nothing for another day."

In the thirties the whole of the farming world depended on horses.

"It was a cruel life for them. They had no rest for themselves, were constantly being driven, working hard. They were woken at five in the morning and it took an hour to feed them, groom them and get them ready. Then it was all slog. They had a terrible life when you think about it. The man working them had no peace either. The horses were easily spooked by planes going over and they suffered terribly from flies. These would drive the horses mad at times. You don't know what flies are like nowadays. In those days they were a constant plague in the summer. You were a bag of nerves when you were in charge of a team of heavy horses."

Edwin Durston

In those pre-war days a farmer reckoned to be able to cope with a mixed hill and moorland farm of eighty acres with his son. He milked ten cows and had a few followers on the ground. This was the average size of farm. A man with three hundred acres needed a bevy of sons to keep it going and they were counted well-off. Before tractors came, hay-making would take from July to September, working all the hours available. The first tractor arrived in the area in 1942 and they were generally accepted, and on most farms, by 1955.

"Before the tractor it would take until late into the evening to cut six acres with two horses, and you would get back absolutely exhausted. If you do it with a tractor now, you will be finished in time for a mid-morning cup of coffee. In the old days, a cow in the ditch might mean all the able-bodied people in the village turning out. A tractor will do it in moments now."

Pre-war, any free time was spent out on the moors shooting with a bunch of his friends. Many were sons of farmers and they had the freedom to wander the place where they would and knew every cover and blade of grass. He mentioned that it used to rain frogs literally in the old days or, as he put it,

"The moors were diggle with them after a thunderstorm." In those days there used to be a great many grass-snakes about.

"They used to lie around under the fuzz and the sound of them moving off could be heard distinctly, like a rustle of dry leaves. I haven't seen any in recent years."

It may seem strange that such a keen shooter should be so conservation-minded, but that often turns out to be the case. He was always interested in what he saw but it was not until just after the war that he saw his first bird book.

"Before the war we used to come back with capfuls of peewits eggs. Everyone ate them locally, they were reckoned to be rich and there were more than enough for everyone and the birds themselves. Now there are none to be found on the moors because of the changes which have taken place. When the moors were flooded, the wild swans came in. They flew over the house and had the most wonderful calls. There were none of they mute swans in those days. The geese came in early in the winter and stayed through. Anyone who had a gun was out after them. I remember one Sunday when the whitefronts were flighting. The waves of geese went over all day, from sunrise

Wild swans out on Catcott Heath

late into the night. Thousands of wigeon came in when there was hard weather at the coast. You would see the sun catching their breasts as they came over the fields. One night there were twenty-six guns out on Catcott Drove and they never even made the passing birds waver. Never seen a sight like it. If we got the water back we would get those birds back again, I reckon."

"When you were hand-milking you saw the birds out on the moors. Then, when the milk-bale came in, you were trapped inside, while the noise of the engine came over everything. Tractors with cabs are even worse. I hate them, they shut you away completely".

Locals who lived out on the moors took up the gun in the winter to make a living. These people ditched during the summer, or dug peat. There was not such work available during the winter flooding, so they did what they could. There were enough wildfowl out there, and people wanting to buy them, to make it worth their while. Snipe shooting was both popular and successful, for the numbers of birds were so great. On the fifteen acre ground out at Catcott they would go and shoot all morning. There were so many snipe they just pitched behind the guns when disturbed. The famous local shoot was Shapwick Manor. In August people used to come from all over the country to Shapwick Station and were picked up and rowed out to the shooting grounds. The old game book is said to have recorded nine hundred snipe shot one year, at a time when numbers were not even dented by such losses. Edwin used to go as a beater before the war and enjoyed 2/6d a day, with pork for lunch and a bottle of pop — complete with a marble in the neck of the bottle to seal in the fizz.

The moors are curious places and strange things have happened to them in recent years.

"Shapwick was always low ground and flooded before Catcott. Now the ground at Shapwick seems to have reared up and Catcott is lower. Before Gold Corner Pumping Station, the moors at Catcott dried out completely in summer, in spite of flooding over the whole winter. We had to dig in the bottom of the ditches for the cows to drink in the hot weather. A tub was let into the hole to keep the water clear. Large numbers of eels and fish were found in the last pools. The herons would eat until they could manage no more and could barely walk. Now herons spend more time chasing mice than catching eels, for they seem to have vanished from the ditches."

Edwin is a true naturalist, with all the curiosity that that implies, knowing all the resident local creatures and picking out immediately anything unusual which appears. This has translated itself into a considerable interest in the conservation movement and a critical eye to what is going on,

"They don't know what they'me doing always."

Nevertheless he tries to help in whatever way he can and keeps a keen eye out for anyone misbehaving themselves on the various reserves run by the STNC at Catcott. One big difference between now and his younger days is the attention paid to predators. The young men used to go round in spring and note every nesting crow and magpie and try and destroy the nests before the eggs hatched. There were regular rook and fox shoots and predators were kept down. Now they are multiplying unchained, for few people take the same interest in them. There must be some effect from this, he thinks.

In the war they had to plough up a great deal of hill-ground, but the results were not always very good, as there was nothing available to deal with the over-abundant wire-worms. However, growing corn introduced new skills and extra work to the area. The corn had to be threshed and this brought in high wages during that period. The wages at that time were probably under 25/- a week, while labourers were being offered 10/- a day for work on threshing. This business required a lot of people. Two on the first rick, one feeding the thresher, one behind, on the sacks, one pitching the dead straw away, two putting it away on the new rick and one dealing with the caving (rubbish). Although it was filthy, dusty and exhausting work, people flocked to earn these high amounts. Prior to that wages had not moved at all and it really was subsistence for many. At a time when a man couldn't get 30/- for his week's labour, Edwin sold three white-fronted geese he shot for that sum.

"How has drainage affected the moors?" I asked.

"You could smell the moor when you went down to it. I haven't noticed that particular smell for the past ten years. The last time was when I cut a bit of meadow in 1980. The soil has changed completely. It has dried out and gone powdery. If a cow got into a ditch before the war, you had to dig out a bay to drag her out. Everything took time in those days. You walked down to the moors twice a day to inspect the herd and to look along the ditches. If you found one in, you had to walk back up to the farm, collect a gang of neighbours and walk down again. Then she had to be dug out, a back-breaking job. You got home at the end of the day absolutely exhausted. Now the soil is dry like dust and has changed, possibly beyond recovery. You couldn't dig out those smooth chunks like you used."

He paused a moment and continued,

"Before the pumping station at Gold Corner, Catcott Moor used to be beneath water from before the end of September, in some years, right through to the end of March. But it grew some marvellous grass, more and better than you get now. During the war the hay was sent off in huge quantities to feed pit ponies, before that it often went to towns to support the many thousands of horses kept there. When the pumping station was installed in 1940, to supply water for Puriton munitions factory, many a farmer wished that Jerry would bomb it to perdition. There are numbers of smaller farmers who bitterly regret the coming of the pumps and would like to see the end of drainage, so that grass yields would increase again, though you don't often hear that said."

"In the old days, tractor wheels would come out wet even when you were cutting hay. On some fields the Lord of the Manor decreed that you couldn't put cattle out on the fields before May, but the yields were still good. Of course everything was not perfect in those days. Before the war the hillground by Catcott was unusable because it had no water."

He went on to say that those who have deep drained in the area have never had the value from the money spent. One set of fields — just bought by the STNC for turning back to its original state — had grants to clear the scrub from it, which used to be a feature when he was a boy, more grants to drain it and plough it, now it has had grants to take it back out of production.

"'Tis a crazy situation. It has never been a workable proposition and the land has sunk so much that drainage has had to be made deeper and deeper. The pumping costs thousands of pounds a year in fuel, breakdowns, spares and general attendance. It has not been a success and, without government funds, would never have been attempted."

"What of the future?"

"I reckon 'tis too late now. I can't see them going back to the water up like it was. There's a lot wrong. The grass used to have a bit of supers and slag put on it and grew good crops. Now it's driven by compounds and is not as good. Natural grass took to being flooded until 25th March, then growing heavily. 'Four months to grow a year', they said. This rye-grass cannot cope with those conditions. In the old days every piece of ground would have a few milkers. I was talking to an old farmer the other day — 'In the old days you could make a living from three cows, now you need a hundred — eighty is not enough. Haven't we advanced?' he said, and I reckon he'm right."

Bill and Freda Ibell

Village School Heads

Bill and Freda Ibell came to this part of the world in 1949 and have stayed ever since, now retired after a lifetime of service as teachers and friends to a great many people. They married in 1937, having trained in the same college, but were separated for much of the war, when Bill joined the Navy, seeing service in Dieppe, Salerno, Sicily and Normandy. Freda continued to teach and bring up her child.

By 1947 Mr Ibell was Deputy Head at a school in Taunton, but applied for the post of Headmaster at Blackford Primary School and was very pleased when he was accepted. The school was founded in the last century, costing £110 to build.

There were about one hundred children in the school when Bill started on 1st January 1949, and he taught there for thirteen happy years. There were three staff in all, with forty-five in the infants and the rest in two other classes. It must have been a huge excitement for the children when the first Christmas Party was held in December that year. Each child was given a green cap as a present, which must have made them feel very important and part of the school family.

In those days, it was the farmers who were the more important members of the community. Some were School Managers, and there was a degree of status. You had to be in the right set to be accepted. Now there is a much more open society.

There was a preponderance of five surnames — Vowles, Duckett, Tucker, Fear and Wall — a reminder of the days when families inter-married. Although most were not very well off, few of the families were very poor and the children turned up for school looking clean and well-fed. However, in one instance where a child was unusually poorly dressed, Freda and Bill looked out some shoes and clothes from their own family's wardrobe. When the mother next came in to school she asked if they could provide some clothes for her, too, although it turned out that she had given away one pair of the shoes they had provided because she said they were no good without laces!

Bill settled down to teach all the usual subjects: reading, writing, arithmetic, geography, science, history, as well as some more unusual choices, such as dance / drama, acting, canework, basket making, clay modelling, embroidery and leatherwork. Up to this time it had been an all-age school, from five to fourteen years, and consequently Bill had to allocate a great deal of his allowance to initiate new reading schemes for the younger children. He also spent money on reference books to build up a library. He was very keen on grammar and reading, being determined to give a good, sound grounding. Back in the last century the number of subjects had been limited and, if the Inspector was not satisfied at the end of his visit, then no money was given for staff or equipment. It was 'payment by results'. In those days, too, the children remained at school until fourteen, most leaving to work on farms. This changed in 1948 with the division into Junior at Blackford and Bagley, and a Secondary Modern at Wedmore.

The numbers went up to about a hundred and twenty in 1951 and they were allocated another teacher. The sanitation was just about adequate, but there was no room for an office and no telephone. When water seeped through under the coal shed Bill turned to and sorted it out himself. Then, as now, there was never much spare money and the County had to be nagged and bullied to provide quite basic needs.

Bill persuaded Freda to join the staff in 1955, working with him for seven years until he was offered the post of Head Master in Street. In the classroom, gradually they moved away from the old stilted written English to a free-flowing style, and reading was much encouraged — even to the extent of taking their books home, which involved the parents, too. Children were not forced to sit at their desks all the time and this freedom of movement helped the shyer children to come out of their shells. They felt able to talk to the staff and they came to realise that school was something to be enjoyed.

There was no problem with discipline. The children were not unruly and there was never any pilfering. In all their years of teaching at Blackford, they could only remember two children who had caused some difficulty and one of them is now a policeman! In fact, although many of the children were not particularly academic, almost all of them have turned out to be good citizens. Perhaps the reason for this lay in Freda and Bill's stress on treating the whole school like one big family: there was respect, certainly, but also a feeling of being involved and sharing, coupled with a tremendous enthusiasm to learn. We know this is true, because our children were a part of this family.

When Bill left for Street in 1962, Freda Ibell became Head of

Blackford Primary, with two other members of staff under her. The school kept to its high standards and Freda paid no attention when the School Inspectors said that the children were to be allowed to write freely — *i.e.* without bothering about punctuation and spelling. However, when a student from Bristol came on teaching practice she went back and reported this. Mrs Ibell was hauled over the coals — she was not to teach tables, punctuation or spelling, the children must not be so restricted! Fortunately for many she interpreted this in her own sensible, pragmatic way and the school continued its high standards.

Harvest Home Princess and attendants, Wedmore

It is interesting that, at this time, parents outside the catchment area were anxious to get their children into Blackford School. The numbers were supposed to remain at about a hundred but, if there were spare spaces, it was possible to allow children from outside the catchment area to join the school. Perhaps these parents, like Freda, appreciated a good grounding in the Three R's!

Times began to change in the area, with the building of the M4/ M5 motorways. New young families were moving in, gradually altering the mainly rural school population to include these incomers, who were very keen that their children should reach Sexey's Grammar School, next-door. Freda was quick to make these newcomers welcome. She held Open Days at the school, and all the children had their work on display, not just the bright ones. Very soon the parents became interested and involved. They could always call in to talk over any worries. There was a close, personal relationship with all these families. Village life became very different, with the advent of Clubs for Badminton, Drama and Bowls. Freda feels that this is an improvement. Then, in 1976, the powers-that-be decided that Blackford should close and the children be moved to nearby Wedmore school. The reasons given were a falling child population and to save money. It was the end of a great era of education, where many children were given that really sound grounding which follows them throughout life. Freda took the opportunity to join Bill in retirement, but many continue to be grateful for their efforts over the years.

The old school logbooks, now held in Taunton, following the closure of the school on 10th July 1976, give a most fascinating glimpse into the past, dating, as they do, from the opening of the school. This gives a picture of the school from well before living memory, yet the words come to life as if the people writing them are still here. Many of the names recorded are as familiar today as they were then.

In beautiful copperplate handwriting the first entry reads: 'Jan 10. School opened on the 7th of January, 1879. Attendance poor, because not generally known in the neighbourhood.' However, by the end of the month this had increased to fifty-seven.

During March and April that year the numbers at school were low due to sickness and five children had died of diphtheria. This outbreak persisted in the village through the summer, although by the time the school closed on 19th July, for a month's summer holiday, it appeared to have abated. In March 1891 a lad died from Typhoid fever. Illness was of constant concern. In early 1891 a doctor visited the school from Dr Barnardo's 'for the purpose of examining the boys who came from that Institution.' Whooping cough is mentioned on occasion and influenza frequently, while 'unsightly skin eruptions' and chicken pox are other causes of many children being absent. The great influenza epidemic at the end of the First World War was marked by the school closing for three weeks and one child dying of double pneumonia.

During the autumn term there are repeated references to 'cautioning the boys against going into the adjoining orchards after apples', and 'attendance low on account of the potato harvest'. This becomes quite an annual theme. During haymaking, apple and blackberry picking and potato harvest, the attendance numbers were very low as children remained at home to help. It is also noted that they stayed at home to look after younger brothers and sisters while mother was out at work. In January 1890 it was noted that 'Arthur and Fred Sweet were again readmitted this morning after being absent for fourteen weeks. These boys live on the Heath, three miles off and are therefore outside the compulsory clauses of the Education Act. They are also both over thirteen.' — an interesting light on how it worked officially. In March 1904, 'three of the Heath children have now returned after a continuous absence of six months.'

The weather was also a strong factor: 'Dec 3 1881. Attendance good excepting children from the Heath who cannot attend without 'rowing' on account of the water.' There are constant references to very heavy, drenching rain in the autumns of these last years of the century, and it is not unusual to read that the Heath children were away from school for as much as four weeks at a time. As soon as rains became heavy, or snow fell, the children did not come to school, particularly from the outlying areas. In May 1899 there was a tremendous overnight storm. The entry for May 7th reads,

> There were only sixty children present (normally over 85) this morning owing to last night's storm....the heaviest ever remembered by the oldest inhabitant... The brook was flooded and a considerable amount of damage was done. The water ran down the street like a river.....The water opposite the church gates was five or six feet deep. Mr Latcham's (Carpenter) house suffered most severely. The water rose in the house to within two feet of the ceiling. It rose so rapidly there was no time for the inmates to leave the house and they were forced upstairs. The trunks of five large elms were carried away

... and floated down the street for a quarter of a mile. A waggon, that was under repair, was also swept away and taken down to the bottom of the village. Walls have been knocked down in several parts of the village and a great deal of damage has been done amongst the stock and hay.

In February 1888 the school had to close for several days after a fifteen-hour snowstorm, accompanied by a gale which caused drifting. In 1940 there was twenty-seven degrees of frost and 'the ink was frozen this morning.'

There are also some amusing moments: Aug 12 in 1881,

Attendance much lower in average in consequence of one of ....'s children having the "itch". Parents being under an erroneous impression that other children were suffering from the same complaint refused to send their children to school.

In spite of the Inspector visiting and being asked to endeavour to get a good attendance, the 'itch' was still being mentioned on 16th September, and appears to have come back again the following March. A final note on the subject is recorded on August 18th, 'Two families of children ... have been absent ever since the first week in March, when they ceased to attend school on account of suffering from 'itch'". During several days of September 1918 the school was closed for 'blackberry picking ... During the present week 427 lbs of blackberries were despatched from this school.'

Interestingly, no reference is made to the war in the notes of the period. On 11th September, the declaration of war against Germany is mentioned as part of a sentence about the arrival of evacuees.

Almost every entry in the Log Book starts with a reference to 'Attendance' — either good or bad, so it was obviously important in the Headmaster's eyes. He then frequently goes on to note that he cautioned the children about 'being late' (even to the extent of keeping them in), 'climbing the walls', 'rude play during the dinner hour' and 'throwing stones' (the Head burnt all the slings he could find amongst the children).

During its ninety-seven years existence, the school rose from its first recorded numbers of twenty-six pupils, to over sixty within weeks, then to a peak of 176 on the roll in 1908. Numbers fluctuated from sixty-five to over 110 during the twenties and thirties while, after the war a brief burst to 115 gradually fell to a final seventy-seven pupils at closure. Now this bustling building is silent, filled with old furniture belonging to a dealer. What tales it has to tell about the folk from the moors who were taught there!

Man of Peat

Mr M.F.Wall was born on the moors in a little single-storey cottage out on Westhay Heath. He left there when four years old but remembers it still, though he is seventy-seven now. He is a tall, youthful-looking man, whose face is little lined, and walks like a man in his fifties. He was eighth out of ten children, nine raised in that tiny cottage. His mother told him that when he was born, on December 15th, she could hear the water lashing up against the outer walls of the cottage. When floods were particularly bad they had to go and stay with friends but most of the old cottages were built on slight mounds to raise them above the water in winter. They kept a boat tied up to the outside.

The people of the moors did a variety of jobs: peat-digging, either for themselves or others, ditching, looking after cattle or cutting willow spars. If they worked for others, then there was little to do in winter except, perhaps, some ditching or hedging on the drier ground. If you had your own peat-digging, then you delivered the turves during the winter.

Mr Wall went to school at Meare until fourteen, then he joined his father in the peat business. In those days they dug peat for burning, though some was ground up by mill for bedding horses. His father worked for a while in a place where the mill was driven by a horizontal steam engine. In 1906 his father, George Wall, found and dug out a prehistoric boat from under the road by Shapwick Station. He was cleaning out a rhyne for the landlord of the Griffin's Head and saw this piece of wood running under the surface. It is now in Taunton Museum.

Mr. M.F.Wall

Burning peat required a lot of care in its preparation, to stop it crumbling and thus becoming impossible to handle. It was extremely hard work. The economics of peat were delicate. The local estate, owned by Colonel Warry, charged £5 for half an acre of land with peat and even so had a job to get rid of all the land. Rent was collected once a year, on Saturday night, at the Griffin's Head.

The peat was dug to a much shallower depth than now, where it is taken right down to the clay. Below three feet and the peat was too crumbly for consistency. They dug three or four 'mumps' (spits) deep with a heart-shaped spade. Each mump weighed about 28 lbs, so it must have been intensely hard work keeping going all day. This was then sliced into three to produce the characteristic peat bricks. It was impossible to start the process before the end of April, because of risks of frost breaking up the peat bricks, and it finished by July, leaving enough time for thorough drying before the winter. The peat was spread in winrows, or hiles, to dry. A hile consisted of seven turves, with seven more on top of them. Next they were moved again and made into ruckles, beehive-shaped piles of bricks, which were a characteristic of the countryside even twenty years ago. The best-quality peat fetched 15/- a thousand and a lot sold for much less than this. It was very popular and used by everyone for their fires, though it was a hard and poorly-paid way of making a living. Before the Second War they were paid 6/- a day, or a little more than a farm worker.

Mr. Wall can remember steam lorries when he was young, but the peat diggers could never afford such a form of transport. They relied on horses and carts, or putts — the latter having much wider wheels to take heavier loads and travel on softer ground. At the end of summer the peat was carted out to the roadside and stacked up to await delivery. Some was taken in winter to the station for delivery to towns and cities, but much was sold on retail rounds run by the diggers.

This form of peat-digging survived until after the Second War. Then digging for horticultural use gradually took over. (Peat turves were still sold for burning twenty years or more ago when we first came here.) Peat-digging for horticulture was an altogether less demanding form of work, once machinery came into use. The smaller producer now rotovates the ground, then scoops the loose peat up

Typical peat diggings

in a tracked Hymac digger. This machine can grab far into soft ground or even in water. From there the peat is stored in a big heap until needed. Larger peat owners, such as Fisons, use huge machines which slice up the peat and place it by the side of long narrow cuts for drying, but the principles are the same.

The season for digging is still limited, but not so much as previously. Drainage has lengthened the season and frost no longer matters, as all the peat is milled. They dig all they can during the summer and then mill and bag as required. I was shown a modern milling and bagging plant. The Walls—his son now runs the business — own thirty-five acres of peat ground, some of which is worked out, but there is plenty of life left still. They sell straight peat in bags, bought-in forest bark as a mulch and grow-bags which are compounded automatically in the bagging plant.

After Mr Wall was married, they farmed some forty acres, milking seventeen or so cows. Then he had trouble with farmer's lung from the hay and decided to give it up in favour of his first skill, peat. He

130

joined his father-in-law some thirty years ago and built the bungalow where he now lives. So far they have not noticed much effect from the anti-peat campaign, though feel it will eventually bite.

I asked about changes he has seen. Before the war, when the land was wet, they would have to clear the water from the cutting before they could start digging in the morning. This was done by hand, with a gadget like a huge spoon, pivoted on a tripod:

"You could scoop the water up and, with a twist, shoot it over the edge."

It was hard work but it was effective and enabled them to get on with the digging. He remembers Eclipse Peat using a mechanical pump when he was a young boy. The engine drove a chain fitted with buckets which picked up the water, like the spoon, and poured it over the side of the cutting. Modern mechanical pumps really only came into general use after the war. The Walls bought a little grey Ferguson tractor in 1947. Before that everything was dependent on what they called 'half-way' horses, bigger than a pony but without feathered legs, sturdy but not too heavy for the soft land. The thing he remembers vividly about these was the clouds of flies they attracted.

I asked about cider. Back in his father's day some farmers still looked upon cider as part of the wages for their men, though it died gradually as machinery took some of the back-breaking labour out of farming. People took little one-gallon cider barrels out to the fields with them. Many drank tea until about ten in the morning, then went on to cider for the rest of the day.

The area has changed in other ways. The old fields, once pink with orchids and bright with yellow rattle, no longer bloom, though small patches remain. This has come about through the intensification of farming. He is very keen on the wildlife around the place and spends time watching it. They have transformed an old peat digging into a fishing and wildlife lake which is both popular with the fisherfolk and enjoyable for the family. He feels that there is plenty of wildlife around still, though perhaps different from previously. Snipe and lapwings are reduced in numbers, but raised water-levels may bring them back, if this ever happened. He went on to say that perhaps it is not so much a question of raising water-levels as ensuring that the pumping is not so violent, leading to empty ditches after a downpour.

It is still a very close community. Perhaps the most remarkable thing is that it has stayed so over these recent years, although there are signs of change. The farms on either side are worked by relations and others live round about. However, Meare and Westhay have grown so much he hardly recognises places where he used to know everyone.

Farmer and Cider Maker

Michael Richards is a third generation cider-maker, in his mid-twenties, who now farms on his own. The story goes back to his great-grandfather, who came to own the Burtle Inn in 1910, after working on the Somerset and Dorset Railway. He kept cattle in a shed at the back of the inn and I was shown a picture with several generations of his family, taken on the flooded road by the Inn, with the water standing from the foreground right into the distance. One of the present houses is visible on the right, the Crossing house in the far distance and another house back in the moor, which has now disappeared. The cattle are knee-deep in the water in that historic photograph.

The Burtle Inn was a cider house in those days, as were most of the pubs around here. Mr Lee made cider on the premises for his pub and other cider-houses. Some of the barrels in use today originate from that period. Great-grandfather Lee moved to the present farm and built the house in 1920.

His grandfather, with whom Michael was in partnership until his death in 1989, farmed originally in Westham, taking over the tenancy from his wife's uncle, whose family had farmed there for generations, where he concentrated on cheese-making and contracting. At one stage he had eight or nine tractors in the yard, doing binding, threshing, ploughing and anything else needed in the area; the war was a particularly busy time.

Grandfather Lee moved to Burtle in the early 1950s and took over the cider-making. At its height they were making 25,000 gallons a year and, in 1985, won the championship at the Bath and West Show for the highest number of points in each of the three categories — sweet, medium and dry draft cider. Some of the sweeter cider was

Michael Richards

carbonated and bottled under the label Moonshine, which I remembered from when we supplied apples to Mr Lee.

The business went on happily until Customs and Excise began looking into the cider producers and started talking about excise tax, as well as VAT. Grandfather didn't want to mess with the paperwork so let it slide to the level agreed as being a hobby, rather than a business — 1,540 gallons a year. At his peak he could process that amount in less than two days. This whole business came to the fore again when Michael took over. He was already one of only two cider makers in Somerset who was notified as a rate-payer. When the Uniform Business Rate came in he was assessed at a very large amount, with nearly as much to pay as one of the biggest producers. He appealed, pointing out that the production was counted a hobby by HM Customs and Excise. He won the case and has restricted his output accordingly.

Many people thought he would pack it in when grandfather died but trade is steadily picking up now and he intends to continue for a few regulars for whom the blend is just right. If he was to pay business rates then production would need to go up to at least ten thousand gallons a year and it would put everything in a very different perspective. This is something which must be left for circumstances to decide in the future. It looks as though cider will continue, but on a small scale, though modern equipment has been purchased and the business has some machinery which would suit a larger concern. One of the constraints must remain Michael's position as a one-man band, employing only casual labour for special occasions such as hay-making, though his parents and sister also help out periodically.

Grandfather gave up milking in the early 1960s and the farm is now turned over to hay-making instead of silage. The farm is 120 acres in all, but thirty acres are rented out under secure tenancies. It is farmed for beef and around eighty cattle are grazed. Most are kept eighteen months to two years and sold for beef. The farm has never had a milk quota,

"Beef and sheep are all right if you operate without the Bank, but many people are in trouble who borrowed heavily to finance their animals." A position which has not faced him so far.

Michael left school at sixteen and was due to go to Seale Hayne Agricultural College but events conspired against him at the time.

He had to join grandfather at short notice to farm some land which had previously been sold as grass keep. Since then he has done a three year day-release course at Taunton and caught up with his contemporaries. The only thing he regrets missing was "the social side of college."

Although his real farming career started at sixteen, he has been mad about it ever since he can remember and kept cattle long before that age. Both he and his grandfather were unusual for farmers, as they were keen on gardening — most farmers look upon this as an unnecessary chore at the end of a busy day. Both of them had success with showing produce and flowers around the various agricultural and local shows.

"What about the village? Is there a good social life round here", I asked.

"Not bad," Michael replied, "there seems to be plenty going on, though the place has changed beyond recognition. But what place hasn't? There are far more people from outside now."

"Now tell me about the business of making cider," I continued.

"You'd better come out and have a look at it all, though it is all a bit dusty at this time of year".

The apples are hauled in during October or November. They are normally bought off the ground and picked up with their own self-propelled machine. Rubber paddles sweep the apples off the ground into rubber rollers. The dust and leaves fall through and the apples are carried to the rear. Generally the apples are bagged off the machine, so they can be weighed at the end for payment but, if the whole crop has been bought, they may be tipped loose into the trailer. The apples are all local and of cider-type. Some new orchards have been planted in the locality, with Yarlington Mill, Bulmer's Norman, Dabinett and Improved Kingston Black — the names have a wonderful ring to them.

The apples are loaded onto an augur in the yard and taken up to a mill. The resulting pomace, looking rather like apple sauce, is put onto a square of slats, lined with a nylon cloth, which sits on a bed mounted on rail wheels. The apples are piled onto the slat, which is surrounded with a low frame, and the whole is known as a cake. A dozen cakes sit on each other to form a cheese. The complete cheese, weighing a ton, is then pushed along the rails to a huge water-hydraulic press which used to operate at a mighty 3,300 psi and still works at over 2,000 lbs. This press was bought by grandfather in 1964 from a firm where it had been used as a paper press. It is driven by a Petter twin diesel of uncertain age. This is not the only engine, as the farm is lit and powered by a diesel generator. When the electricity first arrived, the engineers came over to see grandfather and explained the running charges and that there would be a hefty lump-sum to install it. As a new generator had been bought some eighteen months previously, Mr Lee decided not to have the mains — the charges were too high — and it has worked well ever since, though spares may soon prove difficult.

The apple juice flows out of the bottom of the cheese, down a drain hole in the bottom of the bed, and is pumped into barrels. If the pomace is very wet a little straw may be added to give body, but nylon cloth has largely taken the place of the old straw and apple-based cheeses. The straw used to act as the filter which the cloth now provides. The juice goes immediately into barrels for fermentation. The barrels, the biggest of which is nearly four hundred gallons in capacity, are filled with the juice and the bung left out of the top. The liquor and foam flow out of the top and the final part of the process is controlled by replacement and management of the bung towards the end of the fermentation.

Most of the cider is drunk young, during the first year. Second year cider has a touch of oxidation in it, as I found when I tasted a couple of barrels. The first year was very dry and smooth, the second sharper. I preferred the first. To keep it fresh once it is drawn from the barrel, it is advisable to store the cider in capped bottles in the sort of quantity you drink at a sitting. In this way you will preserve that wonderful freshness which is the hallmark of a good draught cider. I was also shown some fifteen- to twenty-year-old cider which is sold as cider-vinegar for pickling. Sweeter cider is generally preserved for visitors to the area, who prefer it. Barrels are discarded only when they leak, being used year after year. If cider is drawn from three levels in a barrel each glass may taste quite different. Cider is a living product made from varying products and will always be a new and fresh experience.

The biggest concern expressed by Michael Richards was over the future of the Levels and, in particular, what will happen to the water-table. He would like to see the winter levels raised to increase grass growth, but not so much that it would lead to the ground being poached by the cattle in spring. A lot of other farmers would back him in this,

"The ground is drying up and the peat cracking badly. Some is already being lost by oxidation, though I am assured the process can be reversed if something is done soon. The problem is that a very few intensive farmers dictate the policy of the IDBs and NRA in relation to water-levels. Their needs are quite different from those of the majority. The local Internal Drainage Board swears it has not lowered the water-table in recent years, but anyone who knows the area can take you to ditches where the water is very much lower than previously."

"What do you think will happen?"

"The new ESA standards, following the recent review, make certain levels and payments dependent on higher water-table. With the help of this it should be possible to return to traditional methods of farming on the Levels. They are naturally fertile when the water-table is high and should provide higher profits than those dependent on added artificials."

Michael has gone ninety-five per cent organic in his approach and finds his theories are paying off. The mowing ground is treated with dung from the sheds and he has a trial involving calcified seaweed as a natural fertiliser. With compound fertiliser costing £160 per tonne, it is cheaper to buy in grass he told me. Michael is a young man who has given a lot of thought to the needs of farming on the moors in the future,

"The Levels should give low-cost farming with high-yield results, provided the water is managed sensibly. The secret of successful farming now is to do so without too much borrowing."

Agricultural Representative and Councillor

Pat Kerrigan has always been interested in farming and, during 1941 and '42, worked on a farm at Fitzhead, learning the business. There he was involved with everything, including horses. The cattle were kept in sheds all winter, which involved a lot of hard physical labour,

"Straw was chucked in all winter and then, come the spring, dung forked out into the yard, before being loaded into a putt (broad-wheeled cart). Out on the field this was crooked out into heaps. The horses would walk on a few more yards and another heap would be crooked out. Then it would be spurred — spread with a four-pronged pick in a circle to cover the ground". A process which took hours is now done in a matter of minutes with a tractor.

Horses predominated, many were heavy Shires. Coal was still being imported by barge up to Langport by Walter Winchester at the time. Grass seeds were sown with a fiddle. Farming had altered little since Turnip Townsend's time.

When Pat came back from war service in the Royal Marines, in the Far East and Australia, it had all changed and the modern farm was starting to emerge as a result of wartime need to increase food production. On discharge he went to work on a farm up on the edge of the Quantocks. Mr Sayer was given a fifty acre Council holding after the First World War and built it up over the years. Pat spent a happy few years there, getting up at 6.30 to milk the cows. He has memories of marvellous farm breakfasts afterwards, then horses had to be caught up and harnessed, groomed and fed. It was a busy life.

Water for washing and drinking was piped down from a ram up in the woods above. Periodically this would stop and someone had to go up and look for the obstruction, which might be a creature which had found its way in and drowned. There was no electricity. At night they sat around the fire and talked or dozed, lit by a Tilley lamp.

Pat married in 1948 and a year later was offered a job with Horlicks, who specialised in artificial insemination of cows. For the first time he worked on the Levels, across as far as the Brue area. He stayed until 1954. The trouble was that it involved Sunday working, with only one day off during the week — most people worked six days then. He was not seeing enough of his children so decided to look for something else. His brother-in-law knew Rodney Hodge of

Pat Kerrigan

G.T.Hodges, the Bridgwater agricultural merchants, and in due course he joined them and stayed until the company was sold to Spillers.

It was a marvellously happy time. The firm was run like a family. Rodney was so good to his employees, even lending them money or helping them to buy houses. Everyone mucked in together, the directors and the whole firm loaded lorries on Friday evening for Saturday deliveries. The firm participated in everything locally, with people joining skittling teams, visiting markets at Taunton and Bridgwater weekly, attending shows and doing everything they could to become a part of the local and farming scene. They even helped some of their customers over sticky patches or to get off the ground in the beginning. They were all practical people who could do any of the jobs they discussed with the farmers.

The day started for him going in to the office collecting orders and making out paperwork, before making his rounds. In those days they provided a real service for the smaller and larger farmer. Kale, mangold and other seeds were bought in 1 cwt sacks and then packed in quantities to suit the use. Grass seed was mixed by hand with a shovel on the floor, again to exactly the specification required. Both these services have vanished from the field now, with the domination of the big suppliers. Pat's rounds were mainly to existing customers, on a fortnightly circuit. The farmers and their families became friends with whom he would sit round the table over a cup of tea and discuss prices, local happenings and markets. He made out the cheques for the farmers to sign, brought bags of this and that with him in the car. It was a very personal affair, which was lost long ago when three or four majors dominated the market, selling only on price. In those days the arrival of the 'rep' was an event looked forward to by the more remote farms. Pat used to go to one old farmer, at Burrow Bridge, who lived to over a hundred. He gave Pat meals of elvers in season. Many people used to catch them locally in those days.

"The winters of '47 and '63 were particularly severe and long and in '63 the disruption to deliveries was serious. Feeding-stuffs were left on designated roadsides and collected by farmers through a communal service. This worked perfectly and I cannot remember anything going seriously wrong."

In those days most deliveries were in bag and not bulk. The switch from churns to bulk for milk collections brought some welcome changes to farm entrances and tracks; the Milk Marketing Board insisting on high standards for their tanker routes.

The 1950s was a time of change, with many farms switching to electricity for the first time and able to plug in their machinery and modernise the dairy. It was a time when farms were small and had varied enterprises. There were deep litter houses and hens at the end of the garden path, they milked a few cows and added in anything else which could contribute. Many people had started as part-time farmers who bought grass and kept, say, ten cows. They worked hard and added to their herds and rented land. It was still possible to start with little capital other than the ability to work hard — something which is quite impossible nowadays. Because interest rates were low, people did not pay as regularly as they have to now. Some farmers only paid once a year at harvest time, others had a regular three-monthly settlement. Life was at a slower pace, though people worked hard.

Farmers had old cars, the tractors were made to last many years and few took holidays. Many farms were rented and quite small, though they have grown over the years. There were some real characters about. People had more time to develop their eccentricities and believed in themselves, for they had to grow through hard work. The local Shows were great gatherings, when people came in from all the outlying farms to talk to others. There were Ploughing and Root-Hoeing Matches, Hedging and Sheep-Shearing competitions.

Among his customers were a number of trades which were peculiar to the area. Roy Barrington of Newport both grew and bought in teazels. These were used in the worsted business for combing the cloth and have never been improved upon by machinery or artificial substitutes. Pat remembers visiting his farm when the flood waters came up to the back door. Withies were grown extensively around Stathe. Every part was used, from the stems for weaving, to the shredded bark (stripple) as a mulch. The trade became very good after the War, then dropped in the late 1970s, when many acres were grubbed out under heavy competition from Spain and the Argentine. Since then fortunes seem to have revived again. It is a very labour-intensive job but easy to enter or leave.

Then in the early 1980s farmers went through a phase when they

Withy growing, Stathe and Athelney area

made a lot of money. New cars appeared and it seemed quite reasonable to buy high-powered, four-wheel drive tractors, or the latest machinery. Land prices went higher and higher. They borrowed money on that same land and became heavily indebted:

"Those are the ones who are in bad trouble now. They were encouraged by the Banks then, now their markers are being called in. In effect, the rates of interest have pushed the rent of their land up above earning power. Many farmers now work from dawn to dusk for the Bank, not themselves."

Pat went on to say that, at the same time, the farmers also caused their own ruin in other ways,

"They have never liked paying money out, or allowing their suppliers to make money out of them. As a consequence they drove their small agricultural merchant friends out of business."

They started by forming buying groups to by-pass the merchant, leaving him to try and make his living from the left-overs. They bought their fertiliser, cattle-feed and other large-use products in bulk through their co-op,

"But they were not even loyal to that organisation. If they heard of someone under-cutting their own prices, they were off to them, ignoring the principle of the co-operative. So they even destroyed some of these. In the end they were left with three or four major suppliers who took over the small merchants and co-ops, then clamped down on all the old 'perks' offered by the small man."

Business became a hard commercial world, with discounts strictly according to quantity, payment on the nail and no-one to come in and chat with the lonely out on their remote farms.

This brought changes in other ways also:

"Where previously accounting was a bucket-full of bits of paper taken once a year to the accountant, VAT has made people tidy this up and look at their figures more frequently. People are just as friendly now, but they have less time, worry more. They do not enjoy their farming so much."

"What about the way things are going now? Are the Levels going to survive?" I asked him.

"The Levels is a new, invented term. They always used to be known as the moors locally," Pat replied.

Pat could not remember the moors being particularly flooded, though places like North Curry always were in the winter. Most farms were built on a slightly raised piece of ground and did not suffer from this. The great man of drainage — 'a person of vision' — was Eric Kelting. He was the engineer responsible for building Gold Corner Pumping Station,

"He transformed the moors and made possible modern farming."

I asked whether Pat felt that the ESA payments were of benefit, and what his views were in general about change,

"I am not in favour of going backwards, or returning to a mass of weeds. In time there will be another shortage of food and all the land will be required for growing food again. There is so much good land being lost to agriculture, with factories being built, golf-courses and so on. I don't think public money should be put into ESAs. Farms should be farmed sensibly. Look how well people farm on those parts where they have been able to deep-drain a block of land."

"Farmers have always been slow in thinking about marketing their produce. They sell by price rather than through concentration on

The great flat plain of Sedgemoor

method or quality. They think short-term, rather than long. This is where change could be beneficial."

I asked how he had come into local government. The local seat for Sedgemoor District Council, covering from Bawdrip to Stawell, became vacant and there was a by-election,

"Molly told me to try. 'You're always criticising them, go on, have a go.' So I did and, to my surprise, got in — by seven votes. That was in 1984."

And in 1991 he was re-elected, as an Independent, though heavily opposed by the official Conservative candidate.

I asked whether he enjoyed it,

"Yes, it is good to help people, to try to solve problems. Though the situation has become more and more difficult. The people at the bottom of the rung are like drowning men, they cannot pull themselves out."

Pat is on the Housing Committee, among others, and is particularly interested in this part of the activities of the Council. He also serves on Economic Planning and Development, which has been remarkably successful in bringing business into the area and ensuring a supply of new factories and units,

"However, housing is where you see the heartbreaks. Historically Councils were the providers of housing and comfort for those in need."

Now the Council is not allowed to build new houses, except for old people.

"It's impossible to get on the ladder now. If you're down, you stay down. The new housing associations are supposed to take on this mantle but have not succeeded in doing so. It's a heartbreaking situation and I cannot see it changing. Youngsters who marry and want to stay in the area, say to work on their family farm, just cannot afford to do so. It would be better, instead of selling Council Houses, if they offered a lump sum, equivalent to the discounted value of the house, so people could buy outside in the open market, leaving council houses for those who really need them."

"What of the future for farming on the Levels?"

"It's difficult. The villages are filling with people who want the rural life, but object to cow-dung on the roads. The outlook for the farmer in or close to a village is unhappy. They have not really come to terms with the fact that they are no longer the kings of the country castle. Agriculture will change further. Now that they have got rid of all the small suppliers they have little choice and will be squeezed further. There is less choice. They have made a rod for their own backs and I feel sorry for them. I am glad I am no longer actively part of the trade."

*Common hawker, one of the many beautiful
dragonflies found on the Levels*

7 Wildlife and Conservation

Wildlife and Flora

Although it has changed a great deal, with numbers of wildlife considerably diminished, the Levels have always had a reputation for a large number of creatures. Birds are the most obvious of these, clear indicators of a changing habitat when they leave an area. The international Ramsar Conference, set up to look at the world's great wetlands and attempt to do something to preserve them, was supported by our Government. Parts of the Levels were earmarked as being of international importance for wintering waders and wildfowl, and English Nature (successor to the Nature Conservancy Council) intends to bring them forward shortly as special protection areas. One cannot help wondering if that is done as a pious hope rather than a true reflection of the area's position. A great deal has altered since the Convention was signed by Britain in 1973, but little has been done to preserve the status of this particular wetland — indeed the reverse is true.

A wetland habitat has its own distinctive fauna and flora, birds often only found on wetlands or at a sea-marsh location. Amongst such birds breeding on the Levels are curlew, redshank, lapwing, snipe, mallard and teal. That brilliant canary-coloured creature, the yellow wagtail, is found in numbers at several locations; whinchats breed freely and herons hunt the rhynes in spring to feed their hungry hordes. On remote West Sedgemoor, black-tailed godwits breed periodically in country very similar to Holland, where they are a common sight displaying. Here they are great rarities as breeding birds.

In winter there are many visitors. The most spectacular are Bewick's swans, appearing in great herds of over a hundred birds in places, though most seem to have taken now to living in comfort at Slim-bridge where they are fed twice daily by the Wildfowl Trust. These birds are smaller than the familiar mute swan, have black and yellow bills and, perhaps most distinctive, their wings do not sing in flight. Instead they have the most wonderful, wild, musical calls, like bugles speaking to each other. Mute swans are on the increase on the Levels, with herds of over a hundred birds being found in a number of places. Many waders visit the area in winter. The most noticeable are lapwings, often accompanied by the smaller, chunkier golden plover. Both are particularly fine in flight, giving wonderful aerobatic dis-plays. Dunlin, much smaller and quicker-flying birds, may be seen in big flights at times when the moors have skimmings of water on the surface. Their flight is rapid, direct and they all change direction at once, first showing dark backs, then the flash of white undersides. Little flights of ruff may be seen during winter, some starting to

change into the much more exotic plumage of spring display, though none have shown signs of staying to breed so far.

Occasional parties of geese pass over and some-times stop for a day or so, whitefronts usually. In some parts there are a few native Canada geese and occasional twos and threes of greylags which may breed in the remoter spots. Shoveler, pintail, wigeon, teal, goosander and shelduck visit when the conditions are right, with water lying unfrozen inland but the coast in the grip of harder weather. Garganey pass through in spring when

Barn owls are still found on the moor   the moors also ring to a strange triple note. This is the call of the whimbrel on its annual migration through these parts.

Kestrels and sparrowhawks are common, hobbys roam above the wet levels, looking for dragonflies in summer, and marsh harriers hunt the reed beds. Strangely enough, though it is a largely unwooded area, buzzards breed out on the moors. Only days before writing this I watched three buzzards circling high over Tealham Moor, working their way up into the sun — a marvellous sight. Little owls utter their monotonous calls in spring, while the tawny owl, badly hit when all the elms came down with Dutch Elm Disease in the late 1970s, is regaining its former position. I am glad to report that barn owls live and breed in the area and may be seen hunting in daylight during spring.

Otters still roam the rivers and drains of the region. Their spraints, or droppings, may be found under bridges or on mounds beside rhynes. Mink have joined them also, smaller and very tame. At first they were extremely destructive, exploding into the area in a frenzy of killing but, after a while, they have fitted into the food chain and have settled a pair to every few miles. Like everything else there has to be sufficient prey for them to survive; thus, in due course, the balance is restored.

Perhaps the most noticeable change to the wildlife in recent years has been the arrival of roe deer all over the Levels. Ten or fifteen years ago they were unknown. Then the first signs of footprints were seen. Now they can be seen in daylight in a number of parts. The occasional red deer has been sighted but these are a rarity and probably signify the odd animal who has become lost. It is not red deer country. I have heard that muntjac deer are spreading into the area — tiny deer with tusks protruding from their upper lip, no bigger than a middle-sized dog. They take a bit of seeing as they can hide within the smallest bush.

Dragonflies are a speciality of the moors. All that water attracts many types of breeding insects. In early spring the spectacular and uncommon hairy dragonfly may be seen on old peat cuttings, while southern, common and migrant hawkers are all abundant in season. The ruddy darter is uncommon in most parts of the country but numerous on the Levels, while a number of the needle-fine damselfly species may be watched throughout the summer, including such

Lords and Ladies

specialities as white-legged and red-eyed damselflies and the truly spectacular banded agrion which is found on some slow-running streams. Of other insects it is worth mentioning the presence of marsh fritillary butterflies, greater and lesser marsh grasshoppers and many types of hoverfly.

The plant life of the Levels is famous, ranging from sedges of many kinds to various orchids, though those have become less numerous in recent years. The edges of the rhynes and droves show the full range of marsh orchids, purple loosestrife, yellow rattle, marsh woundwort and other flowers which bring such a profusion of colour in spring and summer. There are still buttercup meadows in which the Friesian cows stand out against an impossibly yellow background. Earlier than this, some fields are brilliant with the yellow of flowering dandelions while later the pale lilac of the cuckoo flower is delicate against the white of the dandelion clocks. Yellow is a dominant colour in the early part of the year, with some fields covered with kingcups, while the rhynes are later edged with yellow flag. Bernard Storer's excellent book, *The Natural History of the Somerset Levels*, goes into much more detail of unusual plants and creatures than space allows me here.

Awakening Conscience

Perhaps the most important item to be determined is the status of the Levels in the future. Are they to be gradually absorbed into the standard farming format of the country in general, or are they to be preserved as something unique, worth keeping in their own right? The arguments about this have been raging — and that is not too strong a word — since the early 1980s, when a Government change of direction became apparent.

That was the time when the Wildlife and Countryside Act was passed, giving teeth to the existence of SSSIs. The Countryside Commission was empowered to act in the case of areas declared Sites of Special Scientific Interest and insist on owners and occupiers following paths of action which would not harm the features or creatures which had caused the area to be so declared. In effect this stopped the further drainage and ploughing up of the Levels, for the majority of parts of the area have been declared SSSIs. All this did not go through without considerable opposition. The Nature Conservancy Council (NCC) was the agency in charge of notification and planning. It did not always behave with as much tact and understanding as it might have. Also there was a clause in the Act allowing three months' notice before notification. Put these together and an explosive situation was in the making.

The notice provision meant that some farmers used this period to push through drainage schemes — curiously, actively aided by another Government organisation, the Ministry of Agriculture (MAFF). Not surprisingly, many farmers took umbrage at the thought of other people deciding how they would farm their own land, as they saw it. There were protest meetings and, at one, an effigy of the local NCC man was burned. The situation was further exacerbated by delays in formulating how the payments would be made for those losing profits as a result of what they were asked to do. Then suddenly it was all over and forgotten, except in odd pockets where particular cases were under consideration. Milk quotas, and a growing realisation that there was no future for surpluses of this, that and the other, brought much of the farming community in touch with hard reality. Many people were happy to accept the payments and keep on with a way of life which they enjoyed and which earned them their living.

Later in the decade the Environmentally Sensitive Area (ESA) came along. Virtually the whole of the Levels was declared within the local ESA. Under it farmers were entitled to receive one of two levels of payment in return for voluntary curbs on the more radical forms of farming. Over fifty per cent of the workable area was subject to such agreements by 1991.

If all this had not occurred at the stage it did, we would now be looking at a totally different piece of countryside. When prices for cereals were high, and there was no talk about surplus mountains, there were plans afoot to drain the Levels and turn them into another Fenland larder. Deep drainage and ploughing would have given rise to extremely fertile land and a desert landscape similar to the fenlands could have been produced. The land would undoubtedly have been turned into huge holdings under a few commercial landlords, the fields increased in size and most trees and hedges removed. Most wildlife would have disappeared for ever. Even worse effects would have been seen in our many and varied villages. The smaller farms would have vanished in the monoculture and their owners and tenants no longer live there. The land would have been farmed by relatively few people armed with huge machines. The many busy little villages would have become bases for commuters and would have lost the richness of their present mix. The holiday attractions of the area would have vanished for good. Who goes to the fens for holidays nowadays, or retires there?

Threat to the Water Table

All should have been well, with the traditional ways of farming permanent grassland being preserved. Cows, grass and ditches, with willow-surrounded fields, were the hallmarks of what was seen as the Levels and all this should now be preserved. But one factor — water — had not been taken into account.

The Moors and Levels take their character from the high water-table, with its soft soil and wetland herbage. Traditionally it has been an area of permanent ancient grassland — its fields lush with wild flowers and other herbage in great abundance. In the winter they flooded, sometimes just keeping the grass above the water, which would lie in long runnels on the surface for months on end. This gave a highly productive grass crop which fed some of the highest yielding milk herds in Britain — and all grown without extra artificial fertiliser.

The efficiency of the new diesel pumping stations just after the war enabled the Water Authorities to manipulate water-tables with complete control. The latest electric pumps, controlled by sensors in the river, allow this whole process to work with only occasional attendance. It has become as automated as a carburettor in a car — once running, it will continue as long as there is fuel — and no-one need be there. The whole process of water-table control then becomes a matter of office-bound planning, rather than local adjustment to suit the situation at a particular moment. The pumps cut in as soon as a certain level has been reached on a drain and cut off as soon as another pre-determined level is reached after pumping.

Up to 1989, the Water Authorities were totally bound up with fulfilling drainage activities and, in effect, worked for the farmers on the one hand, and in preventing the flooding of homes on the other, without thinking about the countryside as a place to enjoy, or of the effects on wildlife. You only have to think back to the rivers which were straightened out, canalised and all their trees removed, to realise the truth of this. Then, in 1989, the Government published their Water Act which privatised the provision of water but also put all rivers and main drains in the hands of a centralised National Rivers Authority (NRA). A new set of provisions were added into the duties of all water authorities. They have a duty to further nature conservation — a mandatory requirement, which puts it at the top of their list. Drainage is a discretionary power, further down the priorities. The various Internal Drainage Boards have had the same provisions added to their statutory requirements and duties.

From the time of the Wildlife and Countryside Act, the water

Bewicks swans, winter visitors from Siberia

authorities had stopped further drainage activities within the Levels and also held the water-table at then existing heights, on the various moors under their jurisdiction. As far as they were concerned, they were holding the status-quo and, in conjunction with ESA and SSSI provisions, this should have preserved the nature and farming systems of the Levels, while providing the right conditions for wildlife.

Unfortunately this has not proved true. The deterioration in the Levels as a wildlife site has increased dramatically over the past few years. Part of this has come from changes in technology, not always recognised by the water authorities as factors affecting the state of the soil and its wetness or dryness. Part has come from the cumulative effects of previous actions in lowering the water-table in the past and part from actions of the Internal Drainage Boards. The change from manually-controlled pumping to automatic pumping by electric motors has had a particularly rapid effect. Prior to the changeover, little pumping took place at weekends or during the night, when there were no staff present normally. This allowed the water to rise in the drains and ditches and kept the soil moist. Under the automatic regime, this soaking never takes place. All this has led to a rapid and potentially destructive drying of the soil.

Crisis averted?

Conservation really only came into public consciousness in the early 1980s. Many people had been interested prior to that, but believed they were powerless to make changes against the barrier of authority which would not listen and the powerful farming lobby, with its remit to produce more and more. It was then that the word started to appear in the national press, at first perjoratively but now as a force to be reckoned with. Most people accepted the need to produce more food before that time, though few paused to think why. If the Common Market has done nothing else, it has forced us to look at our heritage and judge more critically what we are doing with it. In the case of the Levels many people are looking at the area and judging that everything is not as it should be. But this view is not confined to 'they conservationists', as they are still known in the countryside. Farmers have also been complaining about the state of their land and more do so each year. Petitions have been raised against the actions of an IDB in lowering the water-table in a particular area. In 1990, the farmers of Tealham Moor complained to the NRA that they were short of water in mid-summer—a situation which had never occurred before.

Those who observed the wildlife found a very worrying situation. A gradual diminution of winter flooding and general lack of moisture in the top few inches had been followed by a reduction in winter bird-visitors for which the area had become internationally famous. Wild duck, Bewick's swans and wading birds of all descriptions, were seen less and less. What had been a spectacle, became the occasional sighting. The position over breeding birds has been as marked. The Royal Society for the Protection of Birds (RSPB) has carried out a series of surveys, as has the NCC. These have shown that, within a year or so, most of the important breeding species will have ceased to breed on the Levels. Snipe are one of the most obvious examples of this. Wading birds need soft ground, for they feed beneath the surface with their long beaks; they need high ditch levels for their young to drink and feed and they need undisturbed fields while nesting, a condition which has vanished in many places with the increase in cutting for silage.

Various red herrings have been raised about this situation. One concerns predators. Why don't 'they' do something about predators, ask some farmers of the conservationists, as if this factor was responsible for the entire problem and ignoring the fact that they, the farmers, own ninety-nine per cent of the land anyway and therefore could be undertaking this control of crows and magpies. It also completely ignores the winter situation, where a day out on the moors may only reveal a few crows where previously thousands of waders and ducks might be seen. No, the problem is unfortunately much more basic, and at the same time complex.

One of 'they old cranes',
as herons are known locally

155

At the heart of the problem lies the winter pen on the moors. This is an artificially low level held by pumping. In general it is kept from December to May some six inches below the summer level, with the objectives of making for easier ditch-cleaning and to allow machinery access to the fields. Wetland grasses, which produce high yields without extra fertilising, need a high water-table to keep up their growth. They are shallow-rooted species and do not perform at their best when moisture is restricted. In the peatlands the winter pen has a major effect on determining the amount of moisture held in the ground over the summer period. The two cannot be divorced; they inter-react upon each other. A dry winter, or low winter pen without flooding, inevitably brings a dry summer. The ground is like a huge sponge which, once dried out, will not readily re-absorb water. Indeed some people maintain that peat dries out to produce a crust below the surface which cannot be wetted again; its properties change chemically and this is irreversible. Other authorities believe it is reversible, but only with huge effort and cost. Whatever the true answer, the situation is very close to crisis in many parts of the Levels at present.

Up to 1991, the Government had ignored the water situation. It lost a golden opportunity for linking water-table with grant when it introduced the ESA payments. I imagine they thought that farmers would see the benefits of the ESA system and would ensure that the water-table met the aims and objectives of the scheme — to preserve the wetland way of life and habitat. However, a vocal and articulate body of farmers are doing everything they can to allow the erosion of the Levels and to continue its transformation into an intensively-farmed landscape. This goes against the intentions of Government, the realities of agricultural over-production and the real advantages ESA schemes offer their fellows to avoid the economic pressures faced by those in unsupported areas.

Change is taking place. New ESA payments are planned for the ten years from 1991, with two tiers out of four involving some form of water-management. But only time will show whether this voluntary scheme will have the desired effect. Will sufficient farmers take up the third tier to ensure the survival of the Levels as a wetland?

Some institutions are altering their attitudes, but with every sign of reluctance. The NRA has reviewed its position in light of its duty to the environment and asked its Flood-Defence Committee to report back on how the water-table in the Levels should be controlled in future. This committee used to be composed of farmers and those in favour of drainage. However, since the Water Act, there have been changes to its membership as some of its electing bodies have realised their powers and responsibilities. The Chief Executive of the powerful Somerset Trust for Nature Conservation is a member now, as is a prominent member of the staff of English Nature, the successor to the NCC.

The Committee has been taking evidence from farmers, the MAFF and the various conservation bodies. In 1991 it issued an interim report suggesting a compromise system of raising water levels in selected parts of the moors only.

There is deep division between intensive farmers, who want lower water-tables to maintain their systems, conservationists, who demand a totally flooded area to suit their birds and flowers and small farmers, many of whom want a higher water-table, but not such as to reduce access to the land in spring. Will the compromise bring back the wetland character of the area, or is it just another stalling move by the powerful 'progressive' farming lobby?

Meanwhile, the deterioration continues, though the NRA is trying to ameliorate the situation, without altering basic policy. For instance, it has reviewed the settings of its automatic pumping sensors and narrowed the distance between on and off. This had an instant and visible effect, though the mean levels of water in the main drains stay the same. The water in the further ditches remains higher, more constant. It would appear that this has had some effect in keeping the fields damper under normal conditions.

One factor which is having an effect, far beyond the acreage involved, is the height of the water-table in relation to deep-drained ground. Something under eight per cent of the area has been drained by the farmers who own or tenant it, yet it is said that a good proportion of the local water-systems is set to suit their method of farming. Clay drains and private pumping stations, operating over a large enough area, enable a farmer to plough the ground, then use it for root or cereal crops, or to re-seed with short leys. To maintain the benefit it is necessary to keep the ground dry throughout the year. Up until recently the main concern of IDBs has been for farming and drainage, not the environment. Some of these IDBs have adjusted their water-tables to suit the needs of ploughed, deep-drained land, not their normal grassland farms. This has had a disastrous effect on the shallow-rooted wetland grasses and reduced their yields. It is said that it is easier for farmers with root and other crops to prove a loss of yield through flooding, since it is measurable, than if it is a grass crop. The IDBs do not wish themselves sued by those members for negligence of their duty.

Another factor is that, because of the system of voting for the IDB members, based on acreage, determined and 'progressive' farmers can take control of an area at the expense of their lesser neighbours. However, the squeeze on farming through high interest rates, EEC policies and world pricing systems, is already having an effect on this. The most progressive drainers are the ones who have spent large sums of capital on their work and are facing reduced demand for these high base-cost crops. But it is still a fact that committees determining the future of drainage on the Levels in 1991 are led by intensive farmers, though they are a small proportion of the owners of the Levels.

It is not a case of arguing the merits of conserving an area or not, based on the feelings of the farming and non-farming communities as a whole. Rather it is a case of conservation having to prove its case against a hard wall of entrenched opinion from those in authority. In 1991 the NRA was still querying whether the Levels were actually drying out — in spite of overwhelming evidence from those who had studied this matter scientifically and the evidence of local residents

Roe deer, newcomers to the levels but increasingly seen

who had watched it happen because they lived there.

One factor mitigates against all these efforts and that is the entrenched attitudes which have been taken up by both conservation and the more extreme farming interests. Each sees the position as black and white, with no question of compromise. The entrenched conservationist will not see anything but the perfect solution, with flooding conforming precisely to their plan to bring birds teeming back into the area. They appear to ignore the rights of the farmer who lives and works on the land. Equally, the 'drainer' insists that no move will be made away from the present situation, not admitting that it is deteriorating visibly.

There is a terrible need to bang heads together and bring about one of those classic British compromises which achieves most of what is desired by each side.

Nature Reserves and Conservation
There is no doubt that the proper solution is to plan for the total state of the Levels and what is likely to happen to them. How much better to have a working, breathing reserve made up of the whole area, through voluntary response from farmer and country dweller, than to have islands only within a desert of conventional farmland.

However, there is a secondary, 'belt-and-braces', approach which answers part of the problem, though it does not take the place of the holistic approach. This secondary course is to preserve wildlife and countryside within a series of nature reserves. Somerset is fortunate in the numbers of these which exist, but they form only a minute percentage of the whole.

English Nature owns some 740 acres on the Levels, some used experimentally for testing the effects of various changes to herbage and fertiliser usage, others bought specially to show what can be done by bringing back intensively-farmed areas to traditional methods. It has declared the five sites they run as the Somerset Levels National Nature Reserve.

The owner of the largest number of reserves is the Somerset Trust for Nature Conservation (STNC), a society with over eight thousand members and continuing each year to expand ownership of reserves. It has a variety of wetland reserves on the Levels, including Burtle Moor, thirty-seven acres; Catcott reserves, 172 acres; Chilton Moor, forty-five acres; Street Heath, nineteen acres; Tealham Moor, ninety-seven acres; Westhay Heath fifteen acres; Westhay Moor, ninety-seven acres; plus just over an acre at Sharpham Moor. Most can be visited and enjoyed, though some are kept closed in the interests of the fauna and flora. Great Westhay Moor is an area of worked out peat diggings which has been engineered and planned to bring maximum wildlife potential to this interesting habitat. It is a pilot for a much larger reserve it hopes will be formed when other areas of peatland become worked out. Every effort is being made to help the public enjoy this area through hides and trails.

The RSPB owns the justly famous West Sedgemoor Reserve of 1,117 acres, which has a permanent warden and is the site with probably the best potential in the county. This was the centre of considerable controversy in the early days of SSSIs and there remains tension between the local IDB and the Society over drainage policy, but it is evolving back into a piece of traditional winter-flooded moorland and attracting large numbers of birds of many species. At the time of writing, further, adjoining land is being bought to increase the area under protection in this region.

Although these 2,340 acres only represent just over three per cent of the total, a great deal is being learned from all these Levels reserves as to the fragility of the system, the steps which can be taken to make them more attractive to native species of plants, insects, mammals and birds, and how to fit wildlife and humans together. They are worth supporting in every way, especially through membership of the societies. They are the key to understanding the problems and what to do about them for the future.

8 What of the Future?

So that is the position in the early 1990s. The Levels are poised on a knife-edge, though showing signs of tipping towards a saner and more balanced approach to their future, both as a farming area and in preserving the traditional countryside. The Government thought it had done its stuff to preserve all this, through the ESA and SSSI schemes, but others felt their short-term needs were more important and frustrated the true intent. What is likely to happen in the future?

There are already signs that the 'drainage' lobby, for want of a better word, is seeing it will have to give way somewhere. There is talk about trying to arrange a higher water-table in certain key areas — though whether these will coincide with ecologically significant parts has yet to be seen. Clearly it is going to be a long period of argument and change being introduced slowly and even reluctantly, but pressures are such, from legal requirements under the Water Act, to an ever more vocal public, that change for the better will occur. What is important is to carry the farming community with the rest.

The ESA payment scheme was reviewed during 1991, at the end of its first five years of operation. Water-levels will be one of the criteria considered for some of the payments. The real question, then, is whether the payment will be made as an earnest of intent by an individual, without having obtained a centrally run policy of actually raising the table, or only where real increases have been achieved. An individual farmer can do little to affect the decision on his own land, but can do so through his IDB and NFU votes. There is a strong feeling among concerned and practical people that payment should be against actual achievement.

IDBs, like the committees of the NRA, are facing change. Local Authorities will be appointing some members in the future. Thus,

161

slowly but surely, a balanced point of view will come about, instead of reflecting mainly large-farmer and 'drainer' points of view. There is talk also of further payment being made to take land on the Levels back from ploughground, or deep drainage, to wetland herbage. This could attract many people to convert back at a time when their investment has proved to be poor. If this occurred, there would be no pressure on the IDBs to manipulate the winter pen further and levels could be raised without controversy.

There is no doubt that the ESA payment scheme is the most potent force available for returning the Levels to a state where it grows excellent grass crops, looks beautiful and supports large numbers of wetland wildlife and flora. I believe that Government recognises this and will push on with plans to improve the prospects of the area in this sense. More and more farmers have come to realise that this scheme also allows them to farm in their traditional manner, while helping shield them from pressures on margins faced generally in the farming community. Those who argue otherwise are doing wetland farmers and the countryside a grave disservice.

The other medium to achieve change is by way of Government's direct representative on ecology and wildlife, English Nature. The SSSI scheme can be used to exert more direct pressure than it has up to now. It has the teeth to do so, but perhaps not the man-power. For example, it would be possible to insist on certain areas having a higher water-table under the provisions of their SSSIs, which are not voluntary but mandatory. Far better though, to achieve all this by voluntary action, through ESAs.

English Nature is only too aware that entrenched views may yet win the day, as regards direction to the NRA and the IDBs in their water-policy, but it is armed now with the various statutory duties to conservation and the environment built into the terms of reference for those bodies. It is able and prepared to insist on those being carried out. The problem is, will it be too late when all the delaying tactics have been employed?

I am an optimist, and a believer in British good sense and the power of compromise. Let us hope my faith is repaid with the continuation of the Somerset Moors and Levels in a form which we can enjoy, from which the farmer will profit and in which wildlife will flourish.

The future of the Levels is bound up with their wetness and the nature of the landscape. What of its people and the places where they live? The great imponderable is what will happen to the villages and towns under the ever-increasing pressures from those who want to live there. Each new town or village plan brings further pressure to fill in gaps and expand into new boundaries. The joy of living in a good mixed population of newcomers and old-established families could vanish. There are already signs of the pressures on many formerly beautiful and tranquil villages. Those concerned with the future of the area need to consider these factors as carefully as the others, if it is to continue to maintain its unique character.

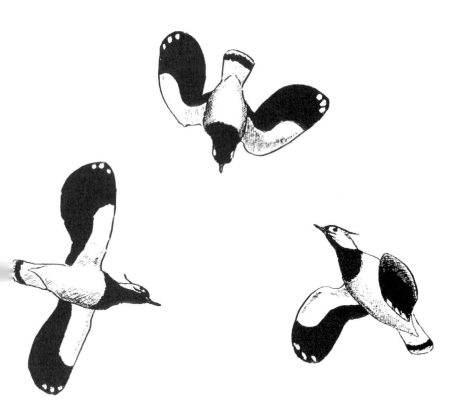

FURTHER READING

The Levels are well-documented and many fine writers have added to our knowledge of this area. Among those we have consulted are:

Robert DUNNING, *A History of Somerset:* Somerset County Library, 1987

Robert DUNNING, *A History of Somerset*: Phillimore, 1983

F.J. PEARCE, *A History of Wedmore*: 1971

John COLES, *Archaeology of Wetlands*: Edinburgh, 1984

Desmond HAWKINS, *Avalon and Sedgemoor*: David and Charles, 1973

Rev. R.W. EYTON, *Domesday Studies*: Reeves and Turner, 1880

J.M. COLES and B.J. ORME, *Prehistory of Somerset Levels*: Somerset Levels Project, 1982

W.R. RICHMOND, *Story of Somersetshire*: Wake and Dean, 1905

Michael WILLIAMS, *The Draining of the Somerset Levels*: Cambridge University Press, 1970

Ray GIBBS, *The Legendary XII Hides of Glastonbury*: Llanerch Enterprises, 1988

Cuthbert ROSE, *Wedmore's Moors and the Enclosure Acts of the Eighteenth Century*: 1982

PLACES TO VISIT

There are many places worth visiting on and around the Levels. Some have been covered in the text but it may be helpful to summarise the more important and interesting of these. At least, it will provide a skeleton upon which to plan a visit. It is impossible to give the full range of opening hours for each, as they may vary from time to time, but an indication is given, together with a telephone number, where available.

Axbridge
King John's Hunting Lodge: Perhaps more of the Mendips than the Levels, but worth a diversion. Recently restored and magnificent Tudor merchant house on the Square, timber-framed and elaborately decorated, it is open in the afternoons during the summer. *Tel 0934 732012.*

Bridgwater
Admiral Blake Museum: This memorial to the town's most illustrious citizen is housed in the very building in which he was born. It contains relics of his life, as well as some from the Pitchfork Rebellion. It is open all the year for part of the week. *Tel 0278 456127.*

Burrow Bridge
Allermoor Pumping Station Museum: Open by arrangement only. Steam pumping engines and parts from mid-1800s. *Tel 0823 69324.*
Gadsbys the basketmakers: Baskets, chairs and other pieces made from local willows. See them being made. Open most of the week, all year. *Tel. 082 369 259*
St. Michael's on Burrow Mump: The church on the top of this strange-shaped hill in the middle of the Levels is a monument to Somerset

soldiers and looks out over miles of ditches, rhynes and willow-fringed fields. There is a free car park at the bottom and it is worth a visit at any time of the year, the scene varying with the season, from winter floods to the lush foliage of high summer.

East Huntspill

New Road Farm: A working farm which shows the life-style and methods so very typical of the Levels. There are many animals to see, including badgers in their sett. Open most days in summer and at weekends in winter. *Tel 0278 783250.*

Glastonbury

Abbey: Behind the ugly car park is a complete haven of peace, set in manicured green lawns. The remains of the Abbey are well-preserved, though varying in extent from one part to another. The kitchen and the cloisters are particularly fine and the atmosphere tranquil. Open all year except Christmas Day. *Tel 0458 32267.*

Chalice Well: a spring at the foot of the Tor which runs red and has a long tradition of healing. The water is impregnated with iron, which oxidises in contact with the air, leaving a blood-red stain. Legend has it that the Holy Grail, or Chalice, which caught some drops of Christ's blood on the Cross, is buried here. Open most weekdays. *Tel 0458 31154.*

Somerset Rural Life Museum: A fascinating insight into rural life over the centuries. The museum is housed in a magnificent tithe barn and outbuildings and is well laid out for a most enjoyable and informative visit. Open all week during the summer and six days in winter. *Tel 0458 31197.*

Tor and St. Michael's Chapel: You cannot visit Glastonbury without toiling up the Tor and looking round the little church tower, from which the last Abbot of Glastonbury was hanged. The views are magnificent and, if you believe the tales, you will feel all sorts of energies flowing along the surrounding ley lines.

Tribunal: One of the oldest buildings in Glastonbury, dating from the fifteenth century, it was the Court House and now holds a most interesting museum. Some of its treasures are taken from the Glastonbury Lake Villages and include a safety pin several thousand years old and a dug-out canoe removed from the peat. This small museum gives an excellent flavour of the Levels in pre-history. Open daily in summer and part of the week during winter. *Tel 0458 32949.*

Meare

Abbot's Fish House: This ancient small building was used by the Abbey for storing fish and was situated on the edge of a long-vanished lake where the monks bred carp. It is particularly beautiful at sunset when the surrounding field is part-flooded. See instructions on the gate for where to obtain the key.

Moorlynch

There is a working vineyard here on the southern slopes of the Polden Hills, midway between Glastonbury and Bridgwater. Prize-winning wines are grown and sold. The estate is open all week during the summer. *Tel 0458 210247.*

Muchelney

Abbey: A definite must for anyone. Muchelney has a great air of peace and permanence, brought about by its associations and the comforting presence of a farm alongside. The Abbot's House is particularly fine and well preserved, even though it has been used as a farmhouse following the Dissolution. Open daily during the summer. *Tel 0458 250664.*

Medieval Priest's House: Owned by the National Trust, this is a late medieval house, home of the priests serving in the nearby parish church with its wonderful painted ceiling. It is set in a beautiful and unspoiled village in remarkably peaceful countryside. *Tel 0458 250672.*

Stathe, Athelney and Stoke St. Gregory

The Withy Trail: Signposted during the summer, this route from nearby Burrow Bridge takes you to see withy-growing and preparation, travelling through some of the most traditional old hamlets, which can have changed but little over the years.

Willows and Wetlands Centre: Set in the premises of Coate, the basket-makers, it shows how the landscape has been made over the centuries, with pictures of typical local wildlife. Exhibits on withy-growing, basket-making and teazel-growing. Open all the week and Saturday mornings. *Tel 0823 490249.*

Street

Clark's Shoe Museum: Set up by Clarks, one of England's oldest shoemakers, in this town of many shoe shops, the museum is of considerable interest. It shows footwear from Roman times right up to the present day. It is fascinating to see how fashionable and practical wear has changed over the years. Open six days a week during the summer.

Wells

Bishop's Palace: Home to the Bishops of Bath and Wells since 1207 and well worth visiting. The Palace inside the moat, the Bishop's garden and St. Andrew's Well with its five underground springs from which the City derives its name, are open on summer Thursdays, Sundays, bank holidays and the whole of August. Look out for the swans which are trained to ring the bell at the gatehouse when they want food. The surrounding grounds outside the moat, used by many local people for walking, are always open. *Tel 0749 78691.*

Cathedral: One of the finest in Britain and recently restored. Among its many interesting features, look for the West Front with its 293 statues, the great inverted arches inside and the unique medieval clock with its moving knights. *Tel 0749 78691.*

Museum: A general collection of local interest, covering the Mendips, Wookey and the surrounding area of Levels. There are some fascinating objects, including lead ingots marked with the name of Vespasian, a Roman Emperor in the first century A.D., looking as if they had just emerged from casting. Open most weekdays, but check times. *Tel 0749 673477.*

Vicars' Close: A row of exceptional fourteenth century houses with tall chimneys which have been preserved largely unchanged. If possible, visit these in spring when the blossom is out. The street is open the whole time, but the houses are private, some being used by the Cathedral School.

Westhay

The Peat Moors Visitor Centre: There is a splendid small museum and Visitor Centre sponsored by, and attached to, the Willows Garden Centre on the road between Westhay and Shapwick. You are free to wander in and see how the peat used to be dug. There are exhibits showing the construction of the old peat tracks of prehistory, together with pictures showing some notable local wildlife. It is an excellent introduction to the Levels and is open nearly every day. *Tel 04586 257.*

Westonzoyland

Battle of Sedgemoor: This is the area around which was fought the Battle of Sedgemoor in 1685, which brought doom to so many local people and is remembered to this day. There is no tidied-up, prettified site to visit, and it has all changed since then, but there is a sense of history in wandering around the nearby fields. Marks on the church door and walls are said to have been made by troops sharpening their swords. Rebels were herded into the church after the battle and some hanged from the building.

Pumping Station: One of the old steam pumping stations has been restored by enthusiasts and is open during the summer. On certain dates it is shown working, in full steam, and at others the gleaming machinery is just there to admire. *For details ring 0823 412713.*

INDEX

(Page numbers in italics refer to illustrations)

Some other books from Ex Libris Press:

WEST COUNTRY LANDSCAPES SERIES:
THE VALE OF PEWSEY
by John Chandler
Detailed and learned but highly readable account of the wide vale between the Marlborough Downs and Salisbury Plain which lies at the heart of Wiltshire.
Uniform with The Somerset Levels
160 pages, several maps and many black and white photographs, Price £6.95

SEEDTIME TO HARVEST
A Farmer's Life
by Arthur Court
Born in 1908, Arthur Court has lived and farmed on the borders of Somerset and Wiltshire all his life. This is his story and the story of his farming career.
126 pages, Map and photographs, Price £3.95

Many more titles available, of both Somerset and general West Country interest. Please ask for our free illustrated catalogue.

Ex Libris books may be obtained through your local bookshop or direct from the publisher, post-free, on receipt of net price, at:
1 The Shambles, Bradford on Avon, Wiltshire, BA15 1JS